THE CANALS OF SOUTH WALES AND THE BORDER

THE CANALS OF THE BRITISH ISLES

British Canals. An illustrated history By Charles Hadfield
The Canals of Eastern England By John Boyes and Ronald Russell
The Canals of the East Midlands including part of London By Charles Hadfield
The Canals of the North of Ireland By W. A. McCutcheon
The Canals of North West England Vols I and II By Charles Hadfield and Gordon Biddle
The Canals of Scotland By Jean Lindsay
The Canals of the South and South East England By Charles Hadfield
The Canals of the South of Ireland By V. T. H. and D. R. Delany
The Canals of South Wales and the Border By Charles Hadfield
The Canals of South West England By Charles Hadfield
The Canals of Yorkshire and North East England Vols I and II By Charles Hadfield

OTHER BOOKS BY CHARLES HADFIELD

Canal Age
Holiday Cruising on Inland Waterways (with Michael Street)
Introducing Inland Waterways
Waterway Sights to See
Waterways to Stratford (with John Norris)
Atmospheric Railways

THE CANALS OF SOUTH WALES AND THE BORDER

by
Charles Hadfield

WITH PLATES AND MAPS

DAVID & CHARLES : NEWTON ABBOT
in conjunction with
UNIVERSITY OF WALES PRESS : CARDIFF

ISBN 0 7153 4027 1

First edition 1960
Reprinted 1960
Second edition 1967
Reprinted 1977

Printed in Great Britain
by Redwood Burn Limited, Trowbridge & Esher
for David & Charles (Publishers) Limited
Brunel House Newton Abbot Devon

Published in the United States of America
by David & Charles Inc
North Pomfret Vermont 05053 USA

Published in Canada
by Douglas David & Charles Limited
1875 Welch Street North Vancouver BC

THIS BOOK

IS RESPECTFULLY DEDICATED

TO THE MEMORY OF

Thomas Dadford senior, Thomas Dadford junior,
Thomas Sheasby senior, Thomas Sheasby junior,
and William Kirkhouse

CANAL ENGINEERS

AND OF

John Hodgkinson and George Overton

TRAMROAD ENGINEERS

CONTENTS

APPENDICES

ILLUSTRATIONS

PLATES

MAPS IN TEXT

PREFACE
TO THE FIRST EDITION

THIS book is the third of a series. In *British Canals*, published in 1950, with a new edition in 1959, I gave a general account of the history of British inland navigation from the beginning of the canal age to the present day. *The Canals of Southern England*, 1955, described in more detail the waterways of the country south of a line from Gloucester to the Thames and London. This present book, the text and appendices of which are arranged in a similar way, deals with the waterways of South Wales, Monmouthshire, Herefordshire and the Forest of Dean. I say waterways, but in this area, while canals were the main traffic lines of their time, they were fed by many miles of associated horse tramroads. I have therefore said something about the more important of these, especially if they were owned by canal companies.

The industrial growth of South Wales was greatly accelerated by canal building. Yet little local research has been done on the subject. There is the section on canals in Miss Enid Walker's unpublished thesis of 1947 offered to the University of Wales on *The Development of Communications in Glamorgan, with special reference to the growth of industry, between* 1760 *and* 1840, written at a time when the minute books of the canal companies were not available to her; there is Mr Harold Pollins's article on the Swansea Canal in the *Journal of Transport History*, Mr F. V. Emery's work on the Pen-clawdd Canal, Mr I. Cohen's papers to the Woolhope Naturalists' Field Club on the Herefordshire waterways, and 'Dean Forester's' unpublished researches into the tramroads of the Forest of Dean. Fortunately, the records of the principal canals of the area, except the Kidwelly & Llanelly, are still in existence, though material for reconstructing the history of the smaller private concerns is little and fragmentary.

Because of her geographical structure, the canals of South Wales did not become a system. Each main line with its attendant waterway or tramroad branches formed a whole without junction with its neighbours, and only in the border country did the beginnings of a network appear. The arrangement of the book has therefore been dictated by the facts, for the affairs of each valley were largely separate, with only the broad trends showing themselves everywhere.

I should perhaps say that I do not conceive myself to be writing economic history, but describing for the ordinary reader interested in canals or in the locality how the canals came to be built where we now find them. There is here, of course, material for the economic historian, but it is for him to describe how canal development fits into the pattern of general economic growth. He is the master: a specialist like myself is only one of his servants.

My helpers have been many. Among them I would wish especially to thank Mr Walter Minchinton and Mr D. S. M. Barrie, who read the whole manuscript; the officials of the British Transport Commission's Historical Records and of Western Region Deeds & Records; the National Library of Wales, the Glamorgan and Monmouthshire Record Offices, the South-West Wales River Board, and of many public libraries, and especially Mr H. A. Prescott of the public library at Llanelly. In addition, my grateful thanks are due to Mr H. D. Emanuel for doing much research for me in the National Library of Wales and the Glamorgan Record Office, Mr A. J. S. Coombe Tennant, the owner of the Tennant Canal, Mr A. D. G. Evans of the Neath Canal company, and Mr G. P. Bideleux of the Bute Estate for making records available, and Mr I. Cohen who has allowed me to use his extracts from Hereford newspapers. Mr C. R. Clinker, Mr C. Stanley Thomas of Neath, Mr Harold Pollins, Mr F. V. Emery, Mr J. E. Norris, Mr D. E. Bick, Mr Donald Green, Mr H. W. Paar, Mr Robert Craig, Mr W. J. Skillern, Mr Ian Wright, Mr R. C. Jarvis and Mr Idris Evans have all been most helpful.

I must also thank the Leverhulme trustees for a grant towards the cost of the research done for me at Aberystwyth; Dr Elwyn Davies and the University of Wales Press for consenting to publish the book, and Mr John Baker of Phoenix House for including it in his list; my step-daughter Miss Laura Miller for typing the manuscript, and lastly, my wife, who has been my chief encourager, and the patient sufferer of my preoccupations.

CHARLES HADFIELD

PREFACE

TO THE SECOND EDITION

A NUMBER of changes have been made in the text of this new edition. I should like to thank Messrs R. E. Bowen, R. S. Craig, H. W. Paar, Alec K. Pope, P. G. Rattenbury, W. J. Skillern and I. L. Wright, who have made suggestions for corrections or additions.

I am grateful to the University of Wales Press for consenting to publish the book in its original form, and, now that it has been transferred to David & Charles, for continuing to include it in their list.

CHARLES HADFIELD

ACKNOWLEDGEMENTS

PLATES V, VI, VII and VIII are reproduced by courtesy of the British Railways Board; Plates III and IV with the permission of Mr Ian Wright, and Plates I, II and IX with that of the Ordnance Survey.

CHAPTER I

Background to Canals

In England there is a long history of river navigation before the canal age and, when they came, canals were mostly planned as branches of these rivers, or connections between one and another. This pattern shows in the waterways of Herefordshire and western Gloucestershire described in this book. About 1780, when local canals were first seriously talked of, the Severn was an important channel of trade, while barges loaded with coal and groceries were being dragged up the Wye. They could usually get to Hereford, and in times of flood on to Hay, but only a little way up the Lugg, and then with difficulty.

In South Wales there was very little inland navigation till the canals came. In general, the Usk was only navigable to Caerleon, the Taff to Cardiff wharf, the Tawe to Morriston above Swansea. The Neath river could be navigated past the old town of Neath to Aberdulais, where a short cut with two locks led through the ironworks and out again to Ynys-y-gerwyn a little higher up the river. Farther west, craft could sail a few miles up the Loughor to near Pontardulais; the bigger coasting vessels could get up the Taf to Laugharne and the smaller to St. Clears, while others could move on the tide up the Towy to Carmarthen.

West again, small boats could go up the Western Cleddau to Haverfordwest and the Eastern Cleddau to Canaston Bridge near Narberth. The Teifi was navigable from Cardigan to Abercych. A tinplate works had been opened at Dol-y-gored near Llechryd in 1765, and a side-cut to the river built about 1772 between Llechryd and Manordeify. It is not clear whether this last was only a water-channel, or was also used for navigation; there is some evidence of timber and iron-ore barges using it. About 1770 the works were moved across the river to Pen-y-gored (Castle Malgwyn), and soon afterwards Sir Benjamin Hammett got control, and built a walled horse towing-path beside the lower river from Pentood

Marsh above Cardigan to the works for barges carrying iron, tin and chemicals. These closed in 1806, but there was some use of the river into the present century. Finally, the Dovey was navigable for little boats from Aberdovey right up to Doldwymyn in Montgomeryshire.[1]

At this time the trade from the tiny ports of Newport and Cardiff was chiefly agricultural. Industrial production was mainly concentrated in the copper, spelter, salt, soap and other works of Swansea, the copper and tinplate works and iron forges of Neath, and the coal trade from the harbours between Neath and Kidwelly and in Pembrokeshire. Here, therefore, were the earliest canals. At Neath before 1700 Sir Humphrey Mackworth built what is often described as a canal, but was really a small dock basin with tide gates near his Melyn works: this gave on to a pill or creek of the Neath river. At Llanelly Thomas Bowen is said to have built a canal at about the same time to ship coal. The first authentic canals in South Wales were, however, Kymer's Canal from his collieries and limeworks to Kidwelly, probably opened in 1769, and a short waterway from collieries at Llwynhendy, east of Llanelly, to Dafen pill built about the same time by Chauncey Townsend. During the next thirty years a number of other small canals were built to connect collieries or works not far from the sea with a shipping place; Lord Milford's abortive Kilgetty Canal from the Pembrokeshire mines; the Earl of Ashburnham's to the Gwendraeth estuary; the Wern in Llanelly; Chauncey Townsend's second canal to Yspitty; the Llansamlet to Foxhole opposite Swansea; the Glan-y-wern to Red Jacket; and the Penrhiwtyn to Giant's Grave. All were in West Wales, and none penetrated more than four miles inland. They were small and unimportant, and had little influence upon the next and decisive stage of Welsh canal development.

On a strip of high ground about a mile wide and eighteen long, from Hirwaun to Blaenavon, with an extension down the Clydach valley to Glangrwyney, small ironworks were set up from the middle of the eighteenth century where iron ore, limestone, and wood obtained from the valleys of the Taff and Clydach for use as charcoal, were all near one another. When shortage of fuel limited or reduced the output, the ironmasters, using the process discovered by Abraham Darby of Coalbrookdale, turned to coal, which could be found close to the ironstone and the limestone. In the 1780's they introduced technical improvements in smelting that caused the expansion of existing works and the erection of new ones. Cyfarthfa, Plymouth, Penydarren, Dowlais, Sirhowy, Clydach, Beaufort, Ebbw Vale, all were in existence by 1790, pressing for better transport for their iron to the sea-coast, and soon to be followed by Blaenavon, Nant-y-glo and Rhymney. At first the iron had been carried on pack-horses, then on the newly built turnpike roads, many of the trustees of which were the same industrialists, colliery owners and landowners who were later concerned with canals.[2] Neither form of transport had the necessary capacity, and the forward-looking men of the time therefore turned to canals.

If one were to name the begetters of the water transport arteries of South Wales, on which her industrial development was founded, one would probably choose Francis Homfray,[3] and his sons Jeremiah and Samuel, who were invited into Wales by Guest of Dowlais. The Homfrays arrived in 1782, and in 1784 took a lease of the iron ore in the property near Merthyr Tydfil upon which they built the Penydarren works. Francis Homfray had owned ironworks at Broseley on the Severn, and a forge at Stewponey near Stourbridge. One of the greatest and most prosperous of the early English canals, the Staffordshire & Worcestershire, ran through Stewponey, and brought the iron manufactures of Birmingham to Stourport to be transferred to Severn craft for the voyage to Bristol.

Thomas Dadford had worked for the Staffordshire & Worcestershire Company in the 70's as resident engineer, and it would be surprising if the Homfrays had not known him. Then he moved to the Trent & Mersey Canal, the northern neighbour of the Staffordshire & Worcestershire, and in 1789 turned contractor to build a part of the Cromford Canal in Derbyshire. While employed by the Trent & Mersey to build the Fradley–Whittington Brook section of the Coventry Canal (subsequently sold to that company), he had probably met Thomas Sheasby, who had been the contractor to complete the Coventry Canal from Atherstone to Fazeley. Sheasby joined Dadford on the Cromford Canal.

A small tub-boat canal had been built at Cyfarthfa near Merthyr Tydfil about 1776, perhaps suggested by that* made about 1767 by Lord Gower at Donnington not far from Broseley. Now it was proposed to build a bigger waterway from Cyfarthfa to the sea at Cardiff. It was authorized in 1790, and the engineer-contractors who agreed to build it were Thomas Dadford senior, his son Thomas, and Thomas Sheasby, the two older men having thrown

* The Donnington Wood or Duke of Sutherland's Tub-boat Canal.

up their Cromford Canal contract to take it on. By 1794 this Glamorganshire Canal was open to Cardiff and by 1798 it had its floating harbour or sea-lock pound where coastal vessels could be loaded. Its Act became in 1791 the model for that of the Neath Canal from Glynneath to Neath, extended soon afterwards to a better shipping place at Giant's Grave.

The beginning of construction on the Glamorganshire spurred on the ironmasters and coalowners eastwards of the Taff valley to get better facilities for themselves by promoting the Monmouthshire Canal, from Crumlin by one branch and Pontnewynydd above Pontypool by another to Newport, with many auxiliary tramroads. By 1796 both branches were open. In the meantime the citizens and industrialists of Swansea and its neighbourhood, supported by many Neath Canal shareholders, had in 1794 been authorized to build the Swansea Canal from Hen-neuadd down the Tawe valley to Swansea; it was completed in 1798.

Between 1794 and 1799, therefore, five great canal lines had been opened for traffic down the Welsh valleys, to Swansea, Giant's Grave, Cardiff and Newport. These seventy-seven miles of canal, with a total of 180 locks and rising at one point to over 500 feet above the sea, had been built for approximately £420,000, and all by the Dadfords, Sheasby and Sheasby's son, with some local help. They were rightly seen by contemporaries as the midwives of a new age. In 1794 a letter written after the opening of the Glamorganshire Canal said:

'the Canal . . . is completed. . . . With the iron treasures of our hills, we hope to grow daily more truly rich than the Spaniards are, with their mines in Mexico and Peru; as ours occasion industry and population, whilst theirs purchase slothful dependence, and are destructive of both.'[4]

Two years later an observer of the opening of the Pontypool line of the Monmouthshire wrote:

'By means of this Canal the treasures of Iron, Coals, and other valuable articles, which have hitherto slept in the bowels of the mountains, will now furnish inexhaustible materials for industry, and become invaluable sources of wealth and population. Monmouthshire must quickly rise into the first importance, and become the seat of extensive trade.'[5]

In 1793 two important canal additions were authorized, though neither was completed for some years. The bigger, the Brecknock & Abergavenny Canal, was to run from the eastern branch of the Monmouthshire at Pontymoile (Pont-y-moel) near Pontypool to

Brecon, serving partly to transport iron downwards from such works as Clydach and Beaufort, and partly to supply Brecon and its neighbourhood with coal from the Gilwern area. The part from Gilwern at the bottom of the Clydach valley to Brecon was finished in 1800, also by the younger Dadford, and fulfilled the second function; the first had to wait for the completion of the canal in 1812, and then became very important. The other canal addition, the Aberdare, was also not opened till 1812 from near that town to a junction with the Glamorganshire Canal at Abercynon: it was partly engineered by the younger Sheasby, partly by George Overton. For nearly thirty years it carried the comparatively small iron production of the Aberdare and Hirwaun works, before blossoming into great activity as the steam coal trade spattered the valley with collieries. Only one major canal was later added to these, that built privately by George Tennant and engineered by William Kirkhouse from a junction with the Neath Canal at Aberdulais past Neath Abbey to a new and better shipping place—Port Tennant—in the estuary of the Tawe below Swansea. It was opened in 1824.

Without reckoning later improvements, a construction cost of about £800,000 on waterways and, at a guess, of some £700,000 on tramroads* sufficed to provide the transport system that moved almost all the iron and coal of South Wales till 1840, and a great deal of it till much later.

Thomas Dadford senior was soon left to do most of the engineering on the Glamorganshire Canal by himself. Thomas junior, after beginning the Neath, settled down to give three-quarters of his time to the construction of the Monmouthshire and one-quarter to the Leominster, and then to building the Brecon–Gilwern section of the Brecknock & Abergavenny. Thomas Sheasby, after nearly finishing the Neath and then abandoning the work, became engineer of the Swansea Canal, where he was succeeded by his son, also Thomas Sheasby. This son later began the construction of the Aberdare Canal, but, having got himself a better job as clerk and engineer of the Severn & Wye Company, moved to Gloucestershire to build the Lydney Canal, and left a tramroad and colliery engineer, George Overton, to finish the Aberdare. Other notable men concerned with Welsh canals were James Green of Exeter, builder of the enlarged Kidwelly & Llanelly, Edward Martin of Morriston, who worked on several canals, including the Swansea, the Pen-clawdd, and the first part

* Some 350 miles of tramroad at £2,000 a mile.

of the Kidwelly & Llanelly, and that ubiquitous surveyor David Davies of Crickhowell.

On the Welsh border Robert Whitworth was the engineer most concerned. One of James Brindley's principal assistants, he was engaged as early as 1777 in surveys for canals in Shropshire and Herefordshire. From 1781 to 1789 he was planning or building the Thames & Severn Canal from Stroud to the River Thames, and probably because of his work in the area he undertook surveys in 1790 for improvements to the navigation of the Wye. Later, in 1795, he took over the building of the Herefordshire & Gloucestershire Canal after its engineer, Josiah Clowes, who had been his assistant on the Thames & Severn, had died, and completed it in 1798 as far as Ledbury from Gloucester. He also did a small survey on the Leominster Canal, the main engineering of which was the work of the younger Dadford, in such spare time as he had from building the Monmouthshire.

The pattern of development in Herefordshire and west Gloucestershire sprang from Hereford's demand for cheaper and more regularly delivered coal, and from efforts by a few local people to develop the Forest of Dean coalmines. The old means of supplying Hereford was by the unimproved River Wye, so first men looked to its improvement. When that did not seem possible, the Herefordshire & Gloucestershire Canal from Gloucester to Hereford was projected. When that failed to get beyond Ledbury, there was talk of a tramroad from the Forest collieries to the Wye shipping place at Lydbrook, and then of an extension all the way to Hereford.

In the end, the river was improved by a horse towing path between Lydbrook and Hereford, while the Forest collieries were given tramroad transport both to Lydbrook on the Wye and to Lydney and Bullo Pill on the Severn by Acts of 1809. The coal trade to the Severn proved far the more important. From Lydney, where a canal and harbour were built to help its shipment, it was moved up the Thames & Severn Canal and to Cheltenham, as well as up and down the Severn. The influence of Hereford was not, however, exhausted. It attracted a tramroad from Monmouthshire in 1829, and the completion of the Herefordshire & Gloucestershire Canal in 1845, after which, for the remaining few years before railways, that town enjoyed two lines by water and one by tramroad for the supply of her needs.

Lastly, the Leominster Canal was a tribute to the energy and over-optimism of its promoters. Because Stourport had become a great inland port for the exchange of coal, ironware, imported goods and all the many products that converged there from Manchester, the Potteries, Birmingham, Stourbridge, Coalbrookdale and Bristol, the promoters saw coal and all the other commodities in the warehouses of Stourport passing along a canal to Tenbury, Leominster and Kington in exchange for the products of the land to be carried to the growing Midland towns. It was not completed, and if it had been it would not have paid; yet the remains of the canal from Leominster to near Mamble still remind us of a once-considerable effort.

Technically, the canals of South Wales were simpler to build than, for instance, those of the north of England which had to cross the Pennines or those in the Midlands that passed from one valley to another. Because they followed the valleys, and did not emerge beyond the valley heads, there were no long tunnels on Welsh canals: indeed, there were only six in all, at Tal-y-bont on the Brecknock & Abergavenny, at Cwmbrân and two at Newport on the Monmouthshire, at Cardiff on the Glamorganshire and at Neath on the Tennant, the longest of them all, at Tal-y-bont, being only 375 yards. On the other hand, rivers had sometimes to be crossed, or the canal carried over tributaries, and many aqueducts were built. The finest are near Trimsaran on the Kidwelly & Llanelly, at Ystalyfera on the Swansea, Aberdulais on the Tennant, Ynysbwllog on the Neath, and at Brynich near Brecon on the Brecknock & Abergavenny: all these, with many smaller structures, remain, but that at Abercynon on the Glamorganshire has been absorbed into a road bridge.

An impressive feature of Welsh canals is, of course, the heavy lockage. There are several flights of locks, such as those at Cwmbrân and Rogerstone on the Monmouthshire. Double locks (two built together and sharing a pair of gates) are frequent, and there was a staircase of three below Nantgarw on the Glamorganshire. On the other hand, inclined planes, so frequent in hilly country on the smaller canals of Shropshire and the south-west of England, were used only on the Kidwelly & Llanelly, where they were installed by James Green who had built several in Devon and Cornwall. No canal lifts were ever built or tried in South Wales. Yet the canal engineers were supreme in the building of their canals along steep hillsides. The upper part of the Crumlin line of the Monmouthshire, the Brecknock & Abergavenny along the lower slopes of Blorenge, the Glamorganshire between Merthyr and Abercynon high above the valley of the Taff, or the upper pounds of the Neath Canal, are outstanding in Britain.

On the border the problems of canal engineering were more ordinary, though often more intractable. The Herefordshire & Gloucestershire had three substantial tunnels, Oxenhall (2,192 yds.), Walsopthorne (400 yds.), and Aylestone Hill (*c.* 440 yds.), as well as two aqueducts over the Frome and the Lugg; the Leominster had short tunnels at Putnal Field and Newnham, and a longer one at Southnet (1,250 yds.) that was never used, as well as two considerable aqueducts over the Teme and the Rea.

Because the principal Welsh canals were all built by the same group of engineers, they were all of about the same dimensions, taking craft some 60–65 ft. long and 8 ft. 9 in.–9 ft. 2 in. broad, except the Swansea, where craft were about 69 ft. long and 7 ft. 6 in. broad. On the border, the Herefordshire & Gloucestershire and the Leominster took the standard English narrow boats 70 ft. long and rather under 7 ft. broad. All these craft carried approximately 25 tons when fully loaded. The Kidwelly & Llanelly used tub-boats on its inclined plane sections and small boats were also used on some of the minor canals. Exceptionally, the sea-lock pound of the Glamorganshire Canal and the Lydney Canal were ship canals, taking craft up to about 400 tons.

If the canal system described in this book was arterial, then the tramroads were the veins.[6] In England mainly grouped in the Tyne–Tees area and in Derbyshire and East Shropshire, they were ubiquitous throughout South Wales and the border: how much so can be learned from a study of such a map as that accompanying Mr Clifford Davies's thesis,[7] which shows the network of lines along the ridge between Merthyr and Clydach in 1836.

The early tramroads* were built with cast-iron edge-rails mounted on iron or wooden sleepers, and the trucks had grooved wheels that straddled the rails.[8] In 1799, however, Benjamin Outram visited the Monmouthshire and the Brecknock & Abergavenny company's tramroads, and recommended their conversion to plateways:

'But if instead of the present railroads, others were substituted on the system I have introduced, the expenses of conveyance might be reduced three-fourths.'[9]

His reports had great influence in South Wales, and not only caused the gradual conversion of these two canal companies' lines

* I use the word tramroad in the text to cover all horse-drawn lines, whatever the type of rail. At the time edge-railways were called rail-ways or rail-roads, while plateways with L-shaped rails were called tramroads, dramroads or rail-roads.

to plateways, but the building soon afterwards of the important Penydarren and Sirhowy tramroads on the new plan, and later of many others. Plateways had the advantage that the weight was in the rail and not in the waggon: Overton[10] gives the weight of a plateway tram as 13 cwt., and that of an edge-rail waggon as 23 cwt. Therefore on the one hand there were less rail breakages with plateways because of the stronger rail at a time when the use of cast-iron made breakages always frequent, and on the other the hauling back of the empty trams up the steep Welsh hillsides to the ironworks and collieries was made easier by their comparative lightness, a factor which far outweighed the rather greater friction.

The system grew. Within ironworks; from works and limestone quarries and collieries to each other; from all of them to the canal lines; and from the canals into the countryside the tramroads ran, till by 1830 there must have been some 350 miles of them within the area of this book. The heaviest concentration lay in the valleys above the Monmouthshire Canal, on the ridge behind, and down the farther valleys to the Brecknock & Abergavenny Canal. By their means the ironworks near the ridge—Blaenavon, Nant-y-glo, Ebbw Vale, Sirhowy, Beaufort—were given a choice of two canals, a choice which caused much trouble and litigation. Hirwaun and Aber-nant had a similar choice by the same means between the Aberdare and Neath Canals. Another group criss-crossed the Forest of Dean and its neighbourhood, carrying coal to the Severn and the Wye, while out into the countryside plateways spread as far as Kington from Brecon, or Hereford from Abergavenny, carrying coal and bringing back timber and food.

Occasionally a tramroad was built to by-pass a canal, at first in rivalry, as the Penydarren paralleled the upper part of the Glamorganshire or Hall's tramroad the Crumlin line of the Monmouthshire, later to supplement a line hard-pressed to carry the traffic or short of water. So the Monmouthshire company duplicated its own Crumlin line of canal with a tramroad which, connected at Crumlin to existing lines to Nant-y-glo and Beaufort (for Ebbw Vale) provided a through plateway from the valley heads to Newport wharves. These Monmouthshire plateways were then adapted for locomotives, then converted to mixed plates and edge-rails, and then to modern railways, till they replaced their parent canals. Elsewhere the old plateways were taken up as new branch locomotive railways were laid down.

The greatest builder of tramroads in our area was John

Hodgkinson, who had been trained by Benjamin Outram as his assistant, but later was to equal if not better his instructor. The Benjamin Outram Hodgkinson who in 1849 had a farm in Hertfordshire and another at Allt-yr-ynn near Newport I take to have been his aptly-named son.[11] His main achievements were the Sirhowy line, the earlier work on the Hay tramroad, the Kington tramroad, and the three lines which together made up a continuous plateway from the Brecknock & Abergavenny Canal near Abergavenny to Hereford. Another outstanding man was George Overton. Probably trained as a colliery engineer, and in his life a partner both in the Hirwaun ironworks and in coalmines, he engineered the Penydarren tramroad and probably the Bryn-oer, with which he was closely concerned, and surveyed the Rumney. Indeed, it was because of his experience that he was chosen to survey the Stockton & Darlington railway line, and took with him David Davies the surveyor. Thomas Dadford junior built the older Monmouthshire tramroads, and John Dadford the Brecknock & Abergavenny company's line up the Clydach valley. Lastly, William Wells was the engineer who surveyed the later Monmouthshire tramroads, from Aberbeeg to Nant-y-glo and from Crumlin to Risca, and built the latter.

A word must be said about the relation of improved dock facilities to canal development. The earliest docks or floating harbours were in the west: Sir Humphrey Mackworth's near Neath before 1700, and Roderick & Bowen's dock at Llanelly in the 1790's that later became the Carmarthenshire tramroad dock. Later the extension of the Kidwelly & Llanelly Canal was to be tied to the construction of Burry Port, opened in 1831. At Swansea the floating harbour of 1852 was contiguous to the canal wharves, and much improved its shipment facilities. Two important canal shipping places in this part of Wales and one less important were all tidal: Port Tennant at the end of the Tennant Canal below Swansea, Giant's Grave at the foot of the Neath Canal, and Pembrey Old Harbour on the Pembrey Canal. The first was superseded by the floating harbour, and then by the docks built on its own site, the second by Briton Ferry docks, opened in 1861 and accessible only to the competing railway, and the last by the opening of Burry Port.

At Cardiff the Glamorganshire Canal had opened its own floating harbour in 1798. Later the company tried to improve the facilities of the port, but in the end it was the Marquess of Bute who opened the first Bute Dock in 1839, with canal and later railway connexions. At Newport the canal company had a considerable financial interest in the Town Dock, opened in 1842, and later connected to the canal by a tramroad, but the canal's own wharves were always to remain tidal. Lastly, the Lydney Canal, itself a floating harbour, was opened in 1813, and served the tramroads of the southern part of the Forest.

The Glamorganshire and the Monmouthshire Canals, and to some extent the Brecknock & Abergavenny and the Swansea, were built upon the iron trade. They made possible the enormous expansion of that trade, as in turn they benefited from it. The trade was slow to start. In 1796 the production of the four works at Merthyr was 16,304 tons; in 1819 the quantity carried down the Glamorganshire Canal was 42,624 tons. On the Monmouthshire Canal there was only one works, Blaenavon, in operation in 1801, to send down 1,091 tons of iron; in 1819 eight works sent down 37,709 tons. This total of 80,333 tons of iron down the Glamorganshire and Monmouthshire Canals in 1819 became 192,602 in 1829, and 372,176 in 1839 as more ironworks came into production, and old ones increased their output; in 1849 it was probably over the half-million.[12] In April 1843 it was reckoned that 117 blast furnaces were in operation in South Wales and Monmouthshire, which produced the raw material for this traffic.[13]

In the '30's substantial imports of iron-ore began, much of it from Cumberland and Lancashire, to be mixed with the local product. This tendency began earlier at the ironworks on the canal behind Cardiff than at those behind Newport, and was probably the result of the cheaper tolls charged on the Glamorganshire Canal.

Some railway plates and rails had always been part of the output of the ironworks, but from 1840 onwards iron rails became increasingly important as a cause of expansion. Then in the '60's the development of the Bessemer process caused a change from iron to steel making, which led to the closing of many canal-connected ironworks, and the concentration of steel production in a few large works served by railways which brought their largely foreign ore and carried away their products.

In the coal trade the earliest development took place round Kidwelly and Llanelly, and then near Swansea and Neath. The canals of the west shipped both bituminous coal and also anthracite for use in maltings, or culm (small anthracite) for lime-burning. A substantial market for culm lay opposite South Wales in Somerset, Devon and Cornwall, where to-day in estuaries like that of the Torridge the traveller can see the giant ruined kilns where once Welsh culm burnt Welsh limestone to make fertile Westcountry fields. By 1801 Swansea was a great coal port, sending out in that year about 153,600 tons.[14] In addition locally-produced coal, canal-borne and other, went to feed her growing copper works.

To the east, Newport's shipments of bituminous coal developed very rapidly once the Monmouthshire Canal was open, favoured as she was by her exemption from the coastwise duties,* which were not repealed until 1831. By 1809 Newport was shipping 148,000 tons of coal,[15] which found a wide market. Bristol was a focal point of trade, and Monmouthshire coal also penetrated up the Avon and the Kennet & Avon Canal: by its competition it had already influenced the promotion of the Somersetshire Coal Canal to enable the Somerset colliery owners to reduce the cost of carriage of their own product and keep it competitive in Bath, if not in Bristol. Not much went higher up the Severn in competition with the Forest of Dean coal, but all along the Somerset, Devon and Cornish coasts the market lay open. Therefore the coal shippers not only took advantage of the existing waterways of the Westcountry, notably those behind Bridgwater,† but they and the Monmouthshire shareholders helped to promote new canals such as the Glastonbury. Then, as the export trade developed, the shippers looked for further markets to Ireland, to the south coast of England round to London, and abroad to the Continent, the Mediterranean, Africa and the New World.

Newport coal had, by its exemption, an advantage over that shipped both from Cardiff or from the Forest of Dean. Until the late '20's, most of the coal carried on the Glamorganshire Canal had been for the use of the local ironworks. Then shipments increased, but it was not till the great steam-coal period began in the early '40's, by which time the coastwise duty no longer existed and the export duty was soon to be repealed,‡ that Cardiff's coal exports leaped up. These were the respective figures for the main canal-supplied South Wales ports in 1833:

	tons
Newport	440,492
Cardiff	171,978
Swansea and Neath	387,176[16]

* See Chapter VII.

† For these Westcountry waterways see my *The Canals of Southern England*, 1955.

‡ It was repealed in 1833, reimposed in 1842, repealed in 1845, reimposed in 1901, and repealed in 1906.

By 1847 the figures were:

	tons
Newport	552,197
Cardiff	513,758
Swansea and Neath	420,022[17]

The expansion of the Forest of Dean coal industry was also hindered by the coastwise duties, as well as by lack of transport. When at the end of the eighteenth century moneyed men began to develop collieries bigger than the small drift mines of the free miners, and a tramroad system was built, the coal had to be despatched mainly to places within the Port of Gloucester; to travel farther to the south it had to be subsidized by the drawbacks on their tolls granted by the Severn & Wye Company for the purpose.

Apart from the main traffic of iron and coal the canals carried limestone and lime, stone for roads and building, and, later, imported iron ore and timber for pit-props. There was also a certain amount of carriage of foodstuffs and domestic goods upwards to the industrial centres: most canals had their market boats, like those that in 1848 ran three times a week between Cardiff and Aberdare.[18] Passenger carrying was rare, and seems to have taken place regularly only on the Tennant Canal.

From about 1800 to 1840 the pattern of canal and tramroad development was both cause and result of steady expansion of iron and other works, of collieries, and of towns and villages in the industrial area. The population of Glamorgan was 71,525 in 1801 and 171,188 in 1841, and of Monmouthshire 45,582 in 1801 and 134,355 in 1841. In Glamorgan and Monmouthshire by the '30's the canals were becoming congested as traffic approached their capacity to carry it, both physically and in terms of water-supply. Because they were controlled mainly by the colliery owners, ironmasters and owners of works whose goods they transported, the companies were very dependent for their whole existence upon large tonnage accounts kept with a small number of freighters, each of whose works was connected to the canal by a wharf or basin, or to a connecting tramroad, and who usually shipped their goods in their own trams and boats manned with their own workmen. It was a vulnerable position.

It was this congestion that provided a main motive for the building of the first competing railway, the Taff Vale, which was opened from Cardiff to Merthyr Tydfil in 1841. Others were the stoppages on the canals caused by repairs, frost or water shortage. In February 1830 Leigh & George of Pontypool were having to send their output by the turnpike road because the canal was frozen:

'What a contrast to all this disagreeable uncertainty', they wrote, 'would be the conveyance by a good rail-road, which not only at all times and seasons might be travelled upon but also at all periods would enable us to reach the port at a cheaper rate. . . .'[19]

Here lay another motive, the belief that the new railways would be cheaper. The early railways proposed to run parallel to the canals were, however, to some extent thought of as supplementary rather than competitive, and, compared to railway development generally in Britain, they came late. The Pontypool and Crumlin lines were opened in 1854, the Vale of Neath in 1851, the Swansea in 1861, and that up the Gwendraeth valley from 1869 onwards. In two cases, those of the Monmouthshire and the Kidwelly & Llanelly, the canal companies themselves built the railways: in the others, the railway companies at first took a share of the new traffic only, so that we see canal tonnages still increasing after rival railways have been opened. The railways built their branches, and provided their sidings, for new collieries and works, while the old continued for many years to use the canal. Sometimes, as in the vale of Neath, the canal conveniently served one side of a valley and the railway the other. It was not till the '60's and '70's that many of the canal-connected collieries and works—especially small ironworks—closed down, and those that were larger or developing began to feel the competitive disadvantage of being served by canals or tramroads, and sought siding or branch accommodation.

Canal companies were therefore able to maintain their tonnages, and their comparatively high dividends, for rather longer than their English counterparts. Few technical improvements were carried out, however, for the physical limitations of Welsh canals made it of little value to introduce steamboats and most difficult to widen the waterway or to build parallel locks, the normal method of speeding up the movement of boats. Improvements did take place on the canal-connected tramroads, notably by the introduction of locomotives from 1829 onwards on some of them, and later by the use of wrought-iron instead of cast-iron plates, and of the combined plate and rail. When decay started in the canal-tramroad system, it spread quickly. In 1860 the Welsh canals flourished: by 1900 they were virtually disused, the exception, paradoxically, being the Swansea, the only important canal that had been bought by an outside railway company, the Great Western, which used it to compete with the Midland-owned line that ran parallel to it.

Outside South Wales the influence of railways on relatively weak waterway concerns was similar to that seen in the same period in southern England. The Wye Navigation became disused after the opening of railways to Hereford in 1854 and 1855. The Herefordshire & Gloucestershire Canal, which had largely superseded the Wye as the carrier to Hereford after 1845, was leased by two railways in 1862, and closed in 1881. The sale of the Leominster Canal to the Shrewsbury & Hereford Railway was authorized in 1845 in order that its bed could be used for the track: the subsequent efforts of the canal proprietors were given to forcing the railway company to carry out the purchase agreement, even though the canal land had not in fact been used. Lastly, the Severn & Wye tramroads were converted by the owning company to railways, and the Lydney Canal became a railway harbour.

A comparison of the following table with that for the canals of southern England* shows that South Wales and its border differed from southern England in two respects: the near-absence of river navigations other than the Wye, and the much greater concentration of canal building into the period 1790–1800.

Canals and Navigations in South Wales and its border by type of waterway†

Date	*Ship Canal*	*Broad Canal*	*Narrow Canal*	*Tub-boat or Small Canal*	*River Nav.*	*Total*
	miles	miles	miles	miles	miles	miles
1760	—	—	—	—	75¾	75¾
1770	—	—	5	—	75¾	80¾
1780	—	—	5	3⅜	75¾	84⅛
1790	—	—	12	4⅝	75¾	92⅜
1800	1	—	143½	5⅞	74½	224⅞
1810	1	—	145¼	5⅛	74½	225⅞
1820	2	5	172½	4⅛	74½	258⅛
1830	2	5	173⅜	2⅛	74½	257¼
1840	2	5	177	1¾	74½	260¼
1850	2	5	190¼	1¾	74½	273½

* In my *The Canals of Southern England*, p. 22.

† The canals and navigations included are those listed in Appendix I that fall within the range of dates quoted. For classification purposes a ship canal is a canal that admitted sea-going ships; a broad canal one with locks at least 12 ft. wide; a narrow canal one with locks less than 12 ft. wide; and a tub-boat or small canal one taking boats carrying a few tons each. See my *British Canals*, 2nd ed., 1959, pp. 55–6, for a fuller description. In the case of some of the small Welsh canals I have had to conjecture the classification.

CHAPTER II

The Canals West of Swansea

THE Burry River flows westwards into Carmarthen Bay. At its mouth three rivers combine to join it from the north; on the west the Taf to Laugharne and St. Clears, in the centre the Tywi (Towy) to Carmarthen, and on the east the Gwendraeth to Kidwelly. On our left as we enter the river is Kidwelly, then Burry Port, formerly Pembrey New Harbour, and then Llanelly, after which the river becomes the Loughor. We pass Pen-clawdd on our right, and so come to the road and rail bridge that joins Llanelly to Swansea, with Yspitty on the left and the small town of Loughor on the right. Except for one unfinished project in Pembrokeshire, all the canals with which this chapter is concerned reached tidal water between Kidwelly and Pen-clawdd.

Kymer's Canal

Thomas Kymer was a rich man who came from Pembroke,[1] and built small docks at Kidwelly. He also owned anthracite collieries and limestone quarries about 3½ miles away up the valley of the Gwendraeth Fawr. For some years he carried coal and culm on the river, but suffered from delays because the river sometimes changed course, and was navigable only on spring tides. After a survey by Richard Evans, in 1766 he obtained an Act,[2] the first for Wales, to make a canal from Kidwelly quay (there was no river connexion) to Pwllyllygoed near Carway.

Kymer's Canal is said to have been opened in 1769.[3] Thenceforward to the end of the century Kidwelly appears to have grown as a small port and shipbuilding town, though the Gwendraeth River to the quay remained navigable only for small vessels.

(*To continue the history of Kymer's Canal turn to p.* 35.)

General Warde's Canal (Dafen)

Chauncey Townsend was a London businessman who came to the Llanelly area about 1732.[4] He had been thinking of canals for the transport of coal as early as 1752, when he was granted the right to cut canals through lands at Maes-ar-ddafen east of Llanelly to help the transport of coal from his collieries.[5] A short canal was then built from these at Tireinon and Llwynhendy to Dafen pill. The sea at that time ran farther inland, and the shipping place was about 300 yards from the present Llandeilo Junction signal box.[6]

Townsend's grandson, giving evidence in 1810,[7] was probably referring to this canal and not that at Yspitty (see below) when he said:

'I also know that, previous to the year 1770, my grandfather had sunk pits, erected a fire-engine, and had made a Canal for leading Coals down to the water side, near Llanelly. . . .'

Such a canal is shown very roughly on *A Chart of Burry Bar & Harbour, Engraved for the Use of Genl. Warde's Colliery and given gratis to vessels loading at it*, 1808,[8] and it seems to be marked on the Ordnance Survey map of 1830 as a short extension of Dafen pill.

General Warde's Canal (Yspitty)

In 1769 Chauncey Townsend also obtained the right to build a canal through the lands of Heol Fach and Haen Pwll Cefn

'for carrying coal, culm, timber, stone and other goods. . . .'[9]

It is possible that this was not to be a new canal, but the extension of an existing one, for a survey of 1772 of Bynea Farm refers to an 'old Canal'.[10] When he and afterwards his widow died, his son-in-law John Smith of Llansamlet* seems to have taken over the principal share in both this and the Dafen Canal. In a grant to him of lands of 1786,[11] there is reference to an existing

'navigable cut or canal through the common called "Dole Vawr y Bynie", in the hamlet of Berwick . . . for the carrying of coals from a part of the said lands to be shipped at the river Burry. . . .'

As John Smith now proposed to open a new colliery near Dafen Bridge and intended to make a new and more commodious shipping place at Yspitty, he was authorized in this deed by the landowner to enlarge his existing canal and extend it westwards. As finally built, this waterway ran from a creek at Yspitty called

* See Llansamlet Canal, p. 45

Townsend's pill, now beneath the railway line, beside and to the south of the Loughor road. It then swung to the west, and split into two, the right-hand branch to a colliery just north of the railway at Bynea, the left-hand branch to Pencrug by Genwen colliery.

On John Smith's death in 1797, he left his property in both canals to his sons Charles and Henry, who sold their interests in 1801 to Major-General Warde.[12] In 1821 there was a plan to extend the western branch of the Yspitty canal from Pencrug nearly to Trostre,[13] but this came to nothing. The shipping place was improved by the Yspitty company in 1823,[14] and in 1829 the collieries were bought by R. J. Nevill, but by then the canal was probably disused, for it is marked as 'Old Canal' on the Ordnance Survey map of that year. It is, however, shown on maps of 1828, 1830 and 1835.

Hopkin's Canal

A manuscript map of about 1825[15] shows a canal running westwards from Townsend's pill for about ½ mile towards Bryn-Carnafon. This may be the same as that referred to by Richard Cort,[16] writing on the possible establishment of copper works at Yspitty:

'In opening a Quarry to the west of the foot of the little canal, which Mr. Hopkins formerly cut, the beds of the rock lie almost flat. . . .'

This was William Hopkin,* who had earlier worked in this district for the Stepney Estate. Cort was probably not referring to this Hopkin's Canal, but to General Warde's two canals, when he went on:

'There are two canals already cut, which may be easily joined, to deliver the coal from the pits to the copper works, at a very moderate expense.'

Pen-y-fan Canal: Wern Canal

Two hundred years ago Llanelly had a very different coastline, while the River Lliedi had its mouth near Sandy to the west of the town and some way inland till the new cut was made in 1839. There is said[17] to have been a canal at Llanelly built about 1750 by Thomas Bowen from coal-pits at Pen-y-fan to Penrhyn Gwyn,

* Father and son lived at Llangennech, and were of the same name.

Machynys, where coal was shipped; indeed a letter of 12 December 1777 to the Customs Collector at Llanelly complaining that shippers favour 'the Canal, the Spitty, and Davenpill Collieries' may refer to it.*

In 1794 Bowen and Roderick sank the Wern colliery and built the mile-long Wern Canal about 1795.[18] From just below what is now Copperhouse Dock, the canal ran past the copperworks, then crossed the present railway line just west of the station, followed Glanmor Road, crossed Station Road, went up Ann Street, turned right into Robinson Street, and followed it into Wern Road, where it ended by Capel Als. A branch probably left the main line at Robinson Street, and ran past what later became the gasworks to end near Murray Street.
by Bowen and Roderick, together with Charles Nevill of the copperworks, this seemingly being also linked to the Carmarthenshire tramroad (see below). In 1811[20] part of the canal and tramroad lying in Heol-fawr (by Llanelly railway station) was leased to Daniell, Savill & Guest, then of the Llanelly copperworks. By that time, however, the canal was probably disused.

Vauxhall Canal

At spring tides the old channel of the Lliedi, which was diverted to scour the channel of the Carmarthenshire dock, seems to have been navigable up to Vauxhall in the centre of old Llanelly, where there appears to have been a small canal.† There is a reference to it in 1798:[21]

'At Foxhole, they have let the water out of the Canal. . . .'

The passage implies that one purpose of the canal was to supply water to help carry vessels down the river, and it may not therefore have been a navigable canal. The 'Gwter Goch', which Sir John E. Lloyd in his *History of Carmarthenshire* refers to as a canal, I take to be the old course of the Lliedi, disused after 1839.

The Llandeilo and Llandovery Canal projects: The Carmarthenshire Tramroad‡

In 1770[22] William Fenton had presented a petition for a canal from the anthracite mines near Pantyffynnon (Ammanford), to the

* I have not included this canal in the Appendices.
† I have not included this canal in the Appendices.
‡ Known at the time as the Carmarthenshire Railroad.

navigable part of the River Loughor at Pen-coed, where the Lead House stood that served the lead mine at Rhandir-mwyn. No action followed, but early in 1793, at the time of the canal mania, a local property-owner, Mr Campbell, presumably of the Cawdor family, called in Thomas Sheasby and also another helper called Cockshutt to survey a canal from Pen-coed to Llandovery, with a branch from Pontardulais up the valley of the Gwili to Mynydd Mawr, and another from Kidwelly up the Gwendraeth.[23] By November a line from the Loughor to Llandovery through Llandeilo was reported upon by the engineers, but the proposal collapsed after February 1794, and was wound up in 1798.[24]

We shall come back to the Kidwelly and Gwendraeth valley project later as the Kidwelly & Llanelly Canal (see p. 35). The projected branch from Pontardulais to Mynydd Mawr or the Great Mountain was revived in 1801[25] with support from General Warde and others, and then became transformed into the Carmarthenshire tramroad, authorized by an Act of 1802[26] from the Burry River at Llanelly, to collieries and limestone works at Castell-y-garreg near Llandybie on Mynydd Mawr. The line was to be 16 miles long. At Llanelly Roderick and Bowen had built the harbour about 1795: it was improved about 1799 by Alexander Raby and became the Carmarthenshire dock. Seven miles from Llanelly to the collieries and ironworks near Cynheidre were opened in November 1803,[27] and about 13 miles in all[28] of the line were built to near Cwm-y-glo by 1804, and were opened with the dock in the following year.[29] The tramroad was a failure, and the company went into liquidation in 1844.[30] The tramroad company's dock and part of the line were then transferred to the Llanelly Harbour Commissioners, and soon afterwards the tramplates were taken up. The track was later used for the Carmarthenshire (Llanelly & Mynydd Mawr) Railway, opened in 1883.

The revival of proposals for a canal down the Loughor valley was probably connected with the tramroad's lack of success. A canal to Lord Cawdor's lead mines beyond Llandeilo was talked of between 1810 and 1812 as the Grand Towy Canal,[31] and in September 1815 there was a notice for a canal or tramroad from Bollwyn in the parish of Llandybie to Yspitty, with a branch to Copperhouse Dock in Llanelly. Another from Copperhouse Dock to Llanedy seems to have been contemplated in 1817 and 1818 when L. W. Dillwyn bought some property north of Pontardulais which he considered would 'become valuable if the Llaneddy Canal should be made, as I have reason to believe it soon will be'.[32] In 1824, again, Richard Cort[33] suggested a canal 8 miles long with only two locks from the Great Mountain by Llandybie to Llanelly.

Earl of Ashburnham's Canal

We must now move to the Kidwelly and Pembrey area, where the next developments were to be. Here there was the Earl of Ashburnham's Canal beginning at a coal level at Ffrwd near Pembrey, with a short branch built later to another at Coed, and served also by tramroads to other collieries near Pembrey. From these levels it ran straight to the far side of the Kidwelly–Llanelly road, and then turned half-right along a course which took it into what was later called the Swan Pool Drain, to a creek called Pill Towyn on the south side of the estuary of the Gwendraeth Fawr.[34] This canal was being built, or perhaps being extended, in 1796, and was completed past the bulwark and into the marsh of the estuary from 1799 to early 1801 for the shipment of coal, the Coed branch being probably built in 1805.[35] There seems also to have been a short canal from a coal level called Bowser's level, situated above the Llandyry–Ffrwd road, to where Pinged Halt now is, where the coal may have been transferred to road waggons.[36]

Kidwelly & Llanelly Canal

We have seen that a canal from Kidwelly up the Gwendraeth valley was suggested in 1793; it was probably anticipation of the effect of the Carmarthenshire tramroad on the collieries in the valley that led to a revival of the idea of extending the useful Kymer's Canal. The first proposal was to improve Kidwelly harbour, and to build a canal with nine locks up the Gwendraeth Fawr valley to a point below Pontyberem, with tramroads on to Cwm-mawr and the Great Mountain, and a canal branch from Spuddersbridge on Kymer's Canal to Llanelly, with canal branches or tramroads to a number of collieries, including Trimsaran. Lords Ashburnham, Dynevor and Cawdor were among the supporters. A prospectus was issued, and in 1812 an Act[37] obtained 'for the improving of the Harbour at Kidwelly, and for making and maintaining a navigable Canal, or Tramroads, in Kidwelly and Llanelly, and other parishes therein mentioned. . . .'
Mrs Mary Kymer and Mrs Hester Kymer were among the sub-

scribers, and the engineers were Edward Martin and David Davies.

The prospectus dated 5 October 1811,[38] issued after a meeting at Carmarthen in September, did not envisage a canal higher up the Gwendraeth valley than Pontyberem. It was considered that 200 tons of anthracite a day might be shipped at Kidwelly, and 100 tons of coal a day at Llanelly, which compared at that time with a daily shipment of about 300 tons from the Swansea Canal, 470 from the Neath Canal, and 750 tons at Newport. The capital required was put at £33,385 plus £5,000 for improving Kidwelly harbour, to be raised by a tax on shipments, and estimated receipts of £4,266 p.a. against expenses of £700 p.a. It was argued that anthracite, available only from Pembrokeshire, was needed for drying malt and hops, and as culm for limestone burning.

By the time the Act was passed, however, the ideas of the promoters had grown. It authorized the Kidwelly & Llanelly Canal & Tramroad Company *inter alia* to restore Kidwelly harbour and the Gwendraeth River; make a canal or tramroad from Kymer's Canal at Spudder's Bridge to the Old Castle House, Llanelly and a basin there; make a canal or tramroad from the upper end of Kymer's Canal up the Gwendraeth valley to Cwm-y-glo beyond Cwm-mawr; improve Kymer's Canal; and make branch canals or tramroads, including one from Kymer's Canal near the quay towards Kidwelly bridge.

The authorized capital was £60,000, with power to raise £20,000 more. The company with James Pinkerton as engineer, then began to build their canal for 2 miles from Kymer's Canal at Spudder's Bridge to Pen-y-bedd on the way to Pembrey, with a lock at Tŷ-mawr. This line passed the end of Bowser's level* and ended by joining the Earl of Ashburnham's Canal about ½ mile from Ffwrd. It seems that part at any rate of the branch from the quay towards Kidwelly bridge was built. It may be that the portion between the South Wales Railway station and the quay was later used for interchange traffic. By 1818 £22,000 had been subscribed. A new Act[39] increased the authorized tolls, enabled the company to levy harbour duties, and released them from further harbour improvements at Kidwelly. Thus refreshed, they proceeded with the work. The completion date seems to have been June 1824,[40] though from that of 1815 on the aqueduct near Trimsaran I assume that the line to the Earl of Ashburnham's Canal was completed about 1816, when it is likely that

* Green's map of 1833 appears to show a physical connexion, but this may not be the case.

the line of the Earl of Ashburnham's Canal along the Swan Pool Drain went out of use.[41] From this Spudder's Bridge–Pen-y-bedd line a short branch about $\frac{3}{8}$ mile long was built to Moat Farm which was continued to Trimsaran colliery by a tramroad. Lastly, from a point near the top end of Kymer's Canal, the company extended their line up the river valley with two locks to Pontyates (*c.* 2 miles), where it was joined by a colliery tramroad from the north-west. At these points construction stopped for many years, presumably for lack of money.

(*To continue the history of the Kidwelly & Llanelly Canal see below.*)

Pembrey Canal

Pembrey Old Harbour had been built in 1819,[42] and towards the end of 1823 a private canal was begun by Gaunt & Co., lessees from the Earl of Ashburnham. The purpose was to bring iron ore from the Kidwelly & Llanelly Canal 'to the furnaces they intend erecting at Pembrey', and anthracite to be shipped from the harbour.[43] It was 2 miles long with one lock near Pen-y-bedd, and ran to a point about 400 yards from the old harbour, to the pier of which it was connected by a tramroad,[44] which branched from that connecting the harbour with Gaunt's Gwscwm works. It was completed about the end of May 1824.[45] It was superseded about 1837 by the extension of the Kidwelly & Llanelly Canal itself, but remained in existence at any rate till 1843, when the harbour and canal were to be leased to A. W. Hillary for 60 years at £220 p.a., the Earl reserving the right to import lime, manure, agricultural produce, building materials, etc., free, and to export his coal at half the usual tonnage. Hillary was entitled to return the canal to the Earl within one year. Much of the canal was later built over by the South Wales Railway.

Kidwelly & Llanelly Canal (cont.)

In 1825 the Pembrey New Harbour Company was incorporated to build what is now Burry Port, the promoters being closely associated with the canal company. Their Act[46] empowered the New Harbour company to build a short connexion between their harbour and the authorized line of the Kidwelly & Llanelly Canal, but not to take land that had been leased by Lord Ashburnham to Gaunt & Co. This seemed to R. J. Nevill of Llanelly to be tantamount to substituting Pembrey New Harbour for Llanelly in the original Act.[47] He took this up with one of the canal company's supporters, James Brogden, at whose suggestion the Carmarthenshire tramroad proprietors gave notice early in 1825 to complete the line of canal from New Lodge (Plasnewydd, between Burry Port and Llanelly) to Llanelly,[48] upon which Nevill bought three £100 canal shares for £30 each, and opened negotiations with the Pembertons, the main promoters of the Pembrey New Harbour Act, for a lease of New Lodge colliery.[49] He also took over Raby's furnace at Llanelly, while his relation Mr Roberts took a colliery between New Lodge and Stradey, all of which moves would be to his benefit should an extension be built.[50]

Between Burry Port and New Lodge the Kidwelly & Llanelly company had at some time built a tramroad with a branch by Cwm Capel to Cenrhos[51] and in 1826 part of the gap was filled, following up the Carmarthenshire company's notice, by a tramroad from the dock at Llanelly to Pwll colliery, built at a cost of £2,770 by the canal company with money advanced by the Carmarthenshire company against shares.[52] Part of this tramroad near Stradey was washed away by the sea in 1846 and not replaced, though the colliery concern tried to compel the company to rebuild it.

Work began on Burry Port in September 1830, and by April 1832, when it was fully opened,[53] £76,000 had been spent, but nothing had been done on the canal. At this time, we may remember, there existed canal communication between Kidwelly and Pontyates up the valley, and between Kidwelly and Pembrey Old Harbour, together with the two ends of a tramroad from Pembrey New Harbour (Burry Port) to Llanelly. In this year the Kidwelly & Llanelly company called in James Green,[54] the West-country canal engineer, who reported in 1833.[55]

He noted that the canals already made by the company were not in active use, and proposed that:

(*a*) the company's canal should be extended from Pen-y-bedd to Pembrey New Harbour (he ignored the Pembrey Canal, presumably because of the hostility between the Pembertons and their supporters in the canal and New Harbour companies, and William Gaunt of the old harbour, and because of the prohibition in the New Harbour Act against taking land leased to him);

(*b*) the New Lodge tramroad should be joined to that at Pwll, so giving through tramroad communication from the end of the canal at the New Harbour to the Carmarthenshire tramroad and dock at Llanelly;

(*c*) the Gwendraeth valley line should be extended upwards for 5¼ miles to Cwm-mawr bridge, with three inclined planes.*

The old canal committee must have ceased to meet, because on 8 April 1834 there was a request from the clerk, Evan James, to the Commissioners to call a general meeting, which was assembled on 12 May, and probably consisted mainly of the promoters of Burry Port harbour.

Work began on Green's proposals. By August 1835 the old line had been deepened and the new line built onwards from Pen-y-bedd to Burry Port,[56] and by July 1837 the connecting section of tramroad also from the Cenrhos branch to Pwll†[57]. By 1 July 1837 £55,918 had been spent on the new works.[58] The Gwendraeth valley line was carried upwards as Green had recommended. From Pontyates it rose by two locks to Pont-Henry, where there was an inclined plane with a rise of 57 ft.;[59] it then ran level to Capel Ifan, where there was a second incline of 56 ft. rise, then level again to the third incline at Hirwaun-isaf, with a rise of 84 ft. The canal ended in a basin on the far side of the road from the present railway station at Cwm-mawr, and was fed from a reservoir at Cwm-y-glo. The incline at Pont-Henry is shown as double-tracked on the railway deposited plan of 1865, and probably that at Capel Ifan was also. The uppermost incline seems never to have been completed or worked, or the canal above Pontyberem to have been used other than as a water channel. Instead, the owner of the collieries at Pontyberem laid a narrow-gauge tramroad along the towpath and up the incline to Cwm-mawr to carry coal for local sale.[60]

Green's inclined planes in the Westcountry were powered either by waterwheels, counterbalancing, or by using the weight of water in a bucket descending in a well. In these Welsh instances our only evidence is Ap Huw's statement[61] that

'The inclines were manipulated by hydraulic pumps which were considered to be great discoveries.'

* For canal inclined planes in general see my *British Canals*, 3rd ed., 1966; for James Green's Westcountry planes see my *The Canals of Southern England*, 1955.

† Another tramroad along the shore from Burry Port to New Lodge seems also to have been built.

Boats carrying about six tons, in gangs of four, worked over the inclines, and craft carrying 20 tons elsewhere on the canal.[62]

Lastly, the company leased Kymer's Canal from Lord Dynevor, a member of its committee, in 1835—presumably he had collected tolls for its use before then—he agreeing to take a single payment each year from the tolls received by the company proportionate to the length of that canal in relation to that of the whole system.[63] They had already raised its banks in order to give it two feet of additional depth. James Green ceased to be engineer on 30 January 1836 having failed to complete the inclined planes for the estimated cost.[64] This was only three days after he had been dismissed by the Grand Western Canal company in Devon owing to the failure of an inclined plane. A month later he ceased also to be engineer to the Burry Port company, when the failure of the walls caused the harbour to be closed for much of 1836.

From the beginning of the company £74,500 is said to have been spent,[65] but this of course excludes the cost of Kymer's Canal. No dividend was paid till about 1859, from which date 30s. to £2 on each £100 share was distributed.[66] In 1863 there was canal-borne traffic from three collieries, two at Pwllyllygod (Carway) and one at Pontyberem. From the bigger at Carway and from Pontyberem 57,504 tons of coal and culm were exported, all the coal and some of the culm at Burry Port, some of the culm at Kidwelly; it was shipped mostly to Cardiganshire.[67] The coastal tramroad between Burry Port and Llanelly does not seem to have been long in use. Part was washed away by a very high tide and rough seas in February 1846.[68]

Kidwelly had been declining as a port since about 1800. The difficulties of navigating the river remained in spite of efforts to lessen them, and only small craft could come up to the quay to load from the canal. The building of Burry Port and the growth of Llanelly helped Kidwelly's decline. There was a proposal late in 1836, worked out by Alfred Thomas, a surveyor with the canal company, to build a tramroad from the canal at Kidwelly to the entrance of the Towy at Ferryside. Coal would then be loaded into trams at the collieries, run down to the canal, and, still in its trams, loaded on to boats to be carried to Kidwelly, then put on the tramroad to Ferryside, where it would be unloaded into barges to be taken to Carmarthen. A company was formed, but the proposal went no farther.[69]

Anthracite sales were slow from Burry Port till the end of the '50's, when they quickened, and produced complaints from some of the colliery owners about the state of the canal. In 1858, therefore, it was closed for 45 days and completely dredged; it was after this improvement that dividends were first paid.

In 1863 one of the local colliery owners supported a proposed railway from Kidwelly to Pwllyllygod and Pontyberem. It did not materialize, but in the following year the Carmarthenshire (Llanelly & Mynydd Mawr) Railway was promoted to build over the line of the old Carmarthenshire tramroad, with a branch to Pontyberem. This would have diverted half the canal's traffic, and was strongly opposed. The minutes of evidence on the Bill are enlivened by frequent references by railway supporters to two bursts that had earlier in the year taken place on the canal, and

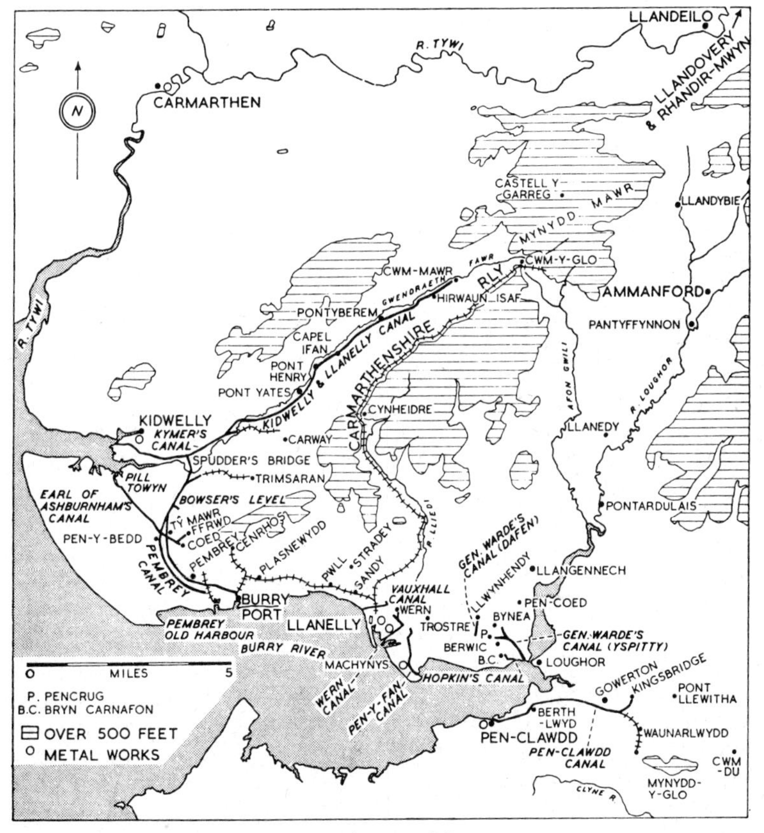

1. The canals west of Swansea

stopped traffic for a time, and scarcely disguised allegations by the canal witness that biped and not quadruped moles had caused the damage.

G. F. P. Sutton, a large canal shareholder, giving evidence against the Bill, said:

'I have no doubt that if we found any necessity for a railway we should adopt one . . . there is no difficulty at all in converting it into a Railway if necessary.'

The success of the Bill made action urgent, and in the following year of 1865 the Kidwelly & Llanelly Canal & Tramroad company became the Kidwelly & Burry Port Railway company, empowered[70]

'. . . to stop up and discontinue the Use of their Canals, and to make a Railway from Burry Port . . . to join the Mountain Branch of the Llanelly Railway in the parish of Llanarthney . . . with Branches'.

Power was also given to buy and convert Kymer's Canal.

In the following year the new company amalgamated with the Burry Port company* to become the Burry Port & Gwendraeth Valley Railway. The terms of the amalgamation provided for £72,400 of the capital of the new company to be allotted to Kidwelly & Llanelly shareholders, and £63,000 to those of the Burry Port company.

The new company built railways from Burry Port to Pontyberem (July 1869) and Cwm-mawr (June 1886), with a branch to Kidwelly (June 1873), mostly over the bed of the canal. Meanwhile the Carmarthenshire (Llanelly & Mynydd Mawr) Railway had been opened in 1883, and the Burry Port & Gwendraeth Valley company built a branch from Burry Port to join it in 1891.

Burry and Loughor Rivers

Before we consider the Pen-clawdd Canal to the east of the river, let us glance at the Burry itself and its continuation the Loughor. Buoys had been laid 'in the entrance to the Bury River, near Llanelly' in 1805.[71] In 1815 an Act[72] was passed to set up Commissioners to 'cleanse, scour, enlarge, and deepen' the Rivers Burry, Loughor and Lliedi, and to provide navigation facilities and pilotage for the export of coal, iron-ore and limestone. A small toll was payable by craft entering the Burry.[73] Various limi-

* The Pembrey New Harbour company had become the Burry Port company in 1835.

tations upon those who could become Commissioners were waived for proprietors of the Carmarthenshire tramroad, Kidwelly & Llanelly Canal, or Pen-clawdd Canal.

Later a company opened a colliery inland from Llangennech on the Carmarthenshire bank of the river above Loughor, and carried the coal by barges towed by a tug to Llanelly for shipment. They found that 'this mode of shipping the coal was attended with unnecessary expense, delay and risk'[74] due to the 'badness of the channel and layer',[75]* and obtained an Act to enable them to build a railway instead and a floating dock. The railway, with an inclined plane, was completed in 1833, and the dock soon afterwards.[76] It is unlikely that there was much navigation above Loughor subsequently.

Pen-clawdd Canal

Before 1800 coal was worked near Pen-clawdd. One means of shipping it appears to have been provided by deepening an existing pill near Berth-lwyd a little above Pen-clawdd.[77] John Vivian had also founded the Pen-clawdd copperworks, and built a small dock. This encouraged schemes for the industrialization of the area, and in 1811, after a survey had been made by Edward Martin and David Davies,[78] an Act[79] was obtained for a canal to run from Pen-clawdd in an easterly direction for 3⅝ miles to a point then called Kingsbridge near the south bank of the Llan River just north of Gowerton and a mile downstream from Pont Llewitha on the Swansea-Loughor road. There were also to be a number of canal or tramroad branches. The authorized capital was £20,000.

A canal dock was built, apparently above the copperworks dock and not below, as seems to have been intended from the deposited plan. This was 642 ft. long by 130 ft. wide.[80] From this point a small canal ran east and then north to Kingsbridge with at least two locks. One tramroad branch was built, from a colliery near Mynydd-y-glo past Waunarlwydd to the canal.

The following notice appeared in the *Cambrian* for 28 May 1814, which indicates that the canal was almost ready:

'Burry River, port of Swansea. To be Sold; Coals, of superior excellence, possessing high bituminous and binding qualities, and durable, calculated for Culinary purposes, Smith's work, etc., and for the Irish and Foreign markets, will be ready for shipping on the 13th day of June next, in the New Dock, at the extremity of

* Meaning, I think, the kind of river bed upon which the craft would have to rest at low tide.

the Penclawdd Canal, from a New Colliery now opened by Lockwood, Morris, and Leyson, at Wain Arglwydd, known by the name of Poor Man's Coal. The Dock is very commodious, having a sufficient depth of water for Vessels of the largest burthen. Great improvements are in progress on the River and Bar, by active Gentlemen appointed Commissioners, by a late Act of Parliament. The Harbour Dues will not exceed One halfpenny per ton. Price of Coal: per Wey—about ten tons—£4. 5s. od. Gratuity to Masters, per wey, 5s. Payable £4. Apply to John Thurston, Ystrad Cottage, at the head of the said Canal.'

No meeting of the company seems to have taken place after 1818. By then the copperworks had closed down, and presumably the colliery also ceased to be worked. In 1825 the canal must still have been in a usable condition, for there was talk by L. W. Dillwyn of building a new tramroad to it.[81] The company seems still to have been in existence in 1840,[82] but by 1861, when the Llanelly Railway & Dock Company (New Lines) Act was obtained, the company had disappeared, and so had memory that the canal had ever been used, for the preamble gave power to enter upon lands taken under the Penclawdd Canal Act 'authorizing the making of certain works which had never been completed or used . . .'. The railway branch to Pen-clawdd was opened in 1867.[83]

Kilgetty Canal

In 1792 the small coalfield in Pembrokeshire exported 60,523 chaldrons of coal. Some of the collieries lay near the sea, but some had their coal carried to the ports by carts. About this date, therefore, Lord Milford began to build a small canal to his colliery at Kilgetty. It is said to have been planned by him, and to have been cut by his own colliers. It does not appear ever to have been finished, and there is no evidence that it was used. The reason was said to be that it was built on too low a level, but this is not convincing.

Study on the ground suggests that the canal started just south of the A 477 road at Stepaside, to which point coal was to be brought by cart or tramroad from the nearby pits. It ran beneath the formation of the later Saundersfoot Railway to Pleasant Valley, and then near the line of the road to the beach. It was probably about a mile long, 10–12 feet wide, without locks, and took small tub-boats.[84]

CHAPTER III

The Canals of the Tawe Valley

THE first canal in the valley was the Llansamlet. The greatest was the Swansea Canal, which ran from that town up the valley, and superseded the little Morris's Canal which had been built near Morriston a few years before. The oldest, I suppose, was at Gwauncaegurwen on the upper Clydach River, where in 1757 a mine was worked by canalized levels, on which boats carried both coal and men.[1] Soon afterwards a similar system was used in England at the mines at Worsley belonging to the Duke of Bridgewater and elsewhere.

Llansamlet (Smith's) Canal

The same Chauncey Townsend who had been active near Llanelly had sunk a pit at Llansamlet near Swansea about 1750. His daughter Elizabeth married John Smith, who succeeded to a one-fifth interest in the colliery, and bought another three-fifths before his death in 1797. This John Smith of Gwernllwynwith, in addition to his canals beyond the Loughor, built one from the colliery down to the Tawe at Foxhole about 1784,[2] replacing an earlier tramroad. The canal began near Gwernllwynwith House, served a number of other collieries along its line, and

'the traffic over it was directed to the wharf at Birchgrove, the spelter works of the Dillwyns, the Middle-bank works of the Grenfells, and Vivian's White Rock works as well as some smaller works en route. It found its terminus just below the present Kilvey church . . .'[3]

and opposite the Swansea Canal wharves. It was three miles long, and must have carried a considerable traffic from Llansamlet colliery alone, which is said to have had an output of 200 to 300 tons a day in 1810.[4]

On John Smith's death the ownership passed jointly to his sons

Charles and Henry Smith, who bought the remaining share in Llansamlet colliery. In 1816[5] it was partly paralleled by a tramroad, 'Scott's Railway', from Scott's colliery beyond Llansamlet to the river above Foxhole. This was also Smith property, like the canal, but both were on ground leased mainly from the Earl of Jersey.

After the sinking of the Charles pit in 1825 the canal was much used to carry coal down to the copperworks,[6] and on 3 April 1833 Charles Henry Smith renewed his lease for another 99 years from the Earl.[7] It was open in October 1844, when Charles Henry Smith made an agreement with the promoters of the Swansea Vale Railway that in certain circumstances:

'No mineral or other produce of the lands of Gwernllanwith . . . shall be conveyed on or over . . . Smith's Canal without the consent of yourselves. . . .'[8]

W. H. Jones, the author of the *History of the Port of Swansea*, thinks it may have remained in use after the opening of the floating harbour in 1852. I myself doubt whether it survived the opening of the Swansea Vale line, which incorporated Scott's Railway, to Graigola collieries in December of that year. A portion of it at Foxhole was, in 1855, bought from the Earl of Jersey[9] and C. H. Smith[10] for the use of the Swansea Vale company's wharves.

Morris's Canal

This canal was probably built about 1790. It was just over one mile long, and ran parallel to the river from coal banks at Landore up to the Fforest Copper Works below Morriston. About 1793 it was described as belonging to Mr Lockwood, Mr Calveley Cotton, Lord Eliot, and Mr Morris.[11]* As Lockwood and Cotton owned the Landore colliery, and Lockwood, Morris & Co. the copperworks, it is probable that the canal was a joint enterprise.

The promoters of the Swansea Canal said that:

'This Canal has been made over a great part of the Manor of Trewyddfa, without the consent of the customary Holders and Homagers, who are entitled to common of pasture thereon, and without the sanction of Parliament.'[12]

The first line proposed for the Swansea Canal incorporated it, but it was 'Insufficient for the purposes of a public Navigation',[13] and an upper line parallel to and a short distance above it was then chosen instead. Finally, it was decided after all to incorporate it in what became the Trewyddfa Canal,[14] built by the Duke of

* John Morris, later Sir John, was the founder of Morriston.

Beaufort and inserted into the line of the Swansea Canal under authority of s. 12 of that company's Act, so that local traffic could continue without payment of tolls to an outside body, while at the same time the duke took a share of those for through consignments.

Swansea and Trewyddfa Canals

Towards the end of the eighteenth century a number of influences were working together to create the necessary conditions for the Swansea Canal:[15] the growth of collieries up the Tawe valley that needed good transport to the river wharves for their coal, much of it for the Westcountry; the possibility of enlarging the Ynysgedwyn ironworks and developing others; the growth of copper smelting that required carriage facilities for the copper ore; the absence of a turnpike road up the valley, a condition that was to remain for another forty years; and the passing in 1791 of an Act to improve Swansea harbour.[16] In 1768, 694 vessels of 30,631 tons register had entered the harbour; in 1793 the figures were 2,028 and 120,822, and colliers were failing to get supplies.[17] At the same time the Tawe valley needed development. The ground was

'little cultivated, owing to the want of Public Roads and Water Carriage. The whole extent of the vale and adjoining country abounds with Limestone, Iron Ore, and Coal, in almost inexhaustible quantities, which have been but little worked (the lower part near Swansea excepted there being but one Iron Furnace and a Tin Work higher up,) but are capable of being brought into full effect by the proposed Canal.'[18]

In 1790 a survey[19] up the valley to Ynysgedwyn above Ystalyfera had been made at the instance of William Padley, a Swansea merchant, by Edward Martin of Morriston, chief mining agent to the Duke of Beaufort, who later became a Swansea harbour trustee and did a number of surveys for Welsh canals,* but it was probably the passing of the Neath Canal Act in 1791, followed by the canal mania of late 1792, that caused a number of Swansea aldermen and burgesses to ask the Corporation to call a public meeting on 5 April 1793. This meeting resolved to start a subscription, to appoint Thomas Sheasby† surveyor, and to ask him to make a survey as far as Devynock.[20]

* Notably the Oystermouth, Pen-clawdd, and Kidwelly & Llanelly.

† He was then a contractor with the elder Dadford on the Glamorganshire Canal, and was building the Neath Canal against time. In addition he took on later in the year a survey of the proposed Llandovery Canal.

Some of the principal figures behind the Neath Canal had existing interests in the Tawe valley: others were obviously interested in its development. Six of the eleven members of the Neath Canal's committee of 1792 were foundation shareholders in the Swansea Canal, holding 69 shares between them, and other Neath shareholders also bought shares in it. Those with common interests included such Neath Canal supporters as Sir Robert Mackworth, the Rev. J. G. Aubrey of Ynysgedwyn, and Alexander Cuthbertson; outside backers like the Wilkinses of Brecon; and the Birmingham interest represented by William Chance, Edward Homer and John Houghton, a solicitor who later became clerk to the Birmingham Canal company. Curiously, some Neath people supported the Swansea Canal first, and soon afterwards appear on the committee of their own: among them are William Gwyn, J. N. Miers, and Rees Williams.

The chief opponents were the Duke of Beaufort and business men such as John Morris who had works in the Landore–Morriston area. The matter of argument was the point at which goods should be trans-shipped from the canal to sea-going craft. The promoters wished the wharves to be low down at the Brewery (behind the present Swansea station), where ships of 600 tons could come.[21] Their opponents wanted the canal to meet the river higher up at Landore, whence vessels even of 200 tons could, it was said, only get on spring tides, but where the duke's lessees had their wharf.[22] Apart from the extra trade to the wharf, a motive was probably to get the first choice of coal for their works: this might otherwise pass them by and be exported.

In September 1793 the Corporation came out strongly for a canal into Swansea itself, and promised to subscribe £1,000 to the right scheme,[23] and when in February 1794 the duke's agent withdrew his own, the duke's, and the Marquess of Worcester's subscriptions, this 'instantly produced a very large additional Subscription, amounting altogether to more than Fifty-two Thousand Pounds, a sum sufficient to defray the expences of the Canal . . .'.[24] The duke's supporters replied that under the Harbour Act of 1791 water should be provided higher up the river, and that 'If the good of the public is intended, let it be a Bill under Commissioners, and not a proprietary one; lower the tolls, and lower the interest to £5 per Cent . . .'.[25]

Swansea won, but the duke was allowed to build his Trewyddfa Canal 1⅜ miles long from Nant Rhydyfiliast to Nant Felin as a section incorporated in the Swansea Canal, and to take tolls so long as they did not exceed those levied by the company. Small craft continued to work up the river to Morriston.[26]

The Act[27] was obtained in May 1794,* authorizing a capital of £60,000 and giving power to raise £30,000 more if required by extra calls, new shares, or mortgages. It empowered the company, or owners of mines or quarries if the company refused, to make tramroads within eight miles of the canal, or canal branches within four.

The proprietors decided not to elect a managing committee, as was usual with canal companies, but to appoint to it all shareholders with at least five shares, a procedure that created a large group with nominal authority, of whom only a few were active. The group included the Portreeve of Swansea, *ex officio* because of the Corporation's £1,000 holding, and from time to time a woman, though no female shareholder dared to attend. The system appears to have worked, for it remained unchanged throughout the canal's life. Again unusually, they decided to build by direct labour. Charles Roberts was appointed engineer for the first nine months, with Thomas Sheasby and later also Sheasby's son to help him; afterwards the elder Sheasby took on alone, though he was at the time involved in a quarrel with the Neath Canal company. Navigation probably began on part of the canal in the third quarter of 1796.

At a meeting on 5 July of that year, it was reported that calls of £60 had been made on each £100 share, on which calls the usual 5 per cent interest had been paid, but that nevertheless there were many defaulters. It was therefore apparently decided to consider as fully paid those shares whose holders had paid all the calls, and to stop interest payments. Shareholders were then asked to pay a voluntary levy of 12½ per cent on them,† and some did. Later, in November 1797, some unissued shares and probably others that had been forfeited were reissued as 'new' shares. Since subscribers apparently paid the full £100 for these, one assumes that the original shares were at that time valued at well above the paid up figure because of the company's prospects. The 12½ per cent levy and the new shares were entitled to 5 per cent interest, but this was paid irregularly for some years, till a loan was raised in 1803 to enable the arrears to be dealt with.

* A side-glance at the way the passing of at any rate one Act was eased is given by an entry in the accounts for 6 September 1794: 'Charges on Act. pd. Frazier to make good his Promise of retaining fee to Editors of Newspaps London £29 8s.'

† These levies were later converted to shares, or repaid in cash.

After forfeitures, 533 shares, including 'new' shares, remained, all of which were considered as fully paid-up for dividend purposes. The total cost of the canal was thus well within the authorized capital of £60,000. On 1 July 1798, when it was almost finished, it had cost £51,601 10s., and was a credit alike to the engineer and the managing committee.

The canal was open to Godre'r-graig in 1796,[28] and fully in October 1798.[29] It was 15⅛ miles long from Swansea to Hen-neuadd (Bridgend),* to which must be added the 1⅜ miles of the Trewyddfa Canal inserted into it. There were 36 locks, taking boats about 69 ft. by 7 ft. 6 in., and loading up to 25 tons. There were no tunnels on the canal, but several aqueducts, the biggest being one of three arches at Ystalyfera.

At the Swansea end an office was opened in the Strand, and wharves were set out, the company ordering:

'That the Wharf or Quay at Swansea be divided into Eight boat lengths each abutting the Canal and River for the purpose of accommodating as farr as the space is capable the General Trade . . . and that the other side of the Canal be divided into similar allotments.'[30]

Here were the beginnings of a very extensive wharf system.

Activity along the banks of the canal began at once. In mid-1799 it was reported that 'Five opulent companies are already formed for working the stone-coal alone, of which 250 tons per day has been brought to Swansea . . .',[31] and a visitor who walked along the towpath from Morriston to Swansea in 1801 found his walk 'pleasant, amusing and instructing; a busy scene the whole way. The pottery, iron, copper, and other works and manufacturers succeeded each other with immense coal wharfs and barges constantly passing up and down through the different locks.'[32]

This activity produced the company's first dividend of 3 per cent declared in 1804, the principal traffic for this year being 54,235 tons of coal and culm.[33] It was also the year of the project for an Oystermouth Canal.

When the Swansea Canal had been completed, there was a movement to extend it to Oystermouth to carry limestone from the Mumbles cliffs and coal from the Clyne valley. At a meeting of the Corporation on 12 August 1803 Edward Martin the

* An earlier 1793 plan shows the canal running higher up the valley to the foot of Cribbarth, but it was later shortened to Hen-neuadd, and two separate tramroads, one with two inclined planes and one with three, built thence to the Cribbarth quarries. The map on p. 55 is, therefore, not quite correct.

engineer, who was a Swansea Canal shareholder and a harbour trustee, explained its advantages. The idea was approved in principle, and Martin was asked to make a survey and estimate, and to consider also the possibility of a tramroad either the whole way or through the town. In March 1804 a Bill for a canal and tramroad was approved by the Corporation.[34]

This extension of the Swansea Canal was opposed mainly on the grounds that it would obstruct the existing unloading facilities and might lead to a new harbour growing up at the Mumbles. However, a sober discussion of its merits in the *Cambrian* soon gave way to fun, when 'Speculator'[35] suggested that old ladies might take to gondolas instead of bath chairs, that poets and authors would find it a lasting theme, and that it would be useful to stock it with fresh fish, while 'H' from Neath parodied a poem which had already been applied to the Salisbury & Southampton Canal,[36] and wrote:

As Swansea's wise sons find the sea is so large,
Though 'Twill carry a ship, 'Twill not carry a barge,
They've wisely determined to cut by its side
A narrow canal, where *small* vessels may glide. . . .

Edward Martin now tried to get the correspondence back to seriousness, and suggested a tramroad as a possible alternative to the whole length of the canal, perhaps using 'Mr Trevithick's very ingenious machine' (see p. 97). The proposed canal remained a joke, and when on 17 March 'Tom Maggott' addressed the Swansea Canal company:

I hope worthy friends
'Twon't clash with your ends,
In the great Navigation concern,
To permit other folks
(Men free of their jokes)
To sport with their money in turn. . . . , etc.

the Editor stepped in and said: 'We wish it to be understood by both parties, that this petty warfare *must* have cease, as we will not insert another line on the subject.'

There was, however, some more correspondence, part serious, part not, followed by a public meeting on 26 March. The Swansea Canal company was not enthusiastic, fearing loss of water, and the meeting reflected a general fear that the trade of Swansea harbour would be affected.

This was the end of the canal project. A tramroad was chosen instead, as far as one can judge because it would serve local purposes without endangering Swansea's trade by encouraging the formation of a new harbour. The Act was passed in June 1804,* and the newspaper in September reported that 'The new Railroad from this town to Oystermouth is already begun . . .'.[37] The Swansea Canal's engineer, now John Royle, had already been instructed to make out 'the allotments and alterations of the Wharfs and communication with the Tramroad required by the Oystermouth Tramroad Act'.[38]

By 1809 the Swansea Canal was in good working order, and remained so, though from time to time the company used to complain of the Trewyddfa Canal's condition, till it became the practice for the Swansea company to maintain the duke's portion and recover the cost. At Swansea the unloading facilities were steadily developed as the trade grew. The end of the canal lay well above the river level. The coal and other cargo was therefore unloaded from the boats on to raised embankments, whence it was transferred into tramroad trucks to be carried a hundred yards to the river wharves, and tipped into the waiting ships. In 1824 the canal first had a competitor when the Tennant Canal was opened to Port Tennant (see p. 78). In 1825, therefore, the river wharves were improved to avoid silting, and between 1826 and 1831 the company made toll reductions.

As in the case of the Neath Canal, control of the company was shared between the freighters and the merchants and professional people of the town, whereas the freighters alone controlled the Glamorganshire, Aberdare and Monmouthshire Canals. This meant that tolls on the Swansea and the Neath tended to be higher, and dividends also, than on those where low tolls were the overriding interest. The canal having been cheaply built, the shareholders did well out of quite modest incomings; indeed, as the canal encouraged the trade of the valley, they began to do really well. Since, however, the canal was closely linked with the fortunes of two dozen works and collieries, its income tended to fluctuate considerably from year to year.

Here are the figures, averaged over three-year periods:

* For the history of the line see Charles E. Lee, *The First Passenger Railway*, 1942.

Years (ending 30 June)	*Average receipts £*	*Average dividend %*
1801–03	2,831	—
1804–06	3,366	4
1807–09	4,780	3⅓
1810–12	6,603	6
1813–15	7,563	10
1816–18	5,942	7⅔
1819–21	7,288	10⅔
1822–24	6,947	10⅓
1825–27	9,755	14⅙
1828–30	9,921	15
1831–33	8,942	12
1834–36	9,002	12
1837–39	10,047	15⅓
1840–42	10,522	14⅙

Unfortunately, no record exists of the tonnages passing on the canal in its heyday, except that in 1810–11 it carried 140,000 tons of coal.[39] If it would be reasonable to assume that three-quarters of the coal and culm shipped at Swansea* came down the canal, then the canal-borne tonnages must have been somewhat as follows:

Years (calendar)	*Average shipments of coal and culm from Swansea*	*Estimated average canal-borne*
1816–18	212,844	159,633
1819–21	208,609	156,457
1822–24	245,109	183,832
1825–27	277,911	208,433
1828–30	..	..
1831–33	..	..
1834–36	..	..
1837–39	514,744	386,058

Of these totals, rather more than half represent anthracite, mostly in the form of culm for lime- or malt-burning.

Short private branch canals had been built to Ynysgedwyn and Ystalyfera ironworks, and to the river at Pontardawe and also above it, opposite Cilybebyll, to communicate with tramroads from collieries on the opposite side. There were also many colliery tramroads serving as feeders to the canal: on the west side the principal lines ran from Cwm-du outside Swansea, and down

* Taken from *Report of Committee on Coal*, 1871, vol. iii.

the Lower Clydach, Twrch, and Giedd valleys; on the east about eight of them crossed the river on tramroad bridges from Ynys-y-mwyn near Clydach up to the head of the canal, while the Brecon Forest tramroad (see p. 59) joined it from near Devynock.[40]

In 1830 a notice was published for a parallel railway or tramroad, and in 1833 Sir John Morris suggested that a waggon road should be made beside the canal for the last five miles, presumably because this section was becoming congested. Pressure is indicated also by a plan discussed by the company in 1840 to make a branch canal from Tircanol down the opposite side of the river to new wharves. However, railway competition stayed away, though in February 1840 the Swansea Vale Railway promoters inserted in the newspaper a notice of a Line from Tŷ-mawr near Ystradgynlais to Swansea harbour.[41]

The canal had served Swansea and its hinterland well. We cannot, of course, correlate too closely the development of the two, but we can note that in 1801 the population of Swansea was 6,831, and in 1841 19,115; in 1801 that of Ystradgynlais parish was 993, and in 1841 2,885. Now for ten years from about 1843 there was continuous depression in the valley, and the canal company felt its effects severely:

Years (ending 30 June)	*Average receipts* £	*Average dividend* %
1843–45	8,975	13⅔
1846–48	10,023	12
1849–51	6,784	8⅔
1852–54	8,177	12⅔ (inc. bonus)

Early in this period there was the first serious proposal for a competing railway. The Swansea Vale Railway had been formed originally to build a local line from Swansea to Graigola and other collieries beyond Llansamlet, but in the railway mania year of 1845 its promoters were considering a line to Abercrave beyond Ystradgynlais.[42] In the same year the Welsh Midland Railway was promoted from near Worcester through Hereford and Brecon to Merthyr, with connexions to South Wales ports, with Joseph Bailey, M.P., the brother of the ironmaster Crawshay Bailey, in the chair.

The Welsh Midland sought to safeguard its route by buying canals along it, and made offers for the Herefordshire & Gloucestershire, the Brecknock & Abergavenny, and the Swansea, all three of whom accepted them. The Swansea proprietors agreed to lease their canal for 99 years from the date of construction of the railway at £4,264 p.a., or £8 per share p.a. on the 533 shares, provided that the Welsh Midland obtained its Act in the following session. They then sought the help of the Welsh Midland promoters and the Duke of Beaufort against the threat from the Swansea Vale; started an economy drive; adopted the new Act empowering them to vary their tolls,* and also announced that 'the Proprietors are prepared to treat with the Traders on the Canal for the reduction of Tolls provided the Traders will come forward and enter into an Agreement with the Canal Company to confine the entire carrying trade of all kinds and descriptions of Goods for a period of years on the Swansea Canal'.[43] They also, in December 1846, reduced tolls: iron castings and bars to 1½d. per ton per mile; pig-iron to 1d.; coal, timber, limestone and most bulk cargoes ¾d., and ironstone and copper-ore imported and carried as back-carriage ½d. per ton. These tolls were the charges made by the canal company for the use of the canal, and were payable quarterly. The carrying was done mainly by boats owned by the various works, and with men employed by them, the cost being additional to the tolls.

* See my *British Canals*, 3rd ed., 1966, p. 203.

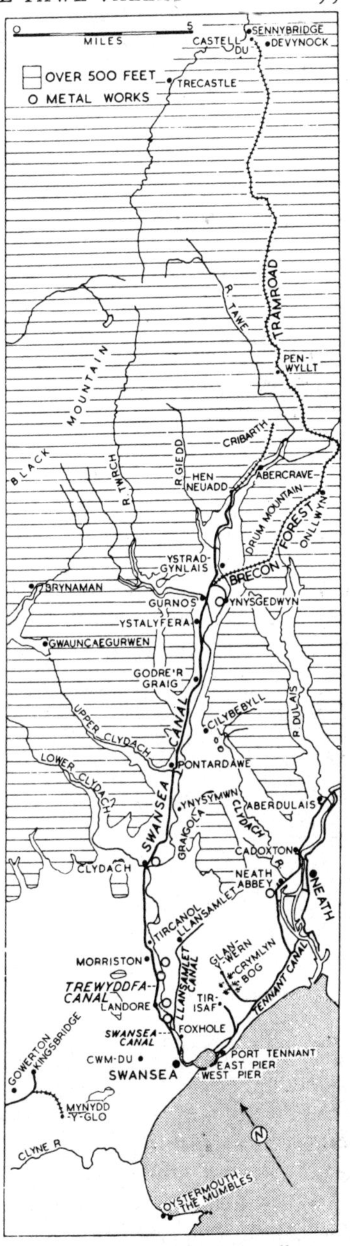

2. The canals of the Tawe valley

Pressure on the Swansea Vale caused that company to agree in 1846 to lease the canal, and then to relinquish the lease to the Welsh Midland when that company got its Act. However, it failed to do so in 1846, and no one thought Parliament would sanction the Swansea Vale arrangement, which was dropped. After brief consideration of the conversion of the canal into a railway, the company entered upon a period that was later to be most prosperous, as it served the considerable expansion of the collieries, tinplate works and ironworks up the valley. As an example of this expansion, the output of the Ystalyfera ironworks rose from 9,893 tons in 1843 to 14,593 in 1847, 23,044 in 1853 and 29,828 tons in 1856.[44] The growth of the valley population also led to the supply of the settlements with their groceries and merchandise by barge, and to women travelling on the barges to do their shopping.[45] In 1849 the tolls were briefly raised, but after protests from the traders they were restored to their previous level. They were again raised in 1853, iron castings and bars to 2d., pig-iron to 1½d., coal and most bulk goods to 1d., and bulk back-carriage to ¾d. Once more the traders protested, and the canal committee recommended the proprietors not to pay more than 10 per cent dividend, but to spend any balance on repairs and improvements to the waterway. In fact, the company accepted the 10 per cent maximum, and at once got round it by paying bonuses. The dividends, which had fallen from 16 per cent in 1846 to 8 per cent in 1852 and 10 per cent in 1853, were supplemented by bonuses of 10 per cent for 1854, 6 per cent for 1855, and 8 per cent for 1856 and 1857, after which the pretence was dropped, and a consolidated 18 per cent was paid for the three following years.

Here are the summarized figures:

Years (ending 30 June)	*Average receipts* £	*Average dividend* %
1855–57	13,271	17⅓ (inc. bonus)
1858–60	13,800	18

In 1852 shipping facilities at Swansea had been much improved when the old tidal wharves were replaced by a floating harbour, the North Dock, a new cut being made for the river. A communicating lock from the canal was built into the half-tide basin above and joining it, to replace the former tidal lock into the river itself. It was probably soon afterwards that the North Dock canal branch was built, making three sides of a square with the main canal as the fourth side. Such a floating harbour in connexion with the canal had been proposed as early as 1830.[46]

Railway competition was now on its way. In December 1852 the Swansea Vale line was opened for 6½ miles from Swansea to Graigola collieries, and in 1856, after opposition from the canal company, who probably hoped to replace the indirect arrangement of 1846 by a direct offer, or at any rate by compensation, got its extension Act. The line was opened to Ystalyfera in 1859 and extended to Ystradgynlais in 1861. Because it ran on the opposite side of the river, it tended to take from the canal the trade that had crossed on tramroad bridges, but for a time to leave that on the canal's side. The canal company during the years 1861–3 considered a railway from Brynaman to the canal to prevent competition there, but nothing was done, and a branch from the Swansea Vale was opened in 1864.

The extension of the Swansea Vale Railway, and soon afterwards the opening of the Dulas Valley Mineral Railway* from Neath to Onllwyn in 1864, brought down the canal company's receipts and dividends:

Years (ending 30 June)	*Average receipts* £	*Average dividend* %
1861–63	8,753	10⅔
1864–66	7,060†	8⅓
1867–69	6,922	8⅔
1870–72	8,526	9⅓

In July 1860 tolls were reduced, iron castings and bars to 1½d., pig-iron, coal and most bulk cargoes to 1d., and iron ore and limestone to ¾d., except for very short hauls.

The writing was on the wall for the canal, and in 1863 the company approached the Neath & Brecon, who were anxious to get an outlet to Swansea for their narrow-gauge traffic that would be uncomplicated by transfer to the broad-gauge lines of the Vale of Neath and South Wales Railways. In November 1864, after the canal company had threatened themselves to build a line up the Swansea valley on or beside the canal,[47] the Neath & Brecon Railway agreed to lease the canal for 999 years at £9,000 p.a., the canal

* The Dulas Valley Mineral Railway, authorized 1862, in 1863 was empowered to change its name to the Neath & Brecon and to extend its line from Onllwyn to Brecon. This extension was opened in 1867.

† Excluding two special payments from the Neath & Brecon Railway of £2,000 in 1864, and £2,200 in 1866.

company having run them up from the original offer of £5,330 p.a.[48] In the same year an independent company in which the Neath & Brecon Railway took an interest (and leased in 1866), the Swansea Vale & Neath & Brecon Junction, got an Act authorizing a junction between the Swansea Vale and the Neath & Brecon, so giving the latter a second possibility of access to Swansea. This line was not opened till 1873, long after the proposed lease of the canal by the Neath & Brecon Railway had fallen through.

In the same year of 1864 the canal company decided to seek powers to build a railway parallel to or near the canal from Swansea through Morriston to Tircanol near Clydach, and to arrange transfer facilities with the Great Western (who had succeeded the South Wales) and other railways. In the end, not enough shareholders would support this move, which was dropped about 1867, at a time when a similar G.W.R. proposal seems to have been under consideration.[49]

The Neath & Brecon paid a deposit of £2,000, and a Bill to authorize the transfer was introduced in 1865 and again in 1866. The latter was withdrawn, however, because the Neath & Brecon would not accept clauses the traders on the canal insisted should go into it, and a further £2,000 was paid to the canal company as compensation.

Meanwhile in 1864, in order to 'revive a long trade on the Canal', meaning to get it back from the railway, the canal tolls on anthracite and culm carried more than 10½ miles had been reduced to a maximum of 8d., and after the Neath & Brecon Bill had been withdrawn a further reduction was made in 1869 to 6d. for coal and culm carried 14½ miles or more, with a reduction also in limestone in 1870.

The fall in receipts in the 1860's had been due not only to railway competition, but also to a falling off in the iron trade before the increasing preference for steel, which severely affected the canal company. In 1859–60, for instance, the receipts from the Ystalyfera ironworks had been £5,321 (38 per cent approximately of the total receipts); in 1867–8 these had fallen to £2,040 (26 per cent approximately of receipts). Indeed, the reduction of tolls showed that there was still a place for the canal in the valley even with full railway competition, and late in the 1860's receipts began to recover.

In 1876 the Ynysgedwyn ironworks closed; in 1886 those at Ystalyfera followed, and the canal then lost its trade in coal upwards from the Primrose colliery at Cilybebyll and iron ore from the docks to the works, as well as the downwards trade in iron.[50]

In April 1871 the canal company appointed a sub-committee to treat with the Great Western Railway or any other railway company for a lease on a return of at least 10 per cent, the shareholders being told that better transport than the present was needed between Clydach, Morriston and Swansea. Agreement was reached with the Great Western Railway in November 1871, and an Act obtained in 1872,[51] by which the railway company paid £107,666 for the Swansea Canal, or £202 per share, and a further £40,000 to the Duke of Beaufort for the Trewyddfa Canal. The sale date was 31 January 1873.

The Great Western Railway's motive in buying the canal was presumably to use it as a means of bringing pressure on the Swansea Vale, following that company's Act of 1866 which authorized the Great Western Railway to lay narrow-gauge on certain lines joining the Swansea Vale Railway, and of 1867 authorizing a junction line from the Swansea Vale Railway to the Great Western Railway.

The Swansea Vale was absorbed by the Midland Railway in 1876, and the Great Western Railway seem then to have worked the canal hard in their rival's territory. Indeed, the receipts for the ten years after railway purchase (1874–83), which include of course the Trewyddfa Canal, were higher at £84,595* than those for the ten last years of independence, £74,329 for 1863–72. The Great Western Railway operated the canal with good success, and profitably to themselves, till the early 1890's. Thereafter traffic was affected by the branches built to valley works and collieries from the Swansea Vale and also by the Great Western Railway's own line opened in 1881 from Swansea to Morriston.

Years	*Average receipts* £	*Years*	*Average receipts* £
1874–76	8,565	1895–97	3,358
1877–79	7,824	1898–1900	4,632
1880–82	8,830 (35 months)	1901–03	4,480
1883–85	8,408	1904–06	3,313
1886–88	6,860	1907–09	2,642
1889–91	7,462	1910–12	2,330
1892–94	6,143		

The canal first showed a working loss in 1895: after that, except

* One month's receipts lacking from this figure.

for 1898–1902, it never showed a profit. As late as 1888 it was passing 385,707 tons of traffic, much of it probably short-haul, and carrying did not entirely cease till 1931.[52] The canal is not now navigable, and is used as a water-channel, except at the extreme top, where it is derelict. By Great Western Railway Acts of 1928 and 1931, and British Transport Commission Acts of 1949 and 1957 the canal below the Llansamlet–Morriston road bridge was abandoned; a short portion at the upper end under a Brecknockshire County Council Act of 1946, a section of nearly two miles between Ynysmeudwy and Ystalyfera by warrant of 14 November 1961, and the remainder of the canal by a British Transport Commission Act of 1962.

Brecon Forest Tramroad

It will be remembered that in 1793 Thomas Sheasby had been told to survey as far as Devynock. In 1805 the canal company[53] ordered their engineer to survey from the head of the canal to Trecastle village to see if communication were possible by tramroad or otherwise. No action followed, but in 1822[54] John Christie of London,[55] who was sheriff of Brecon in 1822[56] and a lessee of mines at Ystradgynlais in 1825,[57] was buying land. He was doing so for a tramroad not connected with the canal, to run from Drum Mountain, about 4 miles from the canal terminus, for 16 miles to Castell Du near Senny Bridge.

In 1828 it was described as having been built 'within a few years at an expense of £40,000'.[58] Its object was the supply of lime to the interior from quarries at Pen-wyllt north of Drum. Limekilns had been built, and coal, timber and stone, as well as lime had been carried. In that year it was offered for sale, Christie having gone bankrupt. The line was then bought by Thomas Arnott and Robert Mercer of London, who leased it with Drum colliery to a group consisting of William Powell, William Watkins and David Jeffreys. In 1834 the line was bought by Joseph Claypon of the Boston (Lincs.) banking family,[59] who renewed the lease for eight years at £600 p.a. and a royalty on coal from Drum colliery. The annual tonnage carried was then about 1,500 tons of lime and limestone, and 2,000 tons of coal, from Pen-wyllt to Castell Du, and it was losing money.[60] About 1832 work began with John Brunton, and later his brother Robert, as engineer on an extension of the tramroad from Drum to the canal which included a considerable inclined plane down the side of Drum Mountain.[61] The purpose of the extension was to enable traffic—coal, timber, slates and seaborne goods—to be carried from the canal into the interior, and limestone to be brought down the tramroad to the Ynysgedwyn works. In a comment in 1833, the *Hereford Journal* considered that with the Hay tramroad, 'a good deal seems to be accomplished towards a straight line of communication between Swansea and Birmingham'.[62] The extension was probably opened in 1834, the junction with the canal being just below Ystradgynlais, at the point where a canal branch runs to Ynysgedwyn.

The tramroad was now 19¼ miles long, with short branches to Pen-wyllt, to the Onllwyn ironworks, and to the Gurnos ironworks. Interchange traffic with the canal first appeared in January 1835, and in that year a fly-boat, the *Brecon Forest*, was put on the canal to run in connexion with the steamer *Mountaineer* from Liverpool, to carry goods for Brecon, Trecastle, Devynock, Llandovery and the interior.[63]

This interchange traffic with the canal seems only to have taken place continuously for two and a half years, from January 1835 to September 1837. Even then the traffic was very small, judging by the tolls paid to the Swansea company, which totalled £46 for 1835, £54 for 1836, and £26 for the first eight months of 1837. Thenceforward takings are minor and occasional, and one can assume that the fly-boat had ceased running. The last toll recorded was for September 1840. There seems, however, to have been some traffic on the tramroad to the Ynysgedwyn, Onllwyn and Gurnos ironworks after that date, though one cannot tell how much, or when it ceased. Claypon died in 1859, and the line was eventually bought from Claypon's trustees, part of the track being used for the Neath & Brecon Railway from Onllwyn to Brecon, which was opened in June 1867.

CHAPTER IV

The Neath Canals

BEFORE 1790 the River Neath was navigable for small vessels to Neath itself, while higher up at Aberdulais there was an artificial cut that passed through the works there. It ran parallel to the river, and was joined to it at each end by a lock. The lower lock is said to have been built by 1700[1] to enable craft of 100 tons to come up-river to the works. The upper lock was probably built between 1740 and 1751, when it was the practice for barges to be loaded at the Ynys-y-gerwyn rolling and tin mills and taken down river and through the upper lock into the Aberdulais works.[2] The locks probably remained in use till the opening of the Neath Canal, for the lower one is referred to in 1791; afterwards Ynys-y-gerwyn bridge connected the works there with the canal, which ran close to those at Aberdulais.[3]

Mackworth's Canal

Between 1695 and 1700* Sir Humphrey Mackworth built a tidal cut about 18–20 ft. wide and 300 yards long from a pill on the River Neath, along which small craft of about 30 tons could navigate to within 400 ft. of the Melyn lead and copper works about a mile below Neath, and soon afterwards added a pair of gates at the entrance, so that the cut could then take craft of up to 100 tons. A tramroad joined the canal and works.[4]

The canal is not shown on a plan of 1720:[5] instead, there is a tramroad to an ore wharf on the river. I assume therefore that by then it was no longer used. A reference of about 1795[6] is presumably to its site, for there is no other evidence that I have seen of its existence after 1720.

* Apparently before 1697, when William Waller said that Mackworth's men may 'bring the oar by water to within a stone's cast of the Work'.

Penrhiwtyn Canal

Lord Vernon built a canal costing about £600 from the end of the pill at Giant's Grave on the Neath River to the Penrhiwtyn furnaces of the Raby company. It was approximately 1⅜ miles long, and was built after 1790[7] and before 1795.[8] About 1795 there was a proposal to join it by a canal ⅞ mile long to Mackworth's Canal at Melyn. However, the extension of the Neath Canal supervened, and in December 1797 the Neath company decided to buy it from Lord Vernon at cost price 'to be added to and made a Part of the intended extension' to Giant's Grave.[9]

Neath Canal

The project for this canal took shape at a meeting on 12 July 1790 at the *Ship & Castle* (now the *Castle Hotel*) at Neath, attended by Lord Vernon and many local people of importance who had been interested in the possibilities of a canal by the passing on 9 June of the Act for the Glamorganshire Canal (see p. 91). The meeting resolved that a canal from Pontneddfechan (Furno-Vaughan) to the town of Neath would be of great public benefit,* that a second canal thence to Giant's Grave 'sufficient to carry ships of burthen will be of equal benefit and utility', and that Thomas Dadford junior be asked to make the survey.[10] This he did, helped by his father and brother John, and a second meeting was held on 13 September. This approved his general line, which seems to have included 22 locks and to have made use of the river for part of its course. The canal was to enter the river at Ynys-bwllog and then use the waterwheel feeder leading to the Ynys-y-gerwyn works. Thence the navigation would pass back to the river, through the Aberdulais cut, and into the river again to Neath.[11] The meeting also instructed the committee to seek an Act incorporating a clause authorizing the construction of tram-roads within 8 miles of the canal, and toll-rates similar to those on the Glamorganshire Canal.†

Dadford's estimate was approved in October[12] at £25,716. Early in 1791, however, Lewis Thomas, Lord Vernon's agent, with two others, after their own survey, proposed a cut on the east side of

* A turnpike road already existed, built under the General Turnpike Act of 1764.

† In fact, the 8-mile clause in the 1791 Act only gave power to owners of mines, etc., to make cuts and tramroads, and not the canal company itself. This was rectified in the 1798 Act.

the river to by-pass the Ynys-y-gerwyn works, and another on the same side past the Aberdulais works, to avoid interference with the works themselves and also with the current needed by the waterwheels.[13] Soon afterwards, it seems to have been decided to avoid the river altogether, though it was then intended to build side-locks into it to give access to the works.

The purpose of the canal was mainly to develop a coal export trade and to bring iron ore down to the Neath Abbey works.[14] The Act of 1791[15] authorized a line from Aber-nant (not to be confused with the Aber-nant near Aberdare) or Glynneath, a little lower down the valley than Pontneddfechan, for about 10½ miles to near Melincrythan pill, Neath, by the Melyn works, and into the river. The canal ran partly on one bank of the river and partly on the other, the crossing being made by a five-arched aqueduct at Ynysbwllog. The authorized capital was £25,000, with £10,000 more if necessary. About 1791 also the River Neath, which was only navigable to the town for small vessels, was improved by the making of the Neath Navigable Cut,[16] apparently with the help of Edward Elton, builder of the Glan-y-wern Canal (see p. 76). Vessels of 200 tons could now come up to Neath, and this may explain why the extension to Giant's Grave was not immediately built.[17]

About £16,000 worth of the capital of £25,000 was Welsh in origin, much of the rest coming from the little group of Birmingham people, William Chance and his associates, who also had glass-works interests at Nailsea in Somerset. Among the shareholders were Sir Herbert and afterwards Sir Robert Humphrey Mackworth; William Kemeys, soon to be a promoter of the Monmouthshire Canal; the ubiquitous Wilkinses of the Brecon bank, the owners of properties up the valley; the elder Dadford; and Neath Corporation, who had a representative on the committee. A curious resolution of the first shareholders' meeting[18] suggested that anyone wishing to sell shares should first offer them to existing shareholders, while the same meeting's appointment of a part-time clerk, at £20 p.a. must be a canal record for economy. It was clearly not a good idea, for Rice Price, who took the job in 1795, was sent to Birmingham to see John Houghton* 'to obtaine such Instructions and Informations about the Duty of the Office of Canal Clerk as are necessary and requisite'.[19] He was to be paid £70 p.a.

* A solicitor who was clerk to the Birmingham Canal company and a shareholder in the Neath.

Thomas Dadford junior was taken on 'as General Surveyor to superintend occasionally the Works' at a daily salary, and began work on the lower section, with Jonathan Gee under him as engineer-contractor. He seems to have built the canal upwards to the Neath side of the proposed Ynysbwllog aqueduct by the middle of 1792, after which his contract to build the Monmouthshire Canal prevented him from doing more. Thomas Sheasby, a fellow-contractor of Dadford's on the Glamorganshire, was then taken on as engineer-contractor. He undertook to build the rest of the canal to Glynneath including the aqueduct by 1 November 1793 for £14,886, of which £2,800 was to be retained at interest for three years after he had handed over the completed canal, as stake money for any work needed.

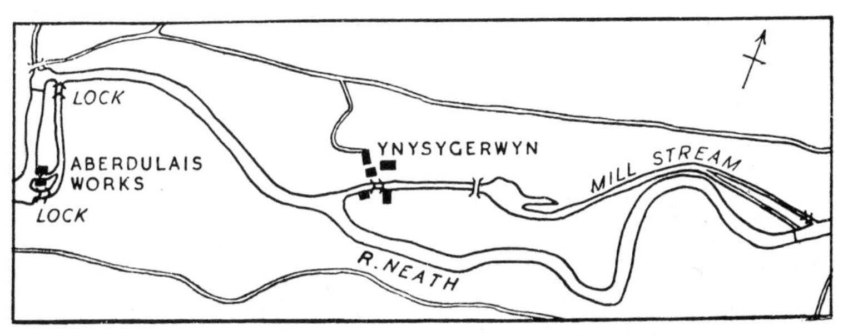

3. Aberdulais in 1791, showing the two river locks

So far, only 191 of the 250 £100 shares had been subscribed, and in July 1793 the remainder were allotted *pro rata* to shareholders, a balance of three being retained by the company itself. Sheasby failed to complete the canal by the agreed time. While arbitration on his accounts was being discussed in 1794 he was arrested at the instance of the Glamorganshire company (see p. 95), and so left the Neath Canal incomplete. The company had therefore to finish off their canal themselves, the lower part being completed about the middle of 1794 (except for the river connexion, which was never made) and the upper part about the end of 1795. For some years after these dates, however, rebuilding of locks and other improvements took place, which is presumably why the preamble to the Act of 1798 refers to the canal as 'nearly completed'. A settlement with Sheasby later on, when he was engineer of the Swansea Canal, and after he had begun an action against the company, gave him a few hundreds for extra work, but not the £2,800 of stake money. The completed canal was 10½ miles long, 30 ft. wide, 4 ft. deep, and had 19 locks, and, as on most other Welsh canals, took boats about 60 ft. by 9 ft., and carrying up to 25 tons.

Towards the end of 1797 the company agreed that powers should be sought for an extension for 2½ miles from the end of the canal just short of Melincrythan pill to Giant's Grave near Briton Ferry, where transhipment to coastal vessels would be easier. Thomas Dadford junior surveyed the line, which included the absorption of the Penrhiwtyn Canal, in September, the authorizing Act was passed in May 1798,[20] Edward Price of Govilon undertook the work, and the extension was completed on 29 July 1799[21] to a termination in a basin on the Neath side of Giant's Grave pill, and close to its mouth. The pill was then scoured out so that vessels could lie there, flood-gates being fitted to the canal to control the scouring. A curious provision of the extension Act was the clause forbidding building at the new end of the canal, lest a rival port to Neath, at that time a town of 2,505 people against Briton Ferry's 188, should grow up.

The Neath Canal was now complete. The main part had been financed by raising £107 10s. from each shareholder; the money for the extension was provided by Lord Vernon, who received £600 for the Penrhiwtyn Canal and a rent-charge of £105 p.a. for his loans. In all, and including payments from revenue, about £40,000 was spent on the canal and its extension, and also on its tramroads, before it was in good working order.[22]

Once the Glamorganshire Canal had been authorized in 1790 from Cardiff to Merthyr Tydfil, and the Neath Canal also in 1791, proposals arose to link them together by a communication that would serve the ironworks and collieries around Aberdare and at Hirwaun. This was to be partly by canal and partly by tramroad, and as there were proposals also at that time for a turnpike road to connect the Neath and Abergavenny turnpikes, meetings of landowners with estates in Glamorgan, Brecknockshire and Monmouthshire were held to invite subscriptions to both.[23] In 1792 John Dadford surveyed a line by canal and tramroad to join the two waterways.[24] The result was the Aberdare Canal Act of 1793 (see p. 118), authorizing a canal from the Glamorganshire to near Aberdare, and a tramroad thence to Aber-nant at the head of the Neath Canal.*

The Act was not, however, implemented, the possibility of a

* The reader may wish here to read the beginning of the account of the Aberdare Canal on p. 118.

branch of the Penydarren tramroad (see p. 96) soon faded, and meanwhile the Aberdare ironworks (John Scale) and the projected Aber-nant works (the Tappendens), as well as Glover's works at Hirwaun, had no convenient transport. It seemed to the Neath company, therefore, that they might take the initiative, and in July 1799 it was 'Ordered that Mr. Jeffreys Wilkins on behalf of the Company be empower'd to offer the Aberdare Compy* the Sum of Five hundred Pounds, to assist them in forming a junction, by a rail way with this Canal, to be paid after the same shall have been compleated.'[25] At the same meeting we may note that Dr Richard Bevan and John Bevan were given permission to make a tramroad from Glynneath to the limestone quarries at Dinas beyond Pontneddfechan, where good fire-clay was also obtainable.

This offer seems to have induced the newly formed Aberdare Iron Company to have a new survey made.[26] The next move came from the Neath company, who at the end of 1800 issued notices for a tramroad from Glynneath to Hirwaun and Llwydcoed collieries near Aberdare. This brought an enquiry from John Scale, and as a result another line was surveyed by Thomas Cartwright and sent to the three firms interested, Aber-nant, Aberdare and Hirwaun, for observations. Meanwhile, the Bevans not having proceeded with the Dinas tramroad, the company asked for tenders to make it themselves. This was enough to make Dr Bevan begin; his tramroad was building early in 1802. Cartwright's plan was for a tramroad that would take in Dr Bevan's, and would run by way of Dinas to Hirwaun and beyond. The canal company proposed to take over from Bevan or to build the first 2 miles, leaving the iron companies to make the rest. Bevan now stopped work on his own account, to await developments.

In May 1802 the Tappendens† of the projected Aber-nant works agreed with the Scales of the Aberdare works that the former should pay the cost, and the Scales should pay tolls for the use of the tramroad. The ironmasters then seem to have suggested an alternative route to the south, over higher ground, which included an inclined plane and a separate tramroad to Dinas. This new line was surveyed by Cartwright and James Birch, one of the Tappendens' partners, and approved. Later the Scales seem to

* The proposed Aberdare Iron company, not the Aberdare Canal company, is I think meant.

† The agreement was made by them outside the terms of their partnership in the Aber-nant Ironworks.

have disagreed with the Tappendens, so that the latter went ahead alone.

As the Tappendens were paying most of the cost, the canal company did not strongly oppose the change of line, though later they were to regret it. Early in 1803 work began, the engineer being Evan Hopkin, and was finished by the beginning of 1805, when the Tappendens were installing the steam-engine, for which they were responsible, at the plane. It began work very ineffectively in March.[27] The tramroad fell just within the 8-mile clause, being 7 miles 1,624 yards long, and cost the Tappendens £17,000 and the canal company £4,350. The latter had built $1\frac{3}{8}$ miles of the total, including the bottom part of the incline, though later the whole incline was transferred to them. It ran from the Canal Head to Pont Walby, where it crossed the river, and then by two inclined planes to the upper part of the Cwm Gwrelych valley, then past Gwrangon-isaf, over the main road, and alongside it to Hirwaun, and on to Llwydcoed and Aber-nant.

The potential trade was good. No action had been taken to build the Aberdare Canal; there were two furnaces at Aber-nant (and one building), two at Aberdare, and one at Hirwaun, where the rolling mills began in October 1805. However, it seemed to the canal company's clerk that the works at Aber-nant and Aberdare 'find Merthyr the best Market for their Iron . . .'.[28] He did not like the arrangement with the Tappendens, and remarked in 1806 that 'in fact we have by confiding so much in these Gentlemen so committed ourselves that we are completely in their Power'.[29] Tappendens had not yet signed a formal agreement with the canal company, calling the latter's original proposals usurious.* The clerk thought 'the whole Business wears a very unpleasant Aspect',[30] but in October 1807 they finally signed an agreement on the original lines, undertaking to pay the canal company 8 per cent p.a. for 42 years on the money spent by it.[31]

Dr Bevan therefore began his own tramroad to Dinas again in 1806, and finished it in 1807.[32] It ran from Dinas to the canal company's line at Pont Walby. His successors still owned it in 1859, but had leased it to Thomas Davis and others, Davis still having it in 1882. In 1860 it was converted from a tramroad to a railway with three rails, giving gauges of 3 ft. 6 in. and 2 ft. 6 in., but still taking trams as well.

* In 1804 Francis Tappenden had borrowed from Wilkins & Co. of Brecon, on the security of the furnace, and most of the money was owing in 1814.([33]) Some of this money may have been for the tramroad.([34])

On the main tramroad the canal company had co-operated with Tappendens, from whom they hoped for the best trade; 'this did not please the other two companies, and this is the Foundation of their Pique'.[35] For a short time, however, all three firms used the tramroad and the Neath Canal, though there were many complaints of the dangerous state of the incline and rope, the small loads that could be passed over it at one time,* and the inefficiency of the steam-engine. Apart from the Tappendens' trade, the Aberdare Iron Company (John Scale) paid £294 in tramroad and canal tolls in 1809,† £391 in 1810, and £266 in 1811; then the payments fell away to £60 in 1812, £31 in 1813, and £8 in 1814. Again, the Hirwaun Iron Company (Bowzer, Overton & Oliver) paid £763 in 1809, £960 in 1810, and £1,156 in 1811, falling to £305 in 1812 and then to nothing.

The reason for the decline was the opening in 1812 of the Aberdare Canal. Scale's and Bowzer's had been talking in 1807 of a tramroad to Merthyr,[36] and early in 1809 it was said that 'the Iron Masters seem intent on making a Tram Road from their Works to the Cardiff Canal'‡ and that 'Mr. Crawshay was willing to advance the Money for the undertaking . . .'.[37] By late in 1809 the Aberdare Canal project had been revived instead of a tramroad, and the Neath Canal's clerk wrote that 'nothing can prevent the traffic from Aberdare leaving our canal but either lower the Tonnage or make a new Road to avoid the Inclined Plane; the Tonnage of Bar Iron on the Glamorganshire Canal has been reduced to 2½d. per ton per Mile while ours is 4d.',[38] though Hirwaun was nearer the sea by the Neath than by the Glamorganshire.

The Neath company wrote mellifluously to the Hirwaun company that 'the Committee are desirous to afford your Company any reasonable accommodation by an Alteration and Improvement of the present Junction Plane',[39] but nothing happened except that the progress of the Aberdare Canal scheme caused a fall of £30 in the estimated real value of Neath shares,[40] and the clerk's private opinion was that 'I think the prospect of the Aberdare Canal is improving in a considerable degree by the proprietors of the Neath Canal declining any alteration in their Tram Road which cannot fail throwing a great Trade to the Aberdare that a good Road would preserve to the Neath Canal.'[41]

* 5½ tons after 1808.
† Years beginning 25 June.
‡ The Glamorganshire.

Early in 1812 the Aberdare Canal had been opened. In 1813 Bowzer's of Hirwaun went out of business. In 1814 Tappendens went bankrupt, and took their guarantee with them. So for practical purposes ended the Neath Canal's connexion with the tramroad, from which only £9 in tolls was received in 1815–16, and £5 in 1817–18. The portion from the Neath Canal to near Rhigos probably went out of use soon afterwards. The Rhigos–Hirwaun section was used until about 1850 to carry coal from Beili Glas near Rhigos village. The remainder of the tramroad between Hirwaun and Aberdare remained in use, and was acquired by the Aberdare Canal company in 1841 from Benjamin Hall, assignee of the Aber-nant works.

Let us now return to the canal itself. In 1798 it was reported that the Foxes of Neath Abbey were getting ironstone from the upper part of the valley by scouring, the usual method of obtaining outcrop ironstone, but one that tended to silt up a feeder to the canal. It was eventually agreed with them in 1807 that a new feeder should be made, but meanwhile the Tappendens had started far worse scouring at Pen-rhiw and Cwm Gwrelych above Glynneath, which caused much silting in the top pounds of the canal. After many protests, the company in 1811 decided to bring an action against Tappendens, which they eventually won, the final excited comment of their Counsel being:

'The important action ag't Mr. Tappenden for scouring . . . has at length been so successfully terminated, and has finally determined the illegality of the measure, notwithstanding the united efforts of the Tappendens and the whole body of iron masters leagued together who were sanguine in their expectations yt Custom would sanction and legalize ye practice. On the success of the Canal Co. upon the Trial of this question depended not only ye well doing but the very existence of ye Canal, as Messrs. Tappendens were enlarging their means of scour'g to such a vast extent (in full confidence of their right) that had the Canal Co. failed in their action the Canal would shortly have been choaked up, the Trade annihilated, and the Canal itself consequently have become of no worth or value.'[42]

As we have seen, the Tappendens then went bankrupt.

The canal had three short branches. One, from near the head of the canal towards Maesmarchog where it joined a tramroad nearly a mile long, to collieries belonging to Capel Leigh of Pontypool, was built about 1800. A second, the Cnel Bach, ran east from a point near Aber-clwyd to the river, where there was a limekiln, and to which coal and iron was brought by tramroad over a wooden bridge from Cwm-gwrach. This branch was built about 1817, and from it, so Phillips tells us,[43] issued in 1824 the ten laden coal barges, under the charge of the veteran bargeman 'Dick Curtis' (Richard Jones, of Ty'r Efail, Rheola) which, accompanied by a brass band, heralded the opening of the Tennant Canal (see p. 78). A third, about 550 yards long from the main line at Court Sart between Giant's Grave and Neath,* gave access to a tramroad running from the Penrose collieries at Eskyn and other early Eaglebush valley pits. It was probably made about 1812, when the Eskyn colliery opened, and gave access for boats crossing the main canal line to loading stages at Court Sart pill, this method of shipment continuing till 1866. All these three branches were made privately, and not by the canal company.

Apart from one dividend in 1799, regular payments did not begin until 1806, though in 1805 the £107 10s. shares had sold for £280.[44] Here are such figures as are available of the dividend and toll record of the canal: they show that the proprietors were fortunate in their cheap construction cost and in a steadily increasing demand for the products they carried.

Years (ending 24 June)	*Average toll receipts* £	*Average dividends (£107 10 0 shares)* £ s. d.
1797–1801	2,117	2 10 0
1802–06	4,015	2 0 0
1807–11	6,541	11 0 0
1812–16	7,043	13 0 0
1817–21	6,570†	21 18 0‡
1822–26	5,904§	16 2 0
1827–31	6,677¶	17 4 0
1832–36		16 0 0
1837–41		18 0 0
1842–46		18 16 0

By 1822, when the canal had reached a steady level of prosperity, its shares were worth about £400 each.[45] As in the case of the

* This branch ran through the site of the locomotive sheds at Court Sart, and almost due east, crossing the main road near Pant-yr-heol church and on to the old road. The pathway between the old and present main roads at this point is the site of the old towing path.

† 1817–20 only.
‡ Including bonus.
§ 1824 and 1825 only.
¶ 1830 and 1831 only.

Swansea Canal, no figures exist for the tonnage carried. In 1811 it was stated that 90,000 tons of coal had been carried the previous year,[46] and it seems likely that by 1820 the canal was carrying about 150,000 tons of coal, which rose later towards 200,000 tons, as well as iron, ironstone and fire-clay. Much of the coal in later years was to originate on the Neath Canal, but then to pass on to the Tennant Canal (see p. 78) for shipment at Swansea or use along its line.

At Giant's Grave there was steady improvement in the wharf accommodation as the trade grew. In 1809 some cottages were built there for the men employed by the canal traders, and in the same year jetties were provided to enable ballast to be taken ashore from ships arriving to load coal. The considerable ballast-banks which can still be seen there are a reminder of a problem that faced all Welsh canals: how to prevent ships' crews from throwing their ballast into the river, as at Newport, or into the canal basin, as at Cardiff.

From 1818 onwards the company supported the formation of a Neath Harbour authority and efforts to get a better harbour, especially after the beginning of work on the Tennant Canal meant that there would soon be an alternative place of shipment at Swansea for the produce of the valley. The river was improved by confining its channel between banks of copper slag and by buoying, so that on spring tides craft of 300 tons and more could reach Neath quays: at neaps they used Giant's Grave.[47]

Tolls on the canal came down sharply. In 1817 iron became 1½d., ironstone and iron ore ½d., and coal other than anthracite and culm ¾d. per ton per mile. Culm was charged 1½d., and formed the main traffic of the canal. Coal and culm tolls were equalized at 1d. in 1830.

In 1836 William Kirkhouse wrote to Charles Tennant: 'I understand they are now talking in earnest about extending the Neath canal to Aberavon . . .'.[48] Kirkhouse, the engineer of the Tennant Canal, had made a plan and survey for such a Port Talbot extension many years before, but no mention of the scheme appears in the canal company's own records.

In 1845 the company noted the growing productivity of the district. There were 'changes taking place by the erection of Iron furnaces for the consumption of anthracite Coal and the Iron Mine* of the district and also the powers which the traders possess for encreasing and disposing of larger quantities of produce'.[49]

* Ore.

Furnaces had been opened at Cwm-gwrach in 1830 and Banwen in 1838, and were to be so at Aber-nant (Glynneath) in 1845 and 1851.[50] In this year of railway promotions the traders on the canal asked for considerable toll reductions in return for a guarantee of the same average receipts, but the company gave only a reduction on iron to 1d. and on ironstone, limestone and building stone to ¼d.

In 1845 the embryo Vale of Neath Railway company approached the canal company through a deputation empowered 'to enter into such an arrangement with them as they in their judgement may deem best for the interests of this Company'.[51] The canal company replied, however, through their clerk 'that the Proprietors did not authorize him to take any steps to bring about an arrangement with this Company'.[52] Therefore except for agreeing with the canal company for a clause in the railway's Act repealing the former's restricting clause upon building at Briton Ferry, the railway company went ahead on its own. It obtained its Act in 1846, and its broad-gauge line was opened in 1851 up the valley and on to Aberdare, with a branch later to Merthyr Tydfil.

The canal remained in a strong position with its existing customers among the collieries and works, for in general it lay on one side of the River Neath and the railway on the other. It was strong enough in 1853 to resist a request for toll reductions put forward on the ground that many collieries had for many years been carried on without profit,[53] and was little affected by the opening of Briton Ferry docks in 1861. In 1875 the clerk could write:[54]

'The Canal has held its own against the Railway for 20 years and upwards and has paid good dividends. It is only the old Collieries that continue to use the Canal, those newly opened all go to the Railway.'

Indeed, dividends kept up very well, as the following figures show, and as late as 1859 shares were changing hands at £170 and as 1873 at £120, or £12 10s. above par.

In the late '70's the older collieries turned over to the railway: the local ironworks had already closed in the '60's. The process began in 1872 when the proprietors of the Ynysarwed colliery began to build a tramroad to the railway over a canal bridge. The canal company then offered facilities for transfer to rail at Court Sart, 'but . . . could not make any reduction in the Tolls'.[55] They fought and won a case to prevent the bridge being used, but were on weaker ground in trying to prevent a new bridge being built,

Years (ending 24 June)	*Average toll receipts*	*Average dividends (£107 10 0 shares)*		
	£	£	s.	d.
1847–51		15	8	0
1852–56		11	6	0
1857–61		17	0	0
1862–66		16	0	0
1867–71		14	12	0
1872–76		7	10	0
1877–81			8	0
1882–86	1,306		nil	
1887–91			8	0
1892–96			14	0

and had in 1876 to agree on payment of 1d. a ton wayleave. Other collieries then followed, notably Aberpergwm and Pwll-faron. In 1878, too late to retain traffic, the toll on anthracite and culm was reduced from 1d. to ¾d., and in 1880 the committee was told by the shareholders to see whether any new traffic could be brought to the canal, or any reduction made in working expenses. Soon afterwards a report was made to the canal company on the possible conversion of the canal to a railway and its extension to Dinas rock, Penderyn, to a junction with a railway from Treherbert, and thence to Cefn Merthyr to join the L.N.W.R., but no action was taken.

By 1883 there was little activity at Giant's Grave, and in the present century there was little more canal traffic than some silica cargoes from Aber-nant and gunpowder from the works at Pontneddfechan. Traffic ceased almost entirely in 1921, though the last toll was taken in November 1934, and the canal is now used only to supply water to works at Neath and Briton Ferry, and as a water channel is well maintained. The tramroad to Pont Walby was extended privately about 1900 for about half a mile to the Dinas silica works. It ceased to be used about 1925.

Giant's Grave & Briton Ferry (Jersey) Canal

Probably about 1815 the Neath Canal was extended privately by Lewis Thomas (Lord Vernon's agent) for 150 yards round the end of Giant's Grave pill to the south side, where a shipping place was built.[56] It was later extended for about 50 yards by the Earl of Jersey, who succeeded to the Vernon Estate, and by 1832 had been further lengthened for about half a mile to the site of the Wern tinplate works, where Rees Williams had a shipping place. Lastly, a further extension took place before 1842, which later enabled the canal to supply coal to the ironworks that were built in 1847.[57]

In 1866[58] the traders complained that the canal 'had gradually become so neglected that it was half filled with mud and allowed such an escape or waste of water as to render it impassable for the navigation of Barges carrying more than half their ordinary load of 24 Tons each'.

I have no evidence to show when boats ceased to navigate the canal. It is now maintained as a source of water.

CHAPTER V

Mr George Tennant's Canals

THE story begins in the Crymlyn bog, that still forbidding part of the area between the estuaries of the Tawe and the Neath Rivers. Mr Rees Jones of Loughor, writing in a copy of Oldisworth's *Swansea Guide*,[1] said:

'Across this bog is . . . an old Canal called by the natives "Clawdd y Saison", or Englishman's Ditch. . . . On clearing the ditch the present adventurers for draining this extensive bog found the skeleton of a boat which had, in all probability, been antiently used for the conveyance of coals to the burrows from the collieries in the neighbourhood, from which circumstance it appears that the exportation of coals was carried on here at an early period, for there is no tradition that this canal had been used for that purpose.'

Glan-y-wern Canal*

Whether the Clawdd y Saeson had ever been a canal or not, one was later built across the bog. In the late 1780's Edward Elton owned Glan-y-wern colliery to the north of it, the coal being 'taken to Swansea River by a tedious and expensive land-carriage and shipped at Foxhole'.[2] Elton decided to build a canal from the colliery for 3½ miles across the Crymlyn bog and eastwards to Trowman's Hole (later called Red Jacket pill) on the Neath River a little above and opposite to Giant's Grave. There was no physical connexion with the river, cargoes being transhipped there from the probably quite small canal boats to river barges lying in the tidal pill.

The land nearly all belonged to Lord Vernon, but with the shipping place it was leased by Edward Elton, who paid the cost of

* Also called the New Chapel Canal, Crymlyn & Red Jacket Canal, Briton or Britton Canal, and Llanywern or Lanywern Canal.

building the canal, which was finished at the beginning of May 1790.[3]

'It was found necessary to take the canal for nearly two miles through the midst of Crymlyn, or Crumlin, bog or morass, the soft spongy ground of which rising up repeatedly after the surface was cut away, seemed to present an insuperable obstacle to the completion of the undertaking. . . . The work may be looked upon as not the least striking instance which this country affords of spirit and perseverance successfully exerted. . . .'[4]

Red Jacket (Neath & Swansea Junction) Canal

'Squire' Edward Elton went bankrupt and died about 1810. Lord Vernon levied a distress on his barges, and on the wharves and coalyards at Trowman's Hole,[5] and it seems that the Glan-y-wern Canal then became disused.

In 1817, however, George Tennant (1765–1832), son of John Tennant, a Lancashire solicitor, who says that he previously knew nothing of canals,[6] took an interest in it. Tennant, who had bought the Rhydings estate in 1816 and later the Cadoxton Lodge estate near Neath, proposed to lease it, clean, widen and deepen it to take river barges of 30–35 tons, and to build a river lock at Red Jacket. He proposed also to build a canal from it to communicate by a river lock with the Tawe just inside the East Pier of the improved Swansea harbour, so joining the Neath and Tawe Rivers and giving the collieries and works of the Neath valley and estuary a better shipping place in Swansea harbour than they had at Neath or Giant's Grave, and encouraging the development of the land between the two rivers.

Tennant approached the big local landowners, but got no financial support; he therefore decided to go ahead on his own. He leased the Glan-y-wern Canal from the Earl of Jersey (who had inherited Lord Vernon's estates in 1814) on payment of toll from the beginning of 1818. With William Kirkhouse[7] as his engineer, he began work late in 1817, and by the autumn of 1818 the new canal was finished to a larger scale than he had formerly intended. It was now 4 miles long from the Neath to the Tawe, with a branch $1\frac{3}{8}$ miles long to Glan-y-wern. Barges of 50 or 60 tons dropping down the River Neath could enter the canal through the river-lock at Red Jacket, and work to Swansea harbour. Coal was available from Glan-y-wern, and timber, bark, fire-bricks and sand passed through, but more coal, lime and iron traffic was needed to give him a return on his capital.

It was necessary that he should connect his waterway with the Neath Canal. He proposed at first to make a lock near Giant's Grave or Court Sart pill to enable craft to lock out of the Neath Canal, cross the river, and enter his waterway at Red Jacket. The Neath company agreed in July 1820 that he could make such a lock at his own expense, and be reimbursed the cost from free carriage on their canal of goods destined for his.[8] By now, however, he had had a bigger and better idea, for what is usually called the Tennant Canal.

Tennant (Neath & Swansea Junction) Canal

It was obvious that to work barges across a tidal river from one river-lock to another was not a satisfactory solution of George Tennant's problem. In addition, he was early in 1820 considering the construction of a tramroad from the Vale of Neath to the source of the Dulais River in order to develop the collieries in the valley, and seems also to have had in mind a branch from this to the Red Jacket Canal. Again, before he bought the Rhydings estate, there had been a water level from the collieries on the Neath Abbey estate past the Rhydings, which provided power for working the mines and then emptied itself into the River Neath.[9] This level Tennant may have turned into a canal, with an inclined plane near Cadoxton to bring the coal down to a shipping place in the river.* He had therefore two possible supplies of coal, and he himself tells us that he was also pressed to provide transport to Swansea by two owners of collieries in the Neath valley.

During 1820, therefore, he decided to extend his canal from the existing line near Red Jacket to run beside the river and past the Neath Abbey ironworks and Neath itself to join the Neath Canal at Aberdulais 'where I had title to an abundant supply of water',[10] and in 1821 began work without an Act.† He had hoped that the

* This canal, and also an inclined plane, 'to connect Redding Canal with the River' is shown on T. Horner's *Plan of the Neath and Swansea Junction Canal*, 1818.([11]) I have not included it in the Appendices.

† Canal building without an Act was rare, because compulsory powers to buy land were usually necessary. The Tennant Canal is the most important example of such a canal: others were the Torrington Canal in Devon, and the Hatherton branch of the Staffordshire & Worcestershire.

big landowners of the neighbourhood, the Duke of Beaufort, Lord Jersey and Lord Dynevor, would take shares, but no money was offered by them, and he began on his own, agreeing in the case of the Duke of Beaufort to pay tolls for passing through his land.

His engineer was again William Kirkhouse. Work began at the Red Jacket end, where the main engineering problem was a deep cutting about 500 yards long near Neath Abbey,* with a maximum

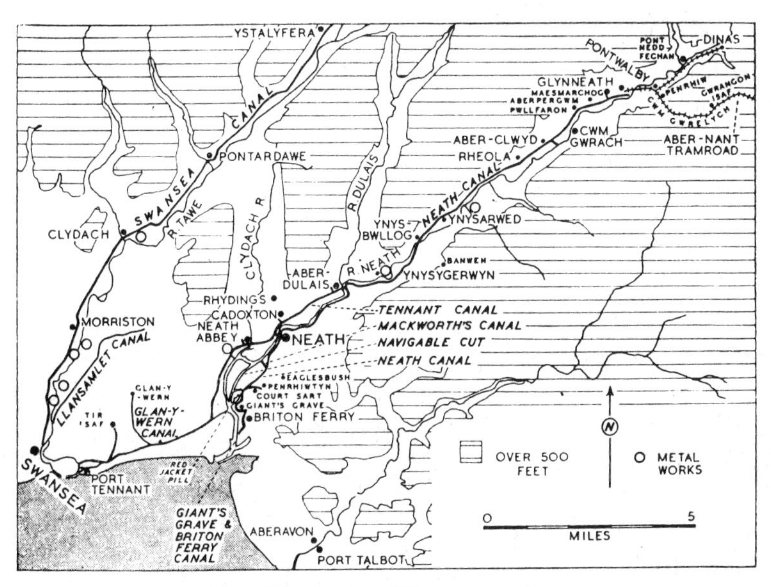

4. The Neath and Tennant canals

depth of 30 ft. This cutting was through a quicksand 'of the finest grain and most subtle nature—and so deep that no tool which could be introduced was long enough to reach the bottom',[12] and the canal had to be held inside an inverted masonry arch. Such was Tennant's enthusiasm that he had begun cutting before he had obtained all his land, or had made an agreement with the Neath Canal company for a junction at Aberdulais, and so he gave hostages to fortune. When in April 1821 construction reached the short tunnel under the Swansea road at Neath, it was held up by the refusal of L. W. Dillwyn to allow permission to cut through

* The Neath Abbey works had at that time a tramroad to the river at Neath.

some land near Cadoxton. Dillwyn was trustee for his son of the estate to which the land belonged, and also a Neath Canal shareholder and committeeman. Tennant had earlier had oral and somewhat vague assurances of his goodwill, but later Dillwyn cooled off, and on 13 December 1821 finally refused to part with the land which was essential to Tennant's purpose. On 26 February 1822 the Lord Chancellor granted Dillwyn an injunction against Tennant, and thenceforward that irritated man sent a stream of visitors to Dillwyn to try to get him to change his mind, among them Lord Jersey and William Crawshay the ironmaster.

They failed, and in August 1822 Tennant noted: '. . . the Traitor must be left to triumph in his Treachery . . .'. One sympathizes also when one reads among the rules he wrote down at the time for his government:

'Avoid all conversation about this man and . . . never mention his name. Be as careful as possible to avoid dispute or controversy with anyone—express no Irritation at any opposition (however unreasonable it may appear) and Time will soften down many asperities in those who fancy their Interests may be affected by my Canal.'[13]

In the autumn of 1822 Tennant, now in a difficult position, put forward to the Neath Canal company proposals for a junction with their canal at Aberdulais so favourable to them and unfavourable to himself that they were accepted without alteration: they included a promise to transfer traffic only at the junction; to charge the same tolls as the Neath company for traders on both canals; and to take water from the Neath Canal only when its own navigation would not be affected.[14] This agreement made, he wrote a conciliatory letter to Dillwyn, who grudgingly was brought to negotiate with 'that terrible plague Mr. Tennant',[15] and in the following year he received from Tennant £3,307 for eight of his Neath Canal shares, the market price of which was £2,400.

The canal was then quickly extended. In May 1823 the 340 ft. long aqueduct across the River Neath on its ten-arched masonry frame was begun, with the only lock on the main line immediately below it, and the junction with the Neath Canal fifty yards above. The length of the whole canal from Swansea was 8½ miles, or 4⅞ miles from the junction with the Red Jacket line.

Apart from Dillwyn, there had been some opposition from the owners of collieries on the Swansea Canal to the prospect of increased competition there. Tennant, with his offer of shipping facilities at Swansea, also accelerated the movement for the improvement of Neath harbour. Elijah Waring, writing to Tennant in March 1824, said:

'Have you heard of the bold push for an improved harbour at Neath? I hear that large subscriptions are made, and making. . . . I find your pamphlet* has annoyed certain persons interested in this harbour not a little . . . you will be most happy . . . at having been the means of calling into exercise the latent talent of the neighbourhood. I am glad, however, to see a little spirit of improvement springing up amongst them, and shd be really sorry to see Neath river quite choked at the entrance as it now promises to be—I know one feeling prevails amongst the Captains trading hither, and that is a strong preference for Swansea when they can make their freights thither.'[16]

George Tennant had built his canal. Here is part of the account of the opening ceremony on 13 May 1824 from the *Cambrian* of the following day:

'We yesterday witnessed with much satisfaction, in which we were heartily joined by some thousands of spectators, the opening of Mr. Tennant's Junction Canal. Ten barges fully laden with coal, accompanied by a brass band, were safely conveyed from the colliery of Mr. Protheroe, in the Vale of Neath, and delivered in the shipping place in our harbour. The health of "George Tennant Esq., and may his Canal return him a large interest for all the capital expended upon it", was drunk with great enthusiasm.'

The opening was also celebrated by a nineteen-verse poem written by Elizabeth Davies, the lollipop-shop keeper of Wind Street, Neath, which was printed by Filmer Fagg at Swansea.†

The construction cost of the whole canal to Swansea, including the Red Jacket Canal, but excluding the cost of land and of the harbour at Port Tennant, seems to have been about £20,000, on top of which George Tennant had saddled himself with costly toll payments to landowners on the cargoes he carried. His son Charles Tennant stated in 1862 that his father had altogether spent £150,000 on his various canal works and on Port Tennant:[17] this figure presumably includes land and maintenance as well as later capital expenditure. He seems never to have had an exaggerated idea of the returns he might get from his canal, and wrote disarmingly:

'. . . his expectations (however vain) have at least had the merit of

* George Tennant: *Neath and Swansea Red Jacket & Neath Canals. Narrative of some Particulars relating to their formation*, etc., 1824.

† Two verses are quoted in my *British Canals*, 3rd ed., 1966, p. 49.

cheering him for six whole years whilst meeting the pay-day of his workmen at the end of every recurring fortnight—conscious that he was injuring no man by the expenditure of his own capital; seeing some prospect of a reasonable return for it, even in his time —and perhaps now and then indulging a secret vanity that his name might hereafter be remembered in Glamorganshire as one who had caused a scratch to be made upon its future map . . .'[18]

He had seen clearly that the improved Swansea harbour would attract traffic from Neath and Giant's Grave, in spite of the greater distance from the valley, and supported his insight by building the longest private canal in Britain after the Duke of Bridgewater's. He died in 1832.

When Swansea harbour had been improved by the building of the East and West Piers by 1809,[19] land inside the East Pier had been let to speculators who built 600 yards of wharves, but did not succeed in their enterprise, and the wharves remained unlet. When Tennant began to build the Tennant Canal, his mind ran beyond the river lock and tidal dock he had already built on the Tawe. His idea was to take over the disused wharf land: 'If this were fenced off with a good Wall with cranes and other accommodation for shipping it would command the Trade of ye Port—call it the "Junction Canal Bazaar" for the deposit and sale of all goods borne on my Canal. . . .'[20] By 1823 he was planning a wet-

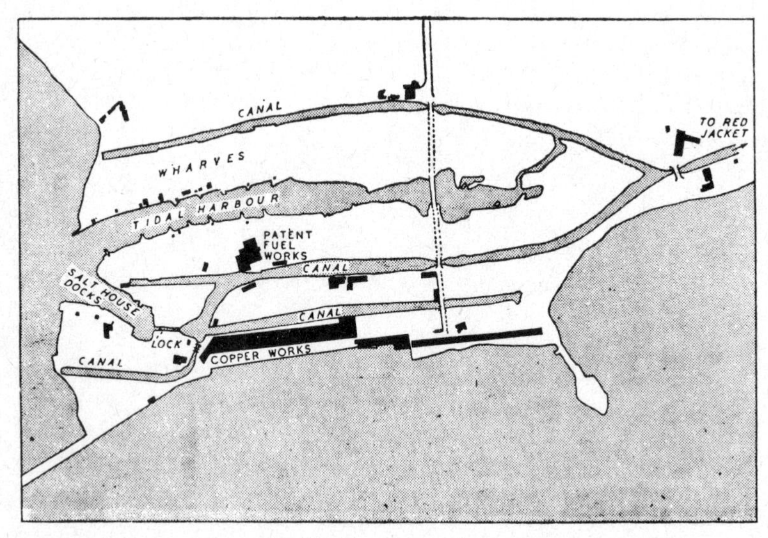

5. Port Tennant in 1853

dock, but this was beyond his resources, and Port Tennant remained a tidal dock enclosed between two arms of the canal, lying inside the East Pier, and approached along a buoyed and dredged channel. The depth of water was about 30 ft. at high tide.[21]

Thirty years later, Abernethy's plan of 1853 shows Port Tennant as before, except that the southern canal arm now forks again, the southernmost branch leading to a termination immediately within the Eastern Pier. On this arm was a branch to the 22 ft. deep river lock, and backwards from this lock branch ran a private canal into Charles Lambert's copper works.[22]

Because he had not been able to build his wet-dock, Tennant's port could only take small craft able to lie on the mud. Here are figures that are available:

Years	*Average number of ships per annum*	*Average registered tonnage per annum*	*Average tonnage per ship*
4 yrs. 1833–36	699	51,971	74⅓
4 yrs. 1837–40	646	46,206	71½
5 yrs. 1841–45	809	56,328	69⅝

In 1853 a plan was drawn up on behalf of Swansea interests for a wet-dock on part of the site of Port Tennant, to be connected with, and supplied with water by, the canal, but it came to nothing. In 1852 the North Dock and in 1859 the South Dock were opened higher up the river. Before long, however, it became clear to the Swansea Harbour Trust that a bigger wet-dock lower down the river was needed, and in 1879 work began on the East, or Prince of Wales's, Dock on the site of the northern arm of the canal at Port Tennant. It was completed in 1881, with access from the canal.

As the following figures show, Port Tennant still catered only for very small coasting ships, and was feeling the competition of the improved Swansea docks.

Years	*Average number of ships per annum*	*Average registered tonnage per annum*	*Average tonnage per ship*
4 yrs. 1863–66	619	47,936	77⅖
4 yrs. 1867–70	494	36,866	74⅗
4 yrs. 1871–74	290	19,712	68
2 yrs. 1875–76	85	6,438	75¾

In the present century the still bigger King's (opened 1909) and Queen's (opened 1920) docks were built on the foreshore and covered the rest of the original Port Tennant. The canal now ran alongside a portion of the north wharf of the King's Dock.[23] George Tennant had been correct in his vision of the future of Swansea. In a paper dated 1 January 1824[24] Tennant had written:

'Swansea is at an angle formed by two arms of inland navigation, extending through more than 40 miles of a populous country, rich almost beyond example, in coal, iron, and minerals of various kinds, as well as in agricultural produce. . . . Let any man, with the map of Great Britain in his hand, say, whether the expectations now expressed be visionary or not; soon or late these things will be accomplished, and why should they be left wholly for a future generation, when the present has the power of accomplishing so much?'

The things of which he spoke, and more, have been accomplished.

Before we return to the history of the canal itself, we must glance at another of Tennant's projects, for a tramroad from the coal-bearing areas in the Dulais valley down to his canal. We have seen that he had this in mind as early as 1820. It was revived in 1825, and after many negotiations Dillwyn agreed on a clause to be inserted in the Bill which compelled a junction with the Neath Canal, whereupon he withdrew his opposition. However, he had 'Reason to fear Mr. Tennant will endeavour to force on the Dylais Tram Road Bill without the clause he had assented to',[25] and when he got to London he was 'astonished to find that Lord Jersey, who is deeply interested, had mustered his friends in the House of Lords and succeeded in pushing the bill by surprise through the House in 5 days, without the clause . . .'.[26] Tennant had got his own back on Dillwyn. This was the Act of 1826.[27] The tramroad was not, however, built. A notice was given in 1841 by two proprietors of collieries on Drum Common for a railway down the Dulais valley to the Neath Canal,[28] which went no farther. In 1862, when the Dulas Valley Mineral Railway (later the Neath & Brecon) was being projected, Charles Tennant opposed it till agreement was reached on a siding to the Tennant Canal.[29]

In 1824, the Neath Canal proprietors heard a rumour that Tennant proposed to continue his canal up the Neath valley by means of a tramroad. They were calmed when told that he had 'publicly declared that no pecuniary consideration will ever induce him to concur in any Scheme which shall have the effect of injuring the Neath Canal by any private Tram Road running for any considerable length of their Line and paralel with their Canal . . .'.[30] No more was heard of it, and in the early '30's the Tennant family became, and remained for some time, modest shareholders in the Neath Canal.

In May 1823, before his canal was fully opened, George Tennant had estimated that he would carry 99,994 tons a year, and earn £7,915 gross. His estimate of tonnage was very accurate, but not of revenue, for he found that he had to carry more cheaply than he had reckoned in order to get the traffic. After a slow start, when the canal carried 37,536 tons in 1827 (revenue £1,372), some 60,000 tons in 1828 (revenue about £2,500), and 70,122 tons in 1830, it reached these average figures:

Years	*Average tons carried*	*Average receipts*	*Average tolls received*	*Average expenditure*
3 yrs. 1831–33	89,432	4,066	3,589	1,595
3 yrs. 1834–36	88,020	4,168	3,376	1,775
3 yrs. 1837–39	91,344	3,393	3,270	955

The picture is one of stability at the 90,000 tons mark, with a slight downward tendency on tolls, and a profit of about £2,500 a year, less the considerable toll payments to the Duke of Beaufort and the Earl of Jersey. The figures of coal and other exports from Port Tennant were for a time much less: George Tennant told Lord Jersey early in 1830 that since the canal had opened the average exports had been 25,733 tons p.a., and commented that a new trade could be only slowly built up.[31]

The canal was in its early years called the Neath & Swansea Junction, but certainly by 1845 it was commonly known by the Tennant name. It was 33 ft. wide at surface, 5 ft. deep on the Red Jacket–Aberdulais section, and 7 ft. on the line from Red Jacket to Swansea harbour, the extra depth providing a reservoir of water to scour out Port Tennant. There was one lock at Aberdulais on the main line, and several, all except one to the river, on the branches. The boats used were the same as those on the Neath Canal, and carried about 25 tons. A peculiarity of the canal was that horse towing services were provided by the canal owner, if required, on payment.*

By the early 1840's some short branches had been built; the

* The only other case I know of was the Regent's Canal, where towing by the company's horses was compulsory for many years after 1847, and later voluntary.

Dulais branch and lock to a quarry in 1840; the Vale of Neath brewery branch at Cadoxton in 1839 at the brewery's expense; a short branch and 18 ft. lock just below Neath into the river, finished in 1828; and a branch into the Neath Abbey works, built by J. T. Price of the works about 1828. In 1839 the Glan-y-wern Canal, which seems for some time to have been little used, was cleaned and re-opened.

The traffic on the Tennant canals in the 1820's and 1830's was predominantly in coal and culm, but also timber, iron ore and sand, mainly off the Neath Canal or from the collieries in the Clydach valley to the Abbey and other works, and for shipment at Port Tennant. There was also some downwards traffic in slag from the works, stone from Red Jacket, and merchandise from Neath. Later, copper ore came inwards to the Lambert works at Port Tennant and to the Crown and Cape copperworks. Upwards there was a small traffic in limestone from Port Tennant to the works, and in oats, malt, flour, timber and miscellaneous goods to Neath; in bricks and stone from Red Jacket to Neath, and in timber from the south end of the Glan-y-wern Canal.

In 1827 a regular packet-boat service for passengers began between Neath and Port Tennant and back, leaving Neath at 9 a.m. and Swansea at 3 p.m., for which Tennant charged the boat owners 3s. a trip with a minimum monthly payment. These boats also carried parcels, shop goods, corn and flour. In 1830 a newspaper advertisement appeared inviting suggestions from 'Engineers and Mechanics conversant with recent improvements in Steam Navigation' for steam packet boats carrying 40–50 passengers and making four trips a day, as a prelude to steam cargo carrying.[32] As there were no locks below Aberdulais, the use of steamboats would have been practicable, but no action followed. The passenger service was still running in 1850, but had stopped by 1857.

In the '40's and '50's the tonnage carried on the canal increased steadily, to a maximum of 225,304 in 1866. An important factor to be added to the general increase of the trade of the Neath valley was the establishment of Charles Lambert & Co.'s copperworks at Port Tennant in the early '50's. The imported Chilean copper ore was smelted with canal-borne coal brought partly from Glan-y-wern and later from Tir-isaf (see p. 87). This traffic gave the Tennant Canal a steady revenue till 1895. In the '60's a patent fuel works was also established at Port Tennant.

Competition with the canal came slowly and in stages. The Tennant family's experiences with the Vale of Neath Railway were unhappy. While the Act was being sought, and afterwards, Charles Tennant on behalf of his mother tried to get compensation for injury to the canal's prospects, but failed.[33] Then in 1851, the year it was opened from Neath to Aberdare, Henry Tennant suggested to the company, which at that time had no outlet to Swansea for coal exports, that it should make use of Port Tennant,[34] by transferring traffic from rail to canal at Aberdulais. Brunel, the railway's engineer, was in favour, but was probably too busy to see Tennant as he had been instructed. By June 1852, however, a branch from the South Wales Railway with which the Vale of Neath had been connected in 1851, provided rail connexion to Swansea Docks, and thenceforward to 1857 Tennant's persistent approaches were only lukewarmly received. The proposal then slept, and in 1861 the railway got another outlet for its coal when the Briton Ferry docks were opened.

In 1861, also, the Swansea & Neath Railway was authorized to extend the Vale of Neath line from Neath to Swansea almost parallel to the canal. This line was opened in 1863, in which year the company amalgamated with the Vale of Neath who had in 1862 leased the harbour railway of the Swansea harbour trustees, and so got access to Swansea docks. Lastly, in 1894 the Rhondda & Swansea Bay Railway was opened across the Neath River and then parallel to the canal and the Vale of Neath Railway to Swansea. Since this line carried Rhondda coal, it probably had little effect on the canal.

Figures are available to show the effect of the worst of the competition on the tonnage carried and the average rate per ton. The former falls steadily after 1866, but the latter does not. This is very unusual, and appears to show that what traffic the canal retained was not available to a competitor, so enabling tolls to be maintained.

Years	*Average tonnage*	*Average receipts*	*Average receipts per ton*
3 yrs. 1863–65	179,844	5,946	7·9d.
3 yrs. 1866–68	206,338	6,342	7·4d.
3 yrs. 1869–71	145,473	4,429	7·3d.
3 yrs. 1872–74	131,819	4,187	7·6d.
2 yrs. 1875–76	110,193	3,567	7·8d.

Two branches were built during the second half of the century. One, the Tir-isaf Canal, 1 mile long from near Port Tennant northwards to Tir-isaf colliery, was seemingly built by the Earl of Jersey, but leased to the Tennants. It was probably opened about 1863, its main function being to carry coal from Lambert's colliery to his copperworks at Port Tennant. The second was a branch from the canal to the river, with a river lock, between Quakers' Bridge and Neath Abbey above the Crown copperworks. It was probably built about 1879, after which the connection between canal and river opposite Neath was closed.

It seems likely that the lock at Red Jacket was little used after the main canal was opened. In 1832 it was out of use, and Kirkhouse reported that 'Mr. T. had a notion of doing away with the Lock entirely & if there was any traffick likely to come that way to have a Capstan with a carriage to take a Barge on it from the River to the Branch Canal . . .'.[35] It seems later to have been used again, then to have gone out of use round about the '80's,* perhaps when the branch by the Crown copperworks was built, and then to have been rebuilt by 1898, perhaps to encourage trade through to the East Dock.

The whole canal had ceased to carry commercial traffic by about 1934 and the Glan-y-wern and Tir-isaf Canals were reported derelict in 1918.[36] Still owned by a Tennant, it is now used only to supply water to works beside its course.

* It is not marked on the first edition of the 25 in. plan.

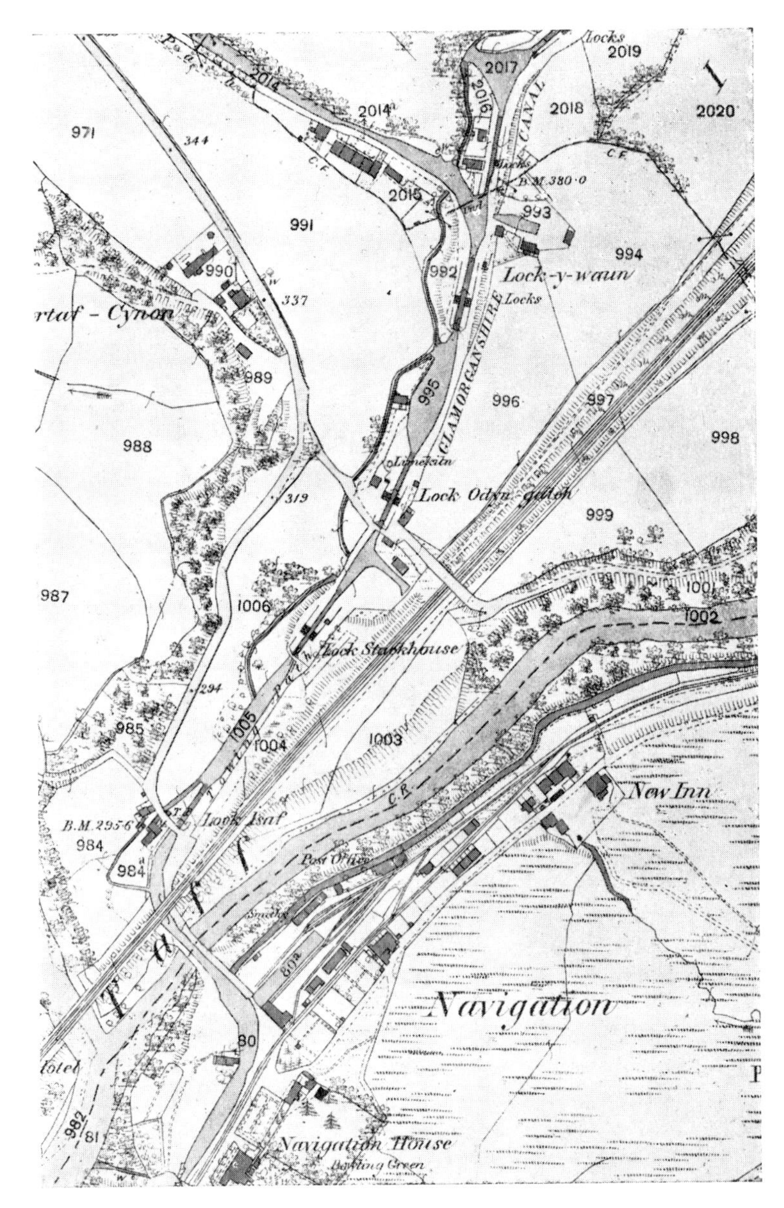

I. Abercynon on the Glamorganshire Canal in 1873. At the bottom of the map is Navigation House, where the Penydarren tramroad and a water feeder from the Taff joined the canal. At the top is the junction between the Aberdare Canal, which runs to the left, and the Glamorganshire Canal, which climbs up to the right on its way to Merthyr Tydfil

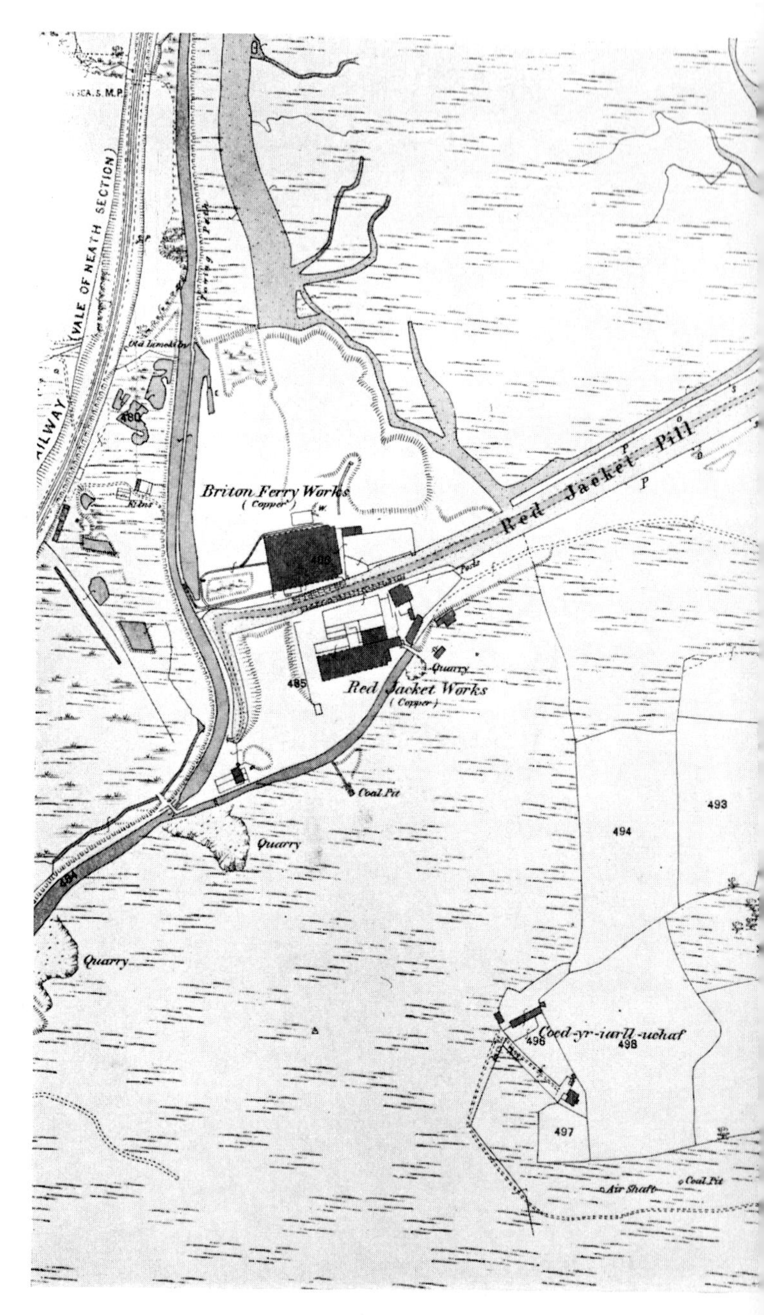

II. Giant's Grave and Red Jacket in 1877. On the left of the map is the T
Red Jacket pill is shown. On the right the Neath Canal curves round Giant's
(Jersey) Canal. The basin between the river and the Neath Canal above C

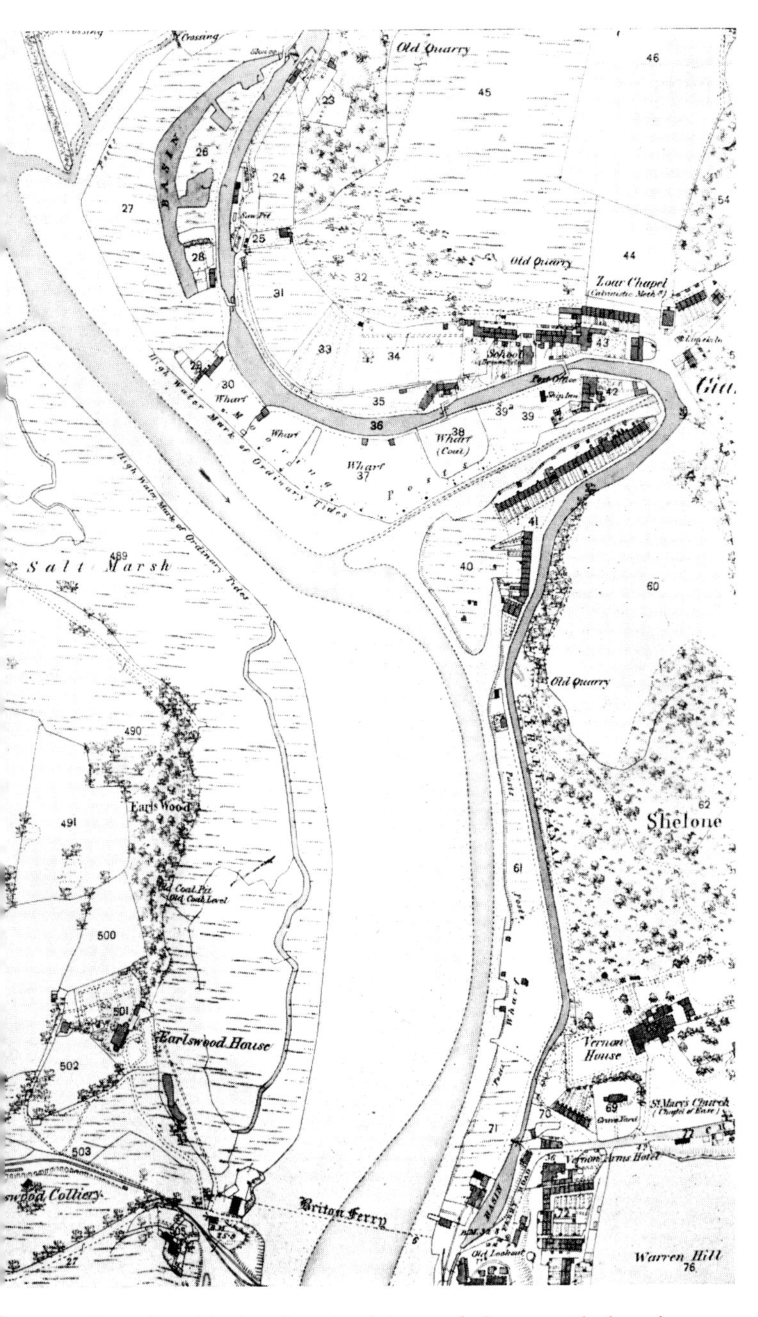

l coming down from Neath and turning left towards Swansea. The branch to
and then continues to Briton Ferry as the Giant's Grave and Briton Ferry
e is probably the original termination before the canal's extension about 1815

III. The sea-lock pound of the Glamorganshire Canal in 1950

IV. The south entrance of the tunnel on the Glamorganshire Canal beneath Queen Street, Cardiff, before demolition. Boatmen pulled the boats through the tunnel by means of the chain on the wall

V. At Allt-yr-ynn (Little Switzerland) on the Crumlin line of the Monmouthshire Canal

VI. Old warehouse at Llanfoist on the Brecknock & Abergavenny Canal

VII. Scene on the Monmouthshire Canal near Mill Street, Newport, before the canal was closed

VIII. The aqueduct carrying the Brecknock & Abergavenny Canal over the River Usk at Brynich near Brecon

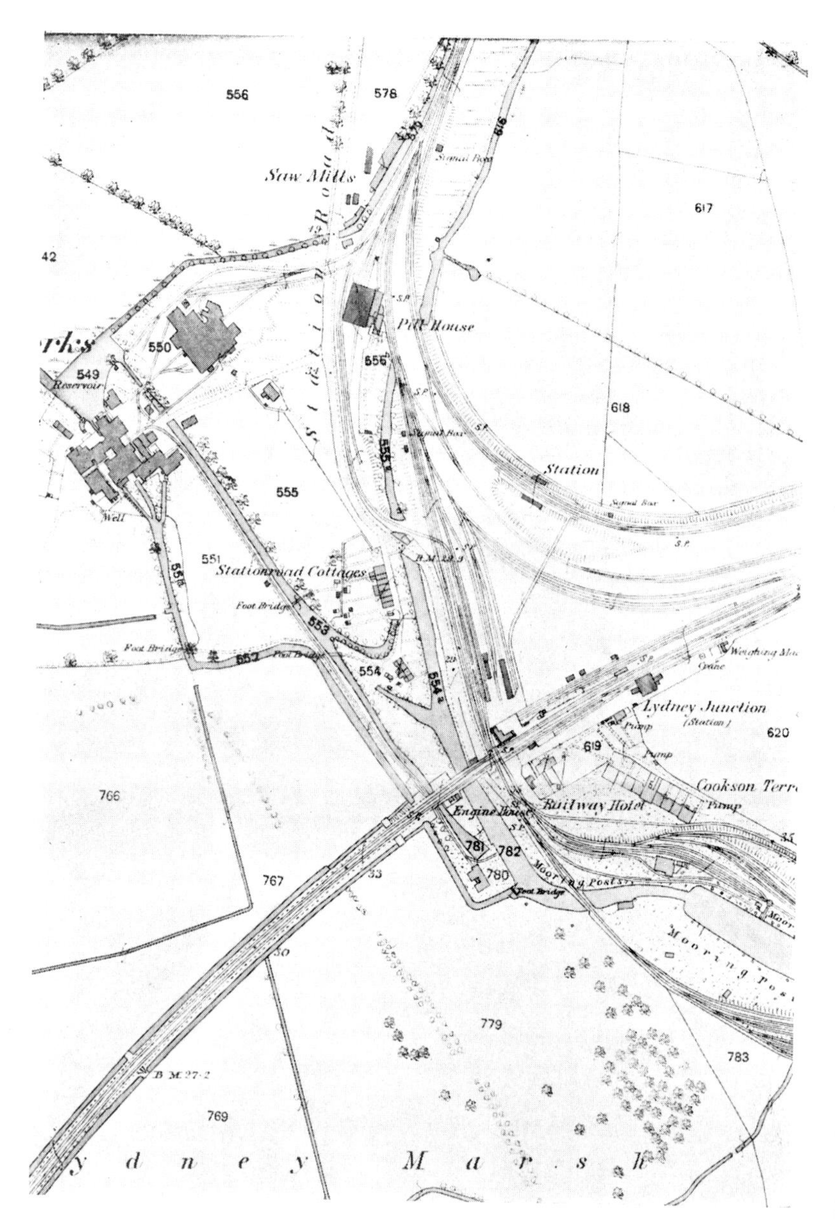

IX. The upper part of the Lydney Canal in 1880. At the bottom of the map the head of the main basin is shown, above which the canal continues to end above the railway, and is joined by a feeder. Pidcock's Canal comes in at the top of the map, past the Saw Mills, and then turns sharply to end at a transhipment point above the railway, and apparently at another below the lines

CHAPTER VI

The Canals of Taff Vale

In 1765 Anthony Bacon, who came from Whitehaven, leased lands at Merthyr Tydfil and built furnaces at Cyfarthfa. About 1777 Richard Crawshay, then of London, became his partner, and in the same year Bacon acquired mineral rights at Plymouth, farther down the valley, and in 1780 at Hirwaun, at both of which places furnaces were leased. In 1783 he leased some of the Cyfarthfa properties to Francis Homfray and his three sons, Thomas Jeremiah and Samuel, who soon disposed of the lease, which later came into Crawshay's hands. Bacon died in 1786, and the Court of Chancery afterwards ruled that his Cyfarthfa property should be leased to Crawshay, who already had a lease on the remainder, his Plymouth property to Richard Hill, formerly Bacon's agent, and Hirwaun to Glover of Aber-carn.

John Guest came in 1759 from Broseley opposite Coalbrookdale on the Severn to manage a furnace at Dowlais established in 1758. When he died in 1785, his son Thomas succeeded him, and became associated there with William Taitt. Meanwhile, when the Homfrays had given up their Cyfarthfa lease in 1784, they had taken over ground at Penydarren and built ironworks there, of which Samuel Homfray became sole manager in 1789. These four works of Cyfarthfa, Dowlais, Penydarren and Plymouth provided the reason for canal-building in the valley,[1] the immediate impetus being the substitution of coal for charcoal in smelting, said to have been introduced at Cyfarthfa and Penydarren about 1787,[2] and the consequent quick increase in output.

Cyfarthfa Canal

The first was a little tub-boat canal 'a few feet in width',[3] which was probably cut in the late 1770's by Anthony Bacon.[4] It ran from a junction with the Canaid brook near the later Cwm pit to Cyfarthfa Yard. Charles Wilkins[5] tells us that:

'It was so arranged as to pass by several of these "coal holes" or "levels", and by a little skill to flow into, but not overflow, the primitive "workings". In each level a small bay was constructed for the convenience of loading the coal. On this canal long strings of iron barges were kept, of a liliputian size, six fastened together, and this convoy of six was entrusted to a couple of men, sometimes a man and a girl, one being on the bank with a shoulder strap, and the other in the first barge furnished with a long boat-hook, which was used in pulling the barge to shore or keeping it away from the banks.'

The course is fully described in F. J. Pedler's *History of the Hamlet of Gellideg* (1930), who states that it was in use up to about 1835–40. The size of the boats is given as 4½ metres by 2½ metres (14 ft. 8 in. by 8 ft. 2 in. approx.).[6]

Glamorganshire Canal

Iron ore, coal and limestone were all found near the four ironworks at the head of the Taff valley in their early days. The pressing need was for better transport for the iron they made. Anthony Bacon, using mule-trains to Cardiff and Swansea, was the leader in getting the poor road from Merthyr Tydfil over the hills through Gelli-gaer and Caerphilly to Cardiff improved about 1767,[7] and soon afterwards he with John Guest and William Lewis were the main industrialists authorized as trustees under the Glamorganshire Turnpike Act of 1771 to turnpike a road down the valley from Merthyr to Tongwynlais below Nantgarw, where it joined the Cardiff District Turnpike. This road was in 1779 separated from others round Llantrisant and made a separate turnpike district, clearly because in the ironmasters' opinion it had not till then had enough attention.[8] The General Turnpike Act of 1785 brought it as trustees Jeremiah and Samuel Homfray and also James Harford of Melingriffith.

Even on improved roads, a road waggon could only carry two tons of iron[9] to the Old Quay on the river at Cardiff for shipment, and it was said that land carriage was costing the ironmasters £14,000 a year.[10] So, led by Richard Crawshay, the men connected with the four ironworks at Merthyr, together with some prominent Brecon people including the proprietors of Wilkins's Old

Bank, the owners of the Melingriffith works near Llandaff, and some from the little port of Cardiff, joined together to obtain the Act[11] of 1790 for the Glamorganshire Canal from Merthyr Tydfil by Pontypridd and Melingriffith to the Bank, a shipping place on the Taff below the Old Quay. It was to be the first major canal in Wales. The authorized capital was £60,000, with power to raise £30,000 more and, alone among Welsh canals, a limitation of dividend to 8 per cent on the capital expended was included, presumably at the instance of some who were going to use it. The original survey of March 1790 had included a branch canal from near Merthyr to Dowlais, with 411 feet of lockage in 1¾ miles, to cost £16,282 in addition to the estimate of £53,465 for the main canal,[12] but this was dropped.

The big shareholders were Richard Crawshay of Cyfarthfa, who subscribed £9,600 and his family another £3,500; William Stevens (£5,000), who was associated with Crawshay; the Harfords of Melingriffith* with £6,000 and a local landowner, John Kemeys Tynte of Cefn Mably, with £5,000. The Homfrays (£1,500) and Richard Forman (£1,000) of Penydarren, the Hills of Plymouth (£1,500), and William Taitt (£1,000) and Thomas Guest (£500) of Dowlais were smaller shareholders, while others were connected with one or other of the ironmasters.

The first committee to be elected was representative mainly of the three ironworks at Merthyr other than Dowlais together with Melingriffith. It met at the *Cardiff Arms Inn* at Cardiff on 30 June 1790, and engaged Thomas Dadford senior, Thomas Dadford junior, and Thomas Sheasby as joint contractors to make the canal for £48,288 exclusive of land, and a bond of £10,000 was taken from them for the performance of their contract. The company did not have an engineer of its own; instead, a group of leading proprietors was asked from time to time to check the work. Construction began in August[14] from the Merthyr end.

Right from the start a quarrel had developed between Crawshay, who had virtually a controlling interest, and Taitt of Dowlais. When the Dowlais branch was dropped, Crawshay told Taitt (according to Taitt) that the Dowlais company must find their own way to the canal. At the same time (according to Taitt), the maximum proposed toll of 3d. per ton per mile on which the capital had been subscribed was raised in the Act to 5d. Taking

* There was already a barge or two working on a short navigable length of the Taff and a works canal feeder at Melingriffith([13]). This is not included in the Appendices.

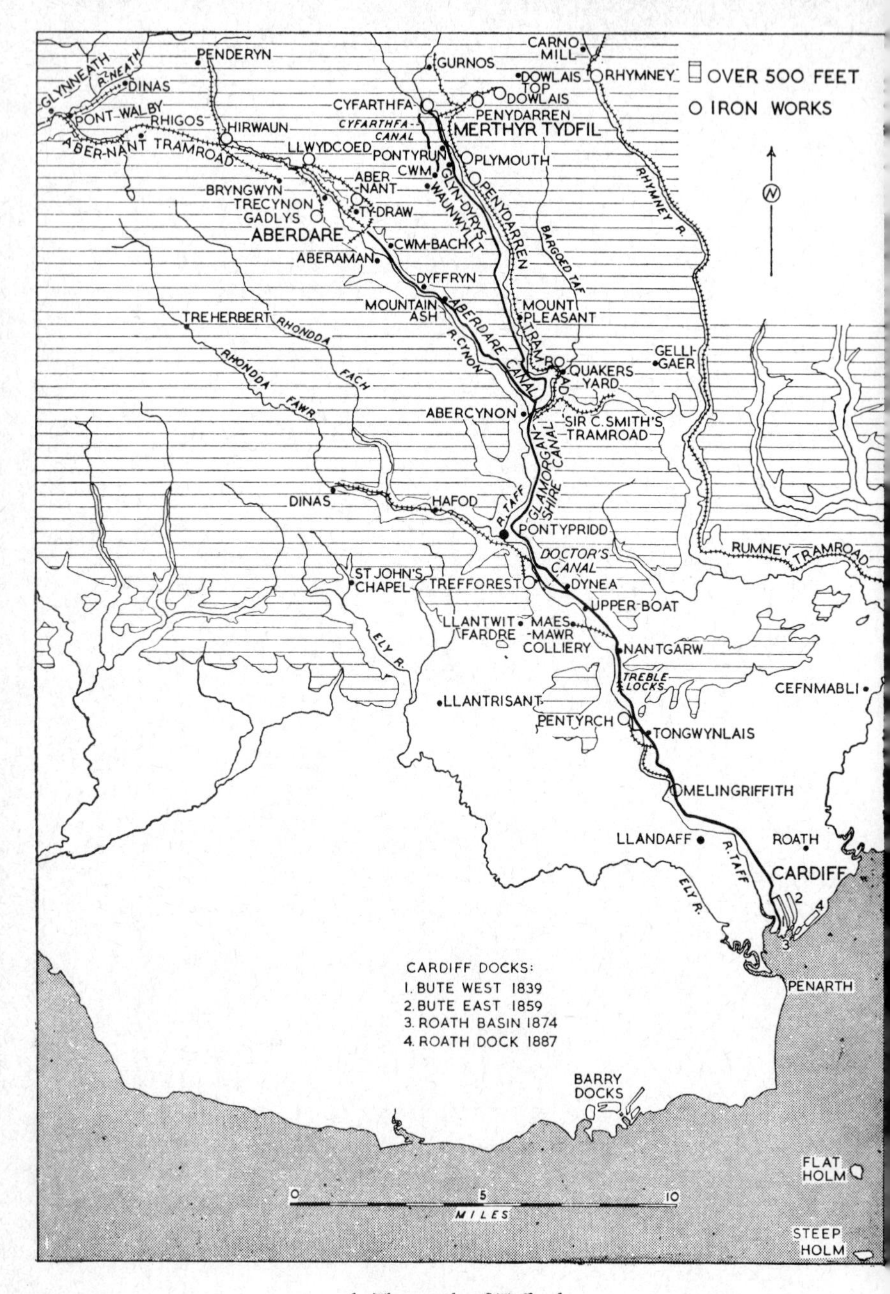

6. The canals of Taff vale

these two considerations together, Taitt protested that the Dowlais company could send, as they were then sending, their iron over the hills on horses' backs as cheaply as they could on the canal. Taitt therefore declared that he would have nothing more to do with the canal, and neither he nor Guest was on the first committee. However, Crawshay returned a soft answer, and the Dowlais company built a tramroad from Dowlais past Penydarren to the canal at Merthyr costing about £3,000,[15] to which the canal company contributed £1,000. It was made by June 1791.

Almost immediately, Homfray and Crawshay also quarrelled 'owing to some difference respecting the making and management of the canal',[16] and Homfray also received a fearful snub from Taitt when he objected to the proposed tramroad, presumably in order to have it nearer Penydarren:

'Your several letters to Mr. Guest about the direction of our Rail Road from Dowlais to the canal surprizes me exceedingly, as I know not what pretence you can possibly have to interfere in that. . . . If you want an accommodation from us, ask it as a favour, but do not think of demanding it as a right. . . .'[17]

This quarrel resulted in Forman of Penydarren leaving the canal committee, so that only two Merthyr works were represented till Taitt rejoined in 1795 for three years.

By June 1791 the dimensions of the first basin at Cardiff had been agreed,* and also an extension of the canal at Merthyr for half a mile to Cyfarthfa. In April 1792 a tramroad from limestone quarries at Gurnos to the canal at Cyfarthfa was authorized by the shareholders, and Crawshay was asked to build it.† About this time the canal was navigable from Merthyr to Pontypridd,[18] and by July seems to have been more or less navigable throughout, but 'not in a state to be taken off Mr. Dadford's hands'.[19]

It was now clear that Dadford's work would cost more than his contract, for he produced a bill for £17,221 for extra work outside it, and said that £5,000 still needed to be spent. Soon afterwards a survey was ordered to see if it were practicable to extend the canal for a mile in Cardiff to the pill called the Lower Layer on what were then described as Cardiff Moors.

The canal was opened on 10 February 1794.

* 'The basin of the canal to contain 16 ft. depth of water, and to be not less than 40 yards wide; the sea-lock to be not less than 30 ft. wide and 90 ft. long; the entrance to the lock to be not less than 36 ft. wide.'([20])

† Another line from the Dowlais tramroad east of Gurnos to Castle Morlais quarries was built by Hill in 1799.([21]) The attribution of a date earlier than 1792 for the Gurnos line([22]) appears to conflict with the evidence of the canal minute books.

'The canal from Cardiff to Merthir-Tidvil is completed, and a fleet of canal boats have arrived at Cardiff laden with the produce of the iron-works there, to the great joy of the whole town. . . . Nothing appears more extraordinary than, from a boat navigating this canal, to look down on the river Taaff, dashing among the rocks 100 yards below. . . . The first barge that arrived at Cardiff was finely decorated with colours, and was navigated from the Mollingriffield works by Mr. Bird, sen. water-bailiff of Cardiff.'[23]

Richard Griffiths of Cardiff, a committeeman, gave an entertainment in celebration, for which the company paid £14 11s. 9d.

The tolls now charged were 2d. a ton per mile for coal, ironstone, iron ore, limestone, lime, manure, bricks, clay and sand, and 5d. a ton per mile for iron, timber, goods and merchandise. The original length of the canal including the extension at Cyfarthfa was 24½ miles, with 49 locks, many of the upper ones being built in pairs, or in one case as a staircase of three. The total rise was 543 ft., most of the locks on the upper part having a rise of over 10 ft., the greatest being 14 ft. 6 in. The main engineering works were a stone aqueduct over the Taff at Abercynon (now incorporated in a road bridge) which also carried the Aberdare turnpike, and upon which the canal company had a toll-gate,[24] and a short 115-yard tunnel in Cardiff. The boats taken were some 60 ft. long by 9 ft. wide, and carried 20, and later 25 tons after the canal had been deepened.

Because an extension had been envisaged, the last quarter-mile to the Bank, and the proposed lock and basin there, were never built. This extension was at first planned to the estuary of the River Rhymney near Roath. Soon afterwards it was decided instead to extend it farther down the Taff, and in 1796 an Act[25] was passed to authorize such a line about a mile long to the river at the Lower Layer pill, with a sea-lock, and to raise another £10,000, this time carrying a maximum dividend of 5 per cent. Now for the first time there occurs a name in the company's records that was to be of crucial importance: in return for his agreement to the extension, the Marquess of Bute and his dependents could use the towing path for horses and cattle, and could carry hay and manure along it free of charge.

This addition to the line, apparently begun before the Act,[26] was opened late in June 1798, 'when a fine sloop of 80 tons burthen, arriving from Bristol, was navigated into the canal. . . . The Basun and Canal for a space of a mile is of sufficient depth to admit of more than 100 brigs, sloops, etc. to ride in perfect safety; and constantly afloat for loading and unloading . . . during both neap and spring tides.' The basin took ships of 150 to 200 tons, though most were smaller. The approach to the sea-lock that gave access to it was by a channel up the Taff, which the canal company took responsibility for buoying, and into which incoming craft dumped their ballast when no one was looking to save the cost of unloading it.

The total cost of the canal, including the extension and basin, was £103,600. This was entirely raised by calls on shares, each of which had therefore a nominal value of £172 3s. 4d., the first £90,000 of capital being limited to an 8 per cent dividend, and the rest to 5 per cent.

A quarrel between the Dadfords and Sheasby and the company followed the completion of the main line in 1794. A breach in the bank occurred in December, and the contractors refused to repair it unless the company advanced money. This was not done, and the contractors, who had not only been completing the works but managing the canal, dismissed their men and withdrew. The company, who considered pressure was being put on them, then ordered that the contractors 'be held to bail at the suit of the . . . company for the sum of £10,000',[27] part of the alleged overpayment of £17,000, and they were arrested.* The extension in Cardiff was therefore built under the superintendence of Patrick Copeland, who in June 1796 had been appointed canal agent or manager. In fact, the company had been wrong about the Dadfords, for when the canal engineer Robert Whitworth was called in to arbitrate, he awarded that only £1,512 out of the £17,000 claimed should be refunded by the Dadfords and Sheasby.

By 1801 much development had already taken place. Thomas Martyn, coming from Caerphilly, wrote:

'We soon crossed the canal and passed some way between that and the river. Upon the left high on the hills were numerous railways leading from coal and other mines, which bring and deposit the bowels of the earth in barges that convey them to immense distances. . . .'[28]

Early in 1798 a tremendous, and lasting, quarrel took place between Richard Crawshay of Cyfarthfa and the other ironmasters. The underlying cause was that the Crawshay group, with its big

* Thomas Dadford junior must have withdrawn from the contract, for he was working full-time on the Monmouthshire and Leominster Canals, and was not affected. Sheasby was arrested, though he was engineering the Swansea Canal at the time. I presume the elder Dadford was too.

shareholding, ran, or appeared to run, the canal in its own way. The quarrel had been building up for some time. There is plenty of evidence in the Dowlais letter-books from 1792 onwards[29] that Crawshay put pressure on boat-owners to carry for him in preference to Dowlais; as early as 1794 Richard Hill was complaining that the canal was taking water from the Taff that was legally his;[30] and in 1797 there had been litigation between the canal company and the Dowlais partners over the number of pounds to be allowed in the hundredweight.[31]

The immediate reason was probably that a letter had been received from Crawshay by the other members of the canal committee protesting against a meeting having been fixed on the Cyfarthfa pay-day, so that his group could not attend. Those present minuted that 'They know no reason why the pay days of Mr. Crawshay or the engagements of his minions should obtruct the Company's public business. . . . They are astonished that any men . . . should be misled by Mr. Richard Crawshay's empty bellowing which here has, and ever will be treated with the contempt it merits.'[32]

Crawshay struck back. At the annual meeting in June he was in the Chair, and seven out of the eleven members of the Committee failed to be re-elected, and were replaced. The dissidents were the leading men of the Dowlais, Penydarren and Plymouth works, and William Lewis of Pentyrch, and on 24 September a parliamentary notice appeared 'for leave to make a Dram Road from or near Carno Mill . . . to or near the town of Cardiff . . .'[33] The plan was for a line from Cardiff to Quaker's Yard above Abercynon, with a branch thence to Merthyr and the quarries beyond, another thence up the valley of the Bargoed Taf and on to the Merthyr-Hereford road, and then east to Carno mill at the head of the Rhymney valley, and another branch from Abercynon by Aberdare to Aber-nant.

Unofficially, the canal company were probably behind the skilfully damaging letter that appeared in the press[34] signed by 'An Humble Inquirer' a week after the notice. Officially, it decided to oppose the project, and wrote to notabilities for their support, which the Monmouthshire Canal company decided to give.[35] On 14 January 1799 the company joined with the Commissioners of the Cardiff–Merthyr turnpike to issue a statement to the local landowners.[36] This said that there was a legal limit on canal dividends; that the canal had been built economically, and 'finished for less Money than any other of its magnitude, and utility, that we have heard of'; that 'It is asserted that by a Dram-Road goods will be carried cheaper than by the Canal. It cannot be believed that horses and Wagons can be made to do this; that the canal toll was 5d. a mile for 25 miles, and 2/– to 2/6 a ton for freightage, or 12/5 to 12/11 a ton altogether'; that with increased trade 'tolls will in time be reduced to perhaps half what they now are without injury to any set of Men'; and that it was 'designed to ruin the Canal Company; and the Deed-Poll holders of the Turnpike Road will never after have 5 per cent for their advance, nor will, it is presumed, the intended Subscribers to this barbarous Horse-Road ever have half 5 per cent . . . the attempt is to terrify the Company, to give up a present Moiety of what they are justly, under the faith of Parliament, entitled to: and on which they subscribed their money'.

On 18 January 1799 the partners of the three ironworks agreed to build the section of tramroad from Merthyr to Abercynon, and a Bill was introduced. At the end of March, while the Bill was before the House, the canal company offered some concessions on tolls in response to an approach from the dissident ironmasters, but these were coupled with a request for an undertaking that the ironworks would carry only on the canal,[37] and were rejected. The Bill was then opposed by the combined Glamorganshire and Monmouthshire Canal companies, and dropped in May, whereupon the tramroad was built without an Act* by Richard Hill of Plymouth works, under the leadership of William Taitt of Dowlais, and with George Overton† as his engineer. This line, usually called the Penydarren tramroad, was opened in 1802 as a 4 ft. 2 in. gauge plateway, 9½ miles long, from a junction with the existing Dowlais tramroad to the canal east of the aqueduct at Abercynon. Here there was a 'spacious basin, surrounded by commodious wharves, where the canal company's business is transacted, and their principal agent resides'.[38] The Penydarren tramroad was owned in the proportion of five shares each to Dowlais and Penydarren, and four to Plymouth. It is well known as the line on which Trevithick's locomotive ran in 1804.[39]

In 1851 Dowlais ceased to use the tramroad when the Dowlais

* If compulsory powers were needed, those of the 4-mile clause of the canal company's own Act could have been used; there is no evidence that they were.

† Overton was a mining and civil engineer, at one time concerned with the Hirwaun works, who later worked for the Glamorganshire Canal Company, was concerned with the Bryn-oer tramroad which served collieries near Rhymney in which he had an interest, and also made the first survey for the Stockton and Darlington Railway.

Railway was built from the works to the Taff Vale Railway, and transferred its shares. The Penydarren works were closed in 1859, and the remaining owner, the Plymouth works, gave up making iron in 1880. The tramroad was then converted into a railway between Merthyr and Mount Pleasant, and the rest abandoned.

The Penydarren tramroad seems therefore to have been the outcome of a quarrel. The often-made statement that it was built because of water shortage in the upper part of the canal may be due to the claims frequently made by Hill of Plymouth that the company was taking water from the Taff which was essential to his works, and to which he was entitled. These claims caused the canal company in 1806 to call in Rennie to report on water supplies. As a result, a reservoir was built at Glyndyrys and a Boulton & Watt steam pumping engine at Pontyrun, which began work in 1809, and which pumped back to the canal the water that had passed through Hill's works. A waterwheel and pump for the same purpose was installed about this time also at the Melingriffith works, with which there was a similar water dispute. About 1821 a reservoir was built below the Treble Locks at Nantgarw in an attempt to improve the Melingriffith supplies, but it was not till 1829, after many years of argument and litigation, that an agreement was reached. In 1832 it broke out again for some years, and when the battle finally ended, Richard Blakemore, who had been associated with Melingriffith since 1807 and who had taken it over in 1812, was said to have spent £20,000 in the courts over thirty years.[40]

Richard Crawshay sat on the canal committee till his death in 1810. His son, William Crawshay I, who had himself had a seat on it since 1798, seems soon after his father's death to have quarrelled with his brother-in-law Benjamin Hall, the company's chairman. It may have been the debt for the Pontyrun engine, which he built, that caused William Crawshay I on 21 April 1813 to write to his son William: 'My determination is fixed not to pay any tonnage to the canal, but to stop the whole till the debt due us is paid. . . . If Hall should advance the tonnage we can then do as we please as to going by the Dram Road. But that would do us no good as he would again advance so as to still divide 8 per cent. . . .' And on 1 July: 'How did the Canal Co. pay their dividend without your tonnage? You will of course continue to deduct all until our debt is wholly paid?'[41] It may have been this quarrel with Hall that disposed William Crawshay to sell his ten shares in the canal to Anthony Bacon for £215 each in part-payment for the Cyfarthfa property. This sale disqualified him from sitting on the canal committee from 1814 to 1818, when he must have bought fresh shares.

In the years from the end of the old tramroad quarrel to 1823, two main questions occupied the committee; to get rid of surplus revenue, and to improve the waterway and especially the basin at Cardiff to accommodate the increasing traffic.

The unusual problem of surplus revenue was the result of the limitation of the company's dividend in its Acts to 8 per cent on the first £90,000 of capital and 5 per cent thereafter. The sum required to pay these dividends was £8,180 p.a., and even in the early years of the canal the profits exceeded this after paying for some capital expenditure out of income. For instance:

Year Michaelmas	*Revenue* £	*Expenditure* £	*Dividend* £	*Balance* £
1804–05	12,592	4,148	8,180	264
1805–06	13,936	5,334	8,180	422
1806–07	13,914	4,224	8,180	1,510

About the year 1805–6, therefore, it was decided to return 20 per cent of the tolls received to the traders. In spite of this a group of traders led by Samuel Homfray applied in 1806 and again in 1807 to the Magistrates in Quarter Sessions to reduce tolls, on the grounds that certain items of expenditure should be disallowed as maintenance and charged to capital, so increasing the disposable balance. These were unsuccessful, but similar appeals in 1808 and 1809 were not, and the magistrates ordered toll reductions.[42]

After a gap of some years, money again became an embarrassment in 1815, when it was agreed to reduce rates by 10 per cent from the beginning of 1816. This move seems to have increased traffic and so revenue, for nine months later it was decided instead of reducing rates again to charge traders no tolls at all for the last quarter of the year, and again for the quarter following. The payment of tolls was then resumed, but at the beginning of 1818, 13s. 4d. in the £ of the December quarter's tolls was returned to the traders, and a reduction of 10 per cent on tolls generally was made, making 40 per cent in all from the Parliamentary rates. Nine months later, in September 1818, 15s. in the £ on the quarter's tonnage was returned, and a further 10 per cent reduction, or 50 per cent in all, was made in tolls. Two years later, in September 1820, a further 5 per cent reduction in tolls was made, and in June 1821 £3,648 was ordered to be returned to the traders.

This picture, pleasant as it was for the owners of works whose traffic was being carried so cheaply and disquieting for those served by other canals whose proprietors took higher dividends, was not completed by any rises in wages for the canal's work-people. The management probably took the view that they should not as canal owners set an example to themselves as ironmasters and colliery owners, for only three months after the last return of money to the traders, the committee asked Crawshay and the clerk to make such wage reductions among all the staff as should seem 'consistent with the honour and liberality of a public body'.*[43] In the following March of 1822 Crawshay reported that he had reduced the wages of the canal staff, and the Committee ordered that 'in future no man be taken into employ above the age of thirty, and that no tools or beer be allowed the men'.[44]

The canal originally had at its entrance a sea-lock communicating with the tidal river, a basin above, and then a stretch of deep water extending back to the next lock in the town. The least of the company's troubles was from silting outside the sea-lock, and from mud brought in when it was opened. Worse was the increasing congestion of ships coming in to load at the iron and colliery companies' wharves above the basin, as successive toll reductions encouraged trade. A symptom of this congestion is a minute of 1818: 'It being necessary that the two men who assist John Morgan at the Sea-Lock be constantly at their post night and day—ordered that John Morgan be allowed 6s. per week for accommodating them with beds, house-room, etc.'[45] To congestion was added the practice of captains of tipping their ballast into the canal before loading, instead of having it carried on wheelbarrows to tipping places beyond the wharves. Because of this practice the sea-lock pound had to be emptied from time to time for cleaning.

Eventually something had to be done more than the lengthening of the sea-lock that took place in 1814. It was agreed in May 1821 to ask an engineer to 'survey the Port of Cardiff as to how it can be improved for the better accommodation of the increasing trade on the Glamorganshire Canal'.[46] George Overton was asked to do so, and he reported in June. He proposed that the canal should be deepened and straightened from the sea-lock to the wharves at Cardiff, where a new basin would be built, so that ves-

* Before the reductions the ruling wages seem to have been 12s. a week for labourers and up to 18s. for masons.

sels of 300 tons could reach the wharves and lighterage to vessels outside the sea-lock would be avoided, and that a branch canal should be built on which the coal wharves would be placed. Overton made it clear that his proposals were expensive, and that they would only be worth while if the company expected an increased trade.

After six months of consideration the company accepted the main recommendation, and ordered that 'in order to facilitate the increased trade on the canal, its line from the sea-lock to the highest wharf below the South Gate Bridge be deepened, widened, and otherwise improved to enable all vessels that can enter the sea-lock to come up to their respective wharfs and take in their full cargoes'.[47] It was not as easy as that. Since 1815 Lord Bute had considered that the canal wharves were encroaching on his land, and he now sought counsel's advice, which was that the canal company had no power to take his land for widening and straightening. He therefore refused his permission, his existing annoyance with the company being reinforced by fear lest 'a very important plan that has been suggested to him for the improvement of his own property at Cardiff' should be frustrated.[48]

The canal company, of which William Crawshay II took over the chairmanship in June 1822, had already decided in April, after an unsuccessful attempt to get Lord Bute to change his mind, that it could carry out the improvements and yet keep within its own land. It now proposed to seek powers to raise the necessary money. Guest of Dowlais and Hill of Plymouth works were in favour, as was the chairman, who felt that either the canal company itself must do something, or must allow Lord Bute to do so.

'A vessel with us last summer took in only 40 tons in 4 days owing to perpetual removals to let others pass her. The captain and many others went away disgusted with the port. The proposed alteration would enable all vessels to take in their full cargoes at the wharf, instead of 2/3 as at present, and totally do away with the expense, delay and inconvenience of lighterage on the other 1/3.'[49]

However, William Crawshay I was against the plan: 'The thing is good, sufficient and prosperous as it is, and will not be rendered more so by any extension—most likely will be less.'[50] It may have been in order to put pressure on the older man as the virtual controller of the canal that Hill and Guest held back their tolls for the last quarter of 1822, together with some lesser folk. The same meeting that authorized a petition to Parliament stopped the defaulters' boats, and family loyalty seems now to have brought young William to his father's side, though he still maintained his opinion, for the proposal to petition was rescinded in March.

This in turn seems to have led to a proposal by the other ironmasters to continue the Penydarren tramroad to Cardiff, for in June William Crawshay II is thanked by the canal shareholders for his exertions against it. The continuation was surveyed by David Davies on a line 15 miles long marked out by George Overton on the opposite side of the valley to the canal, which was later used by the Taff Vale Railway. At Cardiff there was to be a basin connected by a 2¼-mile canal to the Ely River at Penarth. A tramroad branch was also proposed to Llantrisant (5½ miles), with a 4-mile branch from this to St. John's Chapel near Tonyrefail.[51] The canal company strongly opposed the subsequent Bill, which was lost, and a further 5 per cent reduction in tolls was tactfully made.

At the end of 1823 an approach was made to the canal company by the ironmasters, and young William Crawshay and his colleagues agreed to compromise. In January 1824, therefore, the company approved an agreement that gave the proprietor of the Dowlais, Plymouth and Penydarren works respectively a seat on the committee as of right; that provided after the legal dividends had been paid for the tolls being reduced to 1½d. a ton till the balance in hand had fallen to £2,000; and that stated that the canal should be improved to allow vessels drawing 14 ft. of water to come up the wharves at Cardiff. The three ironmasters and Crawshay between them agreed also to advance up to £15,000 for the improvement of the port. Old William Crawshay I, while pleased with the agreement and in favour of some improvements, was against launching out into big schemes at Cardiff: 'A low rate of conveyance is all the Ironmasters want and they ought to obtain it. The improvement and good management of the canal will effect the very lowest rate of carriage possible.'[52] The relative position of each of the great ironworks at this time was as follows: taking 1822–4 together, the gross tonnages paid (before refunds) to the canal company were: Crawshay & Co., £32,338; Dowlais Co., £15,880; Penydarren Co., £11,673; Plymouth Co., £10,657; to which we may add the £2,373 of the Aberdare Iron company and the £1,805 of the Hirwaun company. No other single freighter paid more than £3,000.[53]

A Bill was prepared to authorize the borrowing and the agreement. A sub-committee which included the four firms was formed to see it through, and presumably under what they thought were existing powers, in spite of Lord Bute's earlier attitude, an official of the company was in February asked to 'proceed to take possession of the land of the Marquis of Bute required for canal widening and wharf building'.[54] In June 1824, at the same meeting as a 10 per cent reduction in tolls (70 per cent in all) was made in order to carry out the agreement between the company and the ironmasters, it was minuted that:

'. . . the meeting considers that the decision of the Committee to withdraw the Bill was prudent and warranted by the unexpected claim brought forward by the Marquis of Bute after the execution of the agreement between himself and the Canal Company. The proprietors consider the Marquis's claim to the water of the river Taff as a total infraction of this agreement; that, since the necessary improvement of the port of Cardiff is thus prevented, an immediate amelioration of the sea-lock be entrusted to the committee. . . .'[55]

Simultaneously, Richard Blakemore of Melingriffith sought and obtained an injunction against the canal company to prevent the widening and deepening of the basin, on the grounds that such improvements would use more water, of which his works would be deprived.[56]

Lord Bute's claim to the waters of the Taff seems to have been based on his fisheries, which invested him with the power 'of regulating the port of Cardiff as far as related to anchorage dues etc., and also as far as relates to any improvement which it may hereafter be found necessary to carry into effect for the benefit of the port of Cardiff'. This was stated in 1823 by D. Stewart in his *Report on the River Taff and Fisheries*, who recommended 'that the Canal Co. should not on any account be allowed to take any more water out of the river, nor to increase the size of their canal either in width or depth, without the consent of Lord Bute, and without full compensation for the water so taken'.[57]

So ended an effort by the canal company, which meant the Merthyr ironmasters, to build what might have become the first Cardiff dock. The canal was, however, improved to some extent above the sea-lock pound. Over the next two years from mid-1822 about £3,600 was spent out of revenue, the result being to increase the carrying capacity of the boats from about 20 to 25 tons. To cope with increased traffic the canal was also opened on Sundays.

Lord Bute seems soon to have begun some works of his own, for at the end of 1827 the canal committee asked Crawshay to get in touch with him to represent 'that the erections and docks now being made on his land would render more difficult the improvements of the canal, and to request their suspension *pro tem*'.[58] It was possibly Crawshay himself who in the course of this interview suggested the idea of a ship canal, as distinct from port improvements, to Lord Bute, for the latter, writing to Crawshay in 1847, said: 'I shall also take this occasion to remind you that the Bute Ship Canal was not projected in any rivalry to the Glamorganshire Canal, for in point of fact, you were one of the first persons who suggested to me, viz. in the month of December 1827, that I should make a Ship Canal.'[59] Earlier, he had said: 'Mr. Crawshay is the very man who suggested to me to make the Ship Entrance and Dock . . . and begged me to do so, on the ground that Blakemore had prevented the Canal Co. from cutting a stroke at their own canal.'[60]

Having been given encouragement, Lord Bute called in James Green, the Westcountry canal engineer who had just finished rebuilding the Exeter Canal to small ship-canal dimensions,* to give his views upon necessary improvements to the port of Cardiff. Green reported in April 1828.[61] His criticisms of the current position were that the canal entrance was too high up the river, so that vessels had to follow a winding channel and needed pilots, and that the sill of the entrance lock was at the level of half-tide at moderate springs, so that big vessels could only get out at the top of the tide, and at any high tide there was a crowd of vessels trying to get out through the lock and others trying to get in. He proposed what became the substance of the Bute Ship Canal Act of 1830, foreseeing the new basin as being supplied not only by the Glamorganshire Canal, but by railways 'should it hereafter be found necessary by the increase of Trade to lay down Railroads from the Interior of the Country . . .'.

The ironmasters must have made their views known to James Green, for he writes:

'Since my arrival at Cardiff circumstances have transpired which appear to render it doubtful whether or not the principal Iron Masters of the Port who are also leading Proprietors of the Glamorganshire Canal may so far concur in your Lordship's views of the proposed improvements as to remove their shipping Wharfs from the Old Canal to the new Harbour Basin, and whether the Canal Company may co-operate with your Lordship in carrying the proposed improvements into effect. . . .' He went on: 'I can

* See my *The Canals of Southern England*, pp. 233–4.

have no hesitation in affirming that your Lordship may carry the work into Execution independently of any persons whatsoever and that a most ample supply of water may be obtained from the River Taff within your Lordship's own property. . . .'

Meanwhile the continuing prosperity of the canal was shown by the further 5 per cent toll reduction made in October 1828 (making 75 per cent below Parliamentary rates), followed by one of 2½ per cent in 1830. But in December 1829 notices appeared in the *Cambrian* of Swansea (for Cardiff with less than 10,000 people still had no newspaper) which foreshadowed Lord Bute's Bill of 1830, and a committee was appointed by the canal company to negotiate with him over a canal junction with his proposed wet-dock.

This year of 1830 was crucial to the company, and we may here glance at what is known of its traffic. In 1830 it had carried 201,116 tons of iron and coal. Of this total, 87,367 tons had been iron, shipped as follows:

	tons		*tons*
Dowlais	29,621	Aberdare Iron Co.	7,248
W. Crawshay & Sons	21,312	Blakemore & Co.	2,894
R. & A. Hill	13,046	S. Brown & Co.	664
Penydarren	12,582		

This figure of 87,367 tons of iron compares with 49,382 for 1820 and 68,326 for 1825. Most of the coal, 113,749 tons in all, was shipped by four producers:

	tons		*tons*
Walter Coffin	46,446	T. and G. Thomas	11,400
Sir C. Smith	18,246	Robert Thomas	10,476[62]

The great era of steam coal exports only began in 1830, however, when the first was shipped from Waun-wyllt near Merthyr.[63]

No negotiations with the Marquess are recorded, and in March 1830 William Crawshay complains that Lord Bute has made no offer to indemnify the canal company against the injury he might do them. In July 1830 the Bute Ship Canal Act was passed, to authorize a proposed waterway 1½ miles long and 33 ft. deep, the entrance being a mile lower down the river than that of the canal, with 16 ft. of water on the sill of the entrance lock at half flood tide springs. There was to be a dock basin and two short lateral connexions to the Glamorganshire Canal. The estimated cost of £76,669 was to be borne entirely by Lord Bute.

For some time he took no action. Meanwhile the canal company continued its brisk and endless controversy with Richard Blakemore of Melingriffith and his nephew T. W. Booker: 'Were I disposed to deal in such language and epithets as you and your uncle so continually and unsparingly apply to the Canal Co., I might make my comments on the subject of your communication . . .' wrote Crawshay to Booker in June 1832,[64] while within it a modernization party argued with another led by old William Crawshay, who saw even then that the canal was on the losing side, and advocated only rearguard action. Defend the company's rights, he said, 'and do nothing more than the Act allows us. I believe railways are better than canals and will supersede them . . . I for one will agree to no further outlay or extension. If the thing is radically bad, it can not be made good by quackery.'[65] These views of the father cannot have made the upholding of the canal company's position any easier for the son.

In 1833 the Marquess decided to seek authority for a different plan, and in December, through his agent, sent his draft Bill to William Crawshay II. The company was prevented from taking action themselves by Blakemore's legal barriers, and Crawshay replied: '. . . in my individual capacity, I can venture to say that the Canal Co. will not oppose the objects he states your Lordship to have in mind. Indeed, my Lord, something should be done for the Port of Cardiff. The power is in your hands alone now. . . . I still repeat my opinion that your Lordship would do better to let others take the port-making, yourself keeping every ulterior and collateral advantage.'[66] This acceptance of Bute's plan led to a suspension of Blakemore's hostility, and in March 1834 Crawshay refers in a letter to Booker to the 'dawn of harmony' and 'a suspension of hostilities'.[67]

Lord Bute's plans, recast by William Cubitt, were begun in December 1834 and carried out; the works were opened in 1839. The revised plan provided for a ¾ mile dredged approach to sea-gates leading to an outer basin, whence an entrance lock admitted craft to the main dock, 1,400 yards long and 200 feet wide, which was at that time thought capable of holding 300 craft at once. From this dock there was a connexion through a branch to the canal. This West Bute Dock and its accompanying works cost £350,000, of which £220,000 was in cash and the remainder in materials from the Bute property.

In the years between 1828, when James Green had reported, and 1839, when the first Bute Dock was opened, the growth of the collieries and industries of Taff Vale had been very rapid. The tonnage on the canal doubled from 148,371 in 1828 to 319,718 in 1838, while the growth of shipping using the port was equally striking:

Date	*No. of vessels entering the port*		*Register tonnage*	*Total No. of vessels*	*Total tonnage*
1826	Coastwise	778	61,469		
	Irish	220	16,949		
	Foreign	111	11,592	1,109	90,010
1830	Coastwise	935	65,148		
	Irish	499	42,800		
	Foreign	168	17,468	1,602	125,416
1835	Coastwise	1,925	126,573		
	Irish	661	57,894		
	Foreign	236	28,211	2,822	212,678[68]

In 1839, the year the dock was opened, the canal carried 132,781 tons of iron and 211,214 tons of coal.

This prosperity was reflected in the canal company's tolls. In 1832 there had been a 2½ per cent increase, but in 1833 there was a 10 per cent reduction, bringing them to 85 per cent below the Parliamentary rates, though in 1834 certain tolls, mainly those on general merchandise, were sharply increased. In December 1833 steps were taken to make the canal passable all round the clock, by appointing a double set of lock-keepers, and by lighting the main locks, the tunnel, and the sea-lock. Previously, from 1825, working had been from half an hour before sunrise to half an hour after sunset.

Richard J. Hill of the Plymouth works had been a member of the canal committee since the reconciliation of 1824. In August 1832 old Mr Crawshay described him as having no interest in the canal.[69] He did, however, have an interest in improved transport, for two years later old William Crawshay I wrote to young William: 'The proprietors will never consent to forego their dividends to improve the canal. It is all very well for Hill to propose that; to others it is their source of income and living.'[70] Clearly between March and July the Hills turned their minds to the possibility of a railway, for in the latter month old Crawshay wrote to his son: 'I have no fear of Hill and his rail road, and see no just reason for reducing the dividends.' Another committeeman, however, Thomas Charles, evidently had this fear, for old William refers to him as a 'poor timid curmudgeon', and tells his son to offer for his shares.[71]

We must remember, however, that Crawshay's interest in the canal was as cheap transport and not as an investment. Writing four days earlier to John Morland about the canal as an investment for trust money, he says: 'I certainly look with considerable alarm to the effect of a tram-road upon the property of the Glamorganshire Canal. . . . It has been a very excellent investment hitherto for you and might be so for some years again, but I am anxious to clear myself from any responsibility in having recommended the investment.'[72]

Anthony Hill knew I. K. Brunel, and asked him about the possibility of a railway. He also brought in J. J. Guest of Dowlais, who in October 1833 had taken the chair at a meeting at Merthyr to approve a plan for a railway, the Cambrian, Gloucester & London, from London by Gloucester, Usk, Pontypool and Crumlin to join the Merthyr tramroad.[73] There is a record of a meeting in 1834 between Brunel and Guest to discuss it,[74] after which the engineer made an estimate.

Let us now look at the Glamorganshire Canal, in its day the greatest in Wales, as it was in 1836, synthesizing as well as we may the opinions of the many who gave evidence about it on the Taff Vale Railway Bill.

The canal was operating at something near its capacity, especially below Navigation House at Abercynon. Night working had been introduced not long before; some locks were lit by gas, others by oil lamps. There were thought to be over 200 boats at work. These did about three round trips a fortnight if working through to Merthyr, though the actual passage time if the boat were continuously hauled from one end of the canal to the other was about twenty hours, or ten to twelve hours from Cardiff to Abercynon. The boats were not usually worked continuously, however, for most of the boatmen lived round Nantgarw, and when it could be arranged they moored their boats near the village and went home. Thus goods to Merthyr usually took two days.

There was some congestion all down the canal, but it was worst at the Treble Locks below Nantgarw where working turns* was standard practice, at a narrow place at Melingriffith, and at the tunnel, in which boats could not pass. With normal water boats going down carried 24 tons, falling to 18–20 in short-water times,

* When working turns water was saved by passing boats alternately upwards and downwards through the locks, so making each lockful of water pass two boats. The system caused delays when boats going one way had to wait for those going the other before they could pass the locks.

but boats up carried only 15–18 tons, because the constant working of the locks caused a downwards current in the canal, which made it impossible for a horse to pull as heavy a boat as he could in still water.

At Abercynon (Navigation House, to the east of the Taff, and a few hundred yards below the junction with the Aberdare Canal to the west of the Taff) there was a large basin. Here a colliery tramroad from the Gelli-gaer area (Sir Christopher Smith's) joined the basin, and the coal was tipped into the boats. Here also the Penydarren tramroad met the canal. Down this came all the iron produced by the Dowlais, Penydarren and Plymouth companies, but no public traffic save by favour of these three concerns. Traction had formerly been by horses, 250 trams each carrying 2 tons being used, and three horses taking a train down with about 25 tons of iron. In 1833, after experiments,* locomotives were put on regularly as well as horses, the run from Dowlais taking about four hours, but neither the locomotives nor the horses could pull any substantial load up the tramroad, that for three horses being $2\frac{1}{2}$ tons.

Therefore when about 1834 the ironworks began importing increasing quantities of iron ore, and to some extent cinders, to maintain their growing output, these had to be taken right up the canal to Merthyr where, if intended for Dowlais, they were then hauled up to the works by a locomotive[75] working with a rack and pinion on the Dowlais company's tramroad from the canal. These heavy tonnages of iron ore and cinders moving up the canal had to cope with the existing congestion, the short water more often found on the Merthyr–Abercynon section than lower down, and the lighter loading in any case for boats going upwards. The result was that ore piled up seriously at Cardiff while waiting for transport, and this was probably the trigger that set Hill and Guest off to promote their railway. In 1835, for instance, the Dowlais company sent down nearly 39,000 tons of iron from Abercynon, against 24,000 in 1831, but imported 15,668 tons of iron ore and cinders against 6,156 tons of iron ore in 1827, most of it to be carried right through to Merthyr, and had large quantities waiting at Cardiff. At this time there was only a comparatively small export trade in coal, for the great steam coal days had not arrived, and

* 'The Dowlais Iron Company's steam carriage "Powerful" lately left the Dowlais works for the bason, a distance of 11 miles, with 126 tons of iron attached to it, exclusive of engine, tender and trams, together more than 200 tons. The "Powerful" returned with 47 empty trams and performed the double journey, to and fro, within 12 hours.'([76]) Another engine was the 'Eclipse'.([77])

expansion of coal traffic was not a main motive in promoting the Taff Vale Railway.

The sea-lock pound at Cardiff was also congested. Vessels of 60–70 tons loaded in the upper part nearest Cardiff, where the depth was 8–9 feet, and those of 100–160 tons at the bottom end, in up to 14 feet of water. Those at the upper end had to move down when two-thirds loaded to take on the rest of their cargoes. Coal was transferred from canal boat to collier either from the boat to a stage rigged halfway up the bigger ship's side, then to the deck, and then into the hold, or it was unloaded from boat to wharf, and then put into the ship. Sometimes there was not enough water in the pound to allow the bigger ships to lock out fully laden through the sea-lock. If so, their remaining cargo had to be taken out by lighter, and loaded outside the lock-gates or at Penarth, or the vessel had to wait for a spring tide. Naturally, therefore, the bottom end of the pound became very congested.[78]

There was no complaint of the canal company's charges, which for coal were ½d. per ton per mile against 1¼d. on the Monmouthshire Canal. Richard Blakemore, supporting the canal, called it the cheapest canal in the world, and Guest replied that 'it is a very cheap canal, I admit'. The complaint was of facilities.

In June 1835 R. J. Hill, T. R. Guest, Thomas Charles and Walter Coffin, one of the biggest coalowners, left the canal committee, two more Crawshays and Rees Williams taking their places. In the late summer a meeting of the big canal users was held, at which there was much criticism, and it was after this meeting that Brunel seems to have made his survey. There was then a second meeting, at which William Crawshay II on behalf of the canal company outlined a programme of proposed improvements at a cost of £30,000 to £40,000, including an extension of the canal outwards from the entrance lock, and promised that all further increases of revenue would go to reduce tolls, if the freighters would continue to carry all their trade on the canal. This programme seems to have been tacitly accepted, but what no one had the courage to say face to face with the Crawshays, some were determined to do—they went on with the railway scheme. On 12 October 1835 at a meeting at Merthyr the Taff Vale Railway* was formally inaugurated, with the Hills, the Guests, Walter Coffin and a member of the Charles family on the provisional committee. At this meeting it was resolved: 'that the present means

* For a full account of the railway see D. S. Barrie: *The Taff Vale Railway*, 2nd ed., 1950.

of communication does not afford the requisite facilities . . . it is expedient to establish a communication by means of a Railway, which shall combine the advantages of the latest improvements in the mode of transport.'[79]

The canal company then introduced a Bill early in 1836 for improving the canal. As Chairman of the Standing Orders Committee of the House of Commons, L. W. Dillwyn reported on 1 March that Standing Orders had not been complied with, whereupon the canal company gave him a handsome dinner at the Piazza Coffee House two days later, when he was highly gratified by the strong expressions of obligation and approbation which were bestowed on his attention to county business. On 7 March the Bill's defects had fortunately been cured and it was read a second time 'without the expected opposition', while the Taff Vale Railway Bill was in committee. On 9 May, however, the Canal Bill was defeated in the House by 82 votes to 42, and in the middle of May it was withdrawn.[80] In March Lord Bute had told Crawshay:

'I could not hold the Glamorganshire Canal Co. on a footing to negotiate with me until they had remedied the various encroachments of which I complain. . . . As to their present Bill, I told him that I hardly believed them to be serious; but that if they persevered in it, I must oppose it.'[81]

The Taff Vale Railway company got its Act[82] in the same year of 1836: for the second time the dissident ironmasters had decided to build an alternative to the waterway. The canal company had combined with their old enemy Richard Blakemore, with whom they quickly agreed for a payment of £1,500 p.a. in exchange for the right to take up to 15 tons of water a minute, to oppose the Bill. The railway directors referred later to the 'formidable opposition of the Glamorganshire Canal Company, and Mr. Blakemore', which, they said, 'in the earlier stages of the Bill . . . seriously threatened the ultimate success of the measure'.[83] They therefore paid the canal company and Blakemore £10,000 in compensation, and their opposition was withdrawn. The influence of the Canal Act of 1790 and of that company's opposition was clearly visible in the Taff Vale Act of 1836: that the authorized railway toll for coal was ⅔d., as for ironstone, iron ore and limestone, and 1d. for wrought iron and tinplates, that dividends were limited to 7 per cent, or 9 per cent after tolls had been reduced by a quarter, and that the Act provided for the Justices to make a rate reduction if necessary.*

* These restrictions were later removed.

A second Act in 1837[84] authorized the railway company to buy the Penydarren tramroad for £21,000. Railway branches were also proposed instead of the junctions with the tramroad authorized in the 1836 Act, including one 'for crossing the River near Cyfarthfa, to enable Mr. Crawshay to connect his Works with the Railway, in the manner agreed on between that Gentleman and the Directors before the passing of the Bill . . .'.[85] The railway was opened to Navigation House, Abercynon, from Cardiff in October 1840, and to Merthyr in April 1841.

At Cardiff the railway company had taken powers to make an extension to a dock on the Ely River at Penarth (the old scheme of 1823 will be remembered), and a triangular conflict of interest now developed between the canal company, the railway company with its own small dock, and Lord Bute. In 1838, the year before the Bute Dock was opened, Lord Bute wrote:

'. . . if I keep down my charges so as to meet the competition of the Glamorganshire Canal, the same would obviate any competition which could be brought against me from other quarters.'[86] By 1841 he was more confident: '. . . a change is beginning to assert itself in the character of the Trade. The ship masters are beginning to say to the Iron Masters and others, "we will go to the Bute Dock, you shall come to us, and we will not come to you". . . .' He then refers to the high charges made by bargemasters for transferring cargoes from the canal to the dock 'so that the owners of these barges in fact get the money which I ought to receive. This is a state of things which I do not like to submit to, and the more because many of these barge owners are the very agents of the Iron Masters at their own wharfs. . . . I think that we ought now to get better terms from the Iron Masters than we . . . formerly offered them.'[87] In the same month of 1841 he seems to have given those tenants of his who had wharves on the canal in Cardiff notice to quit,[88] so that they would move to the dock, and wrote also: 'You are not acquainted with Cardiff, or you would be aware that my new Docks are rather looked upon as a rival to the Glamorganshire Canal.'[89] In December 1843 he talked of the railway company entering into 'something of a combination with another party against me'—presumably the canal company—for he goes on: 'I have no objection to see the Dock, the Railway, and the Glamorganshire Canal consolidated into one grand concern.'[90]

Agreement in principle on an amalgamation was reached during the progress through Parliament of the railway's 1844 Bill. This made safe the full value of the railway company's property, saw them 'relieved from a ruinous competition, and the Public Interest most effectually secured by a Railway, Dock and Canal communication, in point of convenience and economy not exceeded (if equalled) by any rival port in the Channel.'[91] William Crawshay II as the canal company's chairman had apparently led the railway negotiators to believe that he agreed subject to the approval of the canal shareholders, but then he 'suddenly, and certainly most unexpectedly, claimed such compensation for presumed personal vested Interests, as at once to put a stop to all further proceedings'.[92] Lord Bute thereupon did not amalgamate his concern with the Taff Vale Railway but instead agreed with them for access to his dock at cheap rates in exchange for the Penarth scheme being dropped. He did not like the company, and in 1845 said of this agreement: 'The crying sin of the Taff Vale Railway has been ever since the first appearance of the Bill in 1836 it was a job for three or four people, whereas the letter and spirit of the agreement on my part is to protect the public against anything of this kind.'[93]

Crawshay's attitude can only have been the result of personal dislikes, for increasingly severe competition from what turned out to be the most prosperous railway in Britain was a foregone conclusion, while Lord Bute's attitude must have been well known to him: 'I will not allow them to dig nor widen their lock or the canal within or without the lock by one inch. This I can prevent their doing.'[94]

Only minor improvements were made to the canal after the Taff Vale Railway was opened. The sea-lock was renovated to accompany the dredging and walling that had already taken place in the sea-lock pound, and some of the canal locks were rebuilt. The opening produced two schools of thought among the canal shareholders: those who considered that high tolls should be charged on goods that could not leave the canal, since the rest of the traffic would go anyway, and those who thought the canal should cut tolls against the railway. A Special General Assembly on 15 September 1841 sharply increased many tolls, and two days later cut them by half: there was a further reduction in September 1844, and another in September 1846. For some time, however, the railway and canal were to find that the traffic offering was ample for both, mainly because the rapidly increasing coal trade provided more tonnage for the canal and also a rapidly growing customer for the railway. The following figures show the comparative position in 1851, ten years after the opening of the Taff Vale:[95]

	Iron	*Iron-ore*	*Coal*
Glamorganshire Canal	190,633	96,408	294,537
Taff Vale Railway	74,701	51,000	580,000

For the year ending Michaelmas 1843 the gross toll receipts were £75,162, of which £60,039 was returned to the freighters. The net revenue including other receipts was £16,682, the expenses £6,805 and the dividends the fixed £8,180. Two years later the gross toll receipts had gone up to £86,245, of which £69,994 was returned.[96] The total tonnage carried, helped by the rapid expansion of traffic from the Aberdare Canal, rose from 319,718 in 1838 to 436,982 in 1848 and 581,578 in 1851, which must have been near the maximum capacity of the waterway, and then fell to 466,983 in 1858. Prosperity did not prevent manœuvrings for position, as when in 1843 a colliery owner was given permission to build a bridge over the canal to carry his coal to a neighbouring ironworks on condition that he agreed not to send any of it by the Taff Vale Railway.

In 1850 the canal company decided to advertise 'that they are desirous of adopting a plan or device for loading coal into vessels lying afloat in the canal from barges alongside, and that they will give a premium of 100 guineas for the best model or exposition of such plan or device'.[97] As a result, a hydraulic tip seems to have been built by W. G. Armstrong & Co., and put into operation in 1851.

In the '60's the canal company's tonnage fell sharply, from 466,983 in 1858 to 315,749 in 1868. There were many causes: the connecting-up of canal-side works and collieries to the railway; the opening of the East Bute Dock partly in 1855 and fully in 1859,* the dock being in turn connected to a branch of the Rhymney Railway in 1857. The tremendous growth of the port of Cardiff as a result of the opening of the docks and the development of the hinterland can be seen from the following figures of traffic handled:

	tons
1840	46,042
1850	873,413
1860	2,225,980
1870	2,804,798

* A canal connexion between the West and East Docks was opened in 1859.

The Roath dock and basin followed, and by 1900 the figure had reached 10,300,000 tons.

There was a proposal in 1864 further to extend the Bute Docks, which was opposed by the canal company, and led to others in 1865 and 1866 that the canal should have its own dock. This activity by the canal company brought an offer from the Bute Trustees to buy the canal. The Crawshays and their supporters were divided. As an investment, their family money would be safer in Consols, but 'To you [Robert Crawshay] as a Freighter, it would not be so desirable. . . . I [William Crawshay II] feel confident that the Trustees would secure us our present dividends upon as good security as consols, but I do not see how we can secure the present low tonnages, if we sell them the canal. . . .'[98] Clearly the offer was refused.

In 1875 the canal company accepted a preliminary proposal from its chairman, now Robert Crawshay since the death of William II in 1867, that the sea-lock pound, the canal at the seaward end, and some additional land be let to a new company, which would build a dock on it and connect it by a railway to the Great Western. The company calculated that they already received £3,500 p.a. for the property, and hoped for a rent of £4,000. After surveys by Richard Hassard, however, they decided in 1877 themselves to build a tidal basin and a dock about 2,000 ft. long and 400 ft. wide on the site of the sea-lock pound and lower part of the canal, and to connect it with the Great Western and Taff Vale Railways. Part of the dock would be equipped with hydraulic coal hoists to ship 1,200,000 tons of coal a year. The cost was estimated at £240,000, and the net revenue at £31,967. The Bill went to a House of Lords committee in 1878, where it was strongly opposed by the Taff Vale Railway and the Bute Trustees. The latter convinced the committee that they could build further coal hoists in their present docks, and that further docks were not needed, and the Bill was lost.

The company was now in a bad way, among the causes being the decay of many ironworks as production turned over to steel, the making of which was concentrated in up-to-date plants connected to the railway. The 8 per cent dividend that had been paid almost from the beginning could not be maintained after 1876, and by 1882 it had fallen to 1½ per cent. In this year the company was authorized to make a short railway branch from the sea-lock pound —its first railway access—and in 1883 work was begun after it had been decided to borrow up to £27,500 on mortgage.

At this point Lord Bute offered to buy all the canal's shares, and this time his offer was accepted on 19 November 1883. He was to pay interest at 6½ per cent on the £100,000 of original capital, and 4 per cent on that raised under the Act of 1796. His reasons were probably many: to prevent the canal company building its own dock or opposing his own Dock Bills (there had been canal opposition to his Bill of 1882); to get water for his docks,*[99] and perhaps as a counter to bargain with the Taff Vale Railway. It was probably as a result of the canal company's agreement to sell that the railway announced in January 1884 a further substantial reduction in their rates on coal for shipment.[100]

In June 1885, the year that his purchase both of the Glamorganshire and the Aberdare Canals took effect, the Marquess of Bute became chairman of the canal company, a new committe was appointed, and the name of Crawshay disappears at last from the records: except between 1814 and 1818, it had been there since the first entry. The new owner called for a report on the state of the undertaking. This was gloomy, and showed that the condition of the canal, locks and buildings was poor. The report ends: 'Of the Sea-Lock Gates, I can only say that they are nearly as bad as they can be, whilst the water lost by leaks is enormous in quantity. . . . Of the whole of the property from Cyfarthfa to Cardiff Sea-Lock I may say without fear of contradiction, there is not a single house but which would be very materially improved by the mason, the carpenter, and the painter.'[101] It was resolved to put the canal into repair, and particularly to make good subsidence damage. The new owner also reconstructed the sea-lock, enlarged and deepened the basin, and provided timber ponds.[102]

From 1887 onwards no dividend was paid, and in 1888 it was decided to promote a Bill to convert the greater part of the canal into a railway. In this year James Abernethy and G. B. Bruce had reported[103] that 'for all purposes of traffic, except a portion near its terminus, the Canal is obsolete . . .'. They pointed out that 'at present the Railway Companies which bring Coal to the Docks at Cardiff have also an interest in taking it to other ports', the Barry Railway to Barry Docks, the Taff Vale to Penarth, the Pontypridd & Caerphilly to Newport. They therefore proposed a line on the course of the Aberdare and Glamorganshire Canals down to Melingriffith, where a junction would be made with the Taff Vale

* The Bute Docks Company subsequently paid the canal company £3,000 p.a. for water.

Railway, with connexions to the Rhymney Railway and Roath dock. Below Melingriffith the canal would remain.

Nothing happened, but in 1896 Parliamentary notice was given to vest the Glamorganshire and Aberdare Canals in the Bute Docks company (which had been formed in 1886 to take over the Marquess's dock undertakings from the beginning of 1887) and to abandon all the Aberdare and most of the Glamorganshire. In 1897 the Bute Docks company was turned into the Cardiff Railway company, but the line subsequently built by it from Cardiff to Trefforest did not use the canal bed.

In 1888 and again in 1898 we know that the company was doing some carrying, but little in proportion to the total tonnage moved.[104] One or two steam boats had been introduced in 1893, but they made small difference owing to the number of locks.[105] By the '90's the canal above Pontypridd was little used, and traffic above it had fallen from 284,041 tons in 1871 to 31,113 tons in 1897.[106] The topmost section fromCyfarthf a to Merthyr had been disused since 1865, and the part from Abercynon to Merthyr was closed on 7 December 1898,[107] and in 1920 was sold to Cardiff Corporation for a water-pipe track. Thenceforward the main value of the canal was as a water feeder. In mid-1915 a burst at Cilfynydd caused the Pontypridd-Abercynon section to be closed, though for some years there had been little traffic higher than Tongwynlais. A final burst at Nantgarw on 25 May 1942 effectively closed the canal except for a part of the sea lock pound.

An Act of 1936 authorized toll changes. In 1943 Cardiff Corporation bought the company and the carrying business closed down, the last boat having passed in 1942. A Corporation Act of that year authorized its abandonment, though it was to be kept open until six months after the end of the war.* The canal company's railway branch from West Canal Wharf to the sea-lock, with a connexion to the G.W.R.'s Riverside branch, was, however, taken over by the Corporation, who worked it until it closed on 23 February 1963.

The Doctor's Canal†

Dr Richard Griffiths was an important figure in Welsh industrial history, for in addition to his other interests he first sent Rhondda

* The barge weighing machine from Cardiff has been re-erected at the Waterways Museum at Stoke Bruerne near Northampton.

† Though built by Dr Griffiths, we find it about 1860 called 'The Rev. G. Thomas's Canal' and then 'Dr Thomas's Canal' by H. R. de Salis in *Bradshaw's Canals and Navigable Rivers*, 1904. It was commonly called 'The Doctor's Canal.'

coal to the outside world. Born in 1756, he took a lease of the minerals under the Hafod Uchaf lands at the end of the eighteenth century. In 1807 he asked the Glamorganshire Canal company whether they would help him to build a tramroad from his colliery at Gyfeillon to their canal by giving him £3,000 worth of free tolls on his first coal shipments, but they refused on the grounds that they had not the power to do so. A year later he proposed to make a canal branch 1 mile long from the Glamorganshire Canal at Denia to Trefforest, and a tramroad thence over the river for 3¼ miles to Hafod, and asked if construction materials could be carried free. This was agreed. The tramroad and river bridge were building in 1809, but it was not till 1813 that the Glamorganshire company would allow him to join his canal to theirs, because they had not been satisfied upon its water supply.

Meanwhile Walter Coffin of Bridgend had bought Dinas farm, higher up the Rhondda valley, in 1806, begun mining about 1807, and had extended his mineral lease in 1810. He in turn built a tramroad for another 2¼ miles from Dinas to connect with Dr Griffiths's line, which was completed in 1812.

Dr Griffiths died in 1826, and his property then passed to his nephews, the Rev. George Thomas and his brother. His tramroad carried a large proportion of the Glamorganshire Canal's coal traffic: Coffin's exports alone were 56,000 tons out of a total of 214,240 tons carried in 1839. It was also the only means of transport up the valley until the road was built.

The Dinas branch of the Taff Vale Railway was opened in 1841, but the canal continued in use to the present century, as did the lower part of the tramroad from Pwll-gwaun colliery. There was a small trade on the canal in 1904, but this had ceased by about 1914. In 1918 it was described as derelict.[108]

Aberdare Canal

Samuel Glover of Birmingham and Aber-carn (later to be served by the Monmouthshire Canal), had leased the Hirwaun works in 1786[109] and had built a tramroad there. These works belonged to John Maybery and Thomas Wilkins, and until his death had been leased to Anthony Bacon. In 1791 the Neath Canal was authorized, from the top of which at Glynneath it was practicable to build a tramroad to Hirwaun. A group of those who were concerned with the Glamorganshire Canal and the development of the Taff valley therefore joined Glover to promote a branch canal and ancillary tramroads from the Glamorganshire at Abercynon to near Aberdare. In 1792 there was a subscription for a survey for a canal from the Glamorganshire to the Neath Canals.[110] There was then no road up the Aberdare valley except a rough horse path and a road was therefore surveyed at the same time by John Dadford.[111] In March 1793 the Aberdare Canal was authorized[112] from Abercynon to Tŷ-draw across the valley from what was then the village of Aberdare, 'and for making or maintaining a Railway or Stone Road, from thence to near Abernant* . . .', as well as other tramroads within eight miles of its line. The Aberdare turnpike road from Abercynon through Aberdare to Aber-nant (Glynneath) was authorized on the same day.[113]

The company's capital was £22,500, with power to raise £11,000 more if necessary. A total of £22,100 was subscribed, some by Samuel and Jeremiah Homfray of Penydarren, Richard Hill of Plymouth works, and John Partridge, soon to be concerned with Melingriffith: they put up £3,500. Much came also from Samuel Glover and other men from Birmingham and Tamworth: they put up £3,200. Two local men, Hugh Lord of Aberaman and John Knight of Dyffryn, put up £1,000 each. Brecon interests, notably the Wilkinses of the Old Bank, who were property owners round Hirwaun, and also the Powells, subscribed £7,600 and the four Dadfords, all concerned in one way or another with Welsh canals, a total of £2,000. Needless to say, Wilkins & Co. were the company's bankers. The list of trustees of the Aberdare Road included Glover, the Wilkinses, the Homfrays, Hill, and Partridge, but also Richard Crawshay of Cyfarthfa and Thomas Guest and William Taitt of Dowlais.

Almost at once it was decided to postpone cutting the canal, but to build a tramroad from the proposed site of the canal basin at Aberdare to 'join Mr. Glover's Rail Road upon Hirwaun Common and from thence to the Lime Rock at Penderin'.[114] The company leased a quarry at Penderyn, and in 1794 another; by September 1794 it appears that James Dadford had built a 3 ft. 2 in. gauge edge-railway from Bryngwyn collieries (south-east of Hirwaun) past the Hirwaun works and on to Penderyn, and perhaps also some way from Bryngwyn towards Aberdare. It was 4¼ miles long from Penderyn to Bryngwyn and cost £4,000. The limestone was used for lime burning (the Company later built kilns on Hirwaun Common) and presumably also in the ironworks. Glover's line

* Aber-nant near Aberdare, not Aber-nant near Glynneath.

had been built in 1780 from the Penderyn quarries to Hirwaun works, so Dadford may well have made use of it.

Glover had given up his lease of Hirwaun works in 1794;* they seem thereafter to have been worked for some time by Anthony and Thomas Bacon. The period after the passing of the Act was not a good one for investment and many of the canal promoters were using their money in subscriptions to the Glamorganshire Canal and in extensions to their own works. The Company therefore confined itself to operating its tramroad and quarries on a small scale. Work on the turnpike road also did not begin till after May 1803, when a new survey was made and new trustees appointed from the Aberdare, Aber-nant and Hirwaun works and it was not finished till about 1810.[115] In 1800, however, Glover leased to John and George Scale of Birmingham and two others the land, usually called Llwydcoed, on which the Aberdare ironworks were to be built and in 1801 Walter Wilkins leased a site at Aber-nant (near Aberdare) to Jeremiah Homfray and James Birch, who in 1802 took the Tappendens from Kent as partners, and built the Aber-nant ironworks.

Even before these leases were signed the Neath Canal company† were making moves towards building a tramroad through Hirwaun to Aberdare to get the potential traffic, and in 1800 the Aberdare Iron Company (as the Scales's concern was called) was itself considering building a tramroad to join the Glamorganshire to the Neath Canal. In July 1800, therefore, the canal company asked Thomas Dadford junior to re-survey the canal, and also recommend improvements to the existing tramroad. Dadford reported on 1 August that the canal could be built for £10,500, from which a tramroad 1½ miles long could be laid to the Aberdare Iron Co.'s works at Llwydcoed for £1,500. On the same day John Scale wrote to the canal company offering to guarantee a revenue of £750 p.a. for the remainder of the Iron Company's lease if the canal company would build the canal and tramroad, and charge 3d. a ton on iron.[116]

They could not face such a toll reduction, and nothing was done about the canal, though a Parliamentary Notice was issued for a 'Canal, Rail or Dram Way' from the Glamorganshire Canal to Aber-nant (Glynneath).[117] In 1801 the Glamorganshire Company

* This date is given by John Lloyd. Glover remained on the Canal Committee until 1799.

† It will be convenient if the reader will look at pp. 66–70 of Chapter IV before reading the next page.

were told that 'The Aberdare Canal Company have promised to unite their cut to us as per plan originally made',[118] and as late as 1802 the Aberdare company were thinking of building the tramroad from Llwydcoed to Werfa (near Rhigos), with the idea of continuing to Dinas.[119] This last proposal had been authorized by the company in August 1801, the three ironworks having agreed to guarantee 8 per cent on its cost and that of the existing lines, and the Aber-nant works agreeing to build a private branch from it. Nothing came of the proposal, and the Aber-nant proprietors instead built a tramroad to Glynneath in co-operation with the Neath Canal company, which was opened in 1805.

In 1806 the three companies agreed to convert the Aberdare Canal company's tramroad from edge-rails to a plateway, and to make and maintain a new bridge at Hirwaun and a new junction with the Aber-nant–Glynneath line, for a payment of £2,500 from the canal company. A few months later they declined to carry out the agreement, and in July 1807 the portion from the Aber-nant–Glynneath line to Bryngwyn collieries was leased to the Hirwaun company (now Bowzer, Overton and Oliver) for £40 a year and its maintenance. In 1808, however, the three companies agreed to convert the rest to a plateway at their own expense and to raise the bridge at Hirwaun on receiving an equal weight of old rails in exchange for the new tramplates.

The company had managed to pay a 1 per cent dividend on the 221 issued £100 shares, of which about one-third was paid-up, in 1804 and 1808 from its takings on the tramroad, but now the Wilkinses and their associates, who held the largest block of shares, decided the time had come to press on with the development of the valley, and in August 1809 it was agreed to build the canal, and a tramroad from it to the Aberdare ironworks at Llwydcoed.

The course was re-surveyed by Martin (presumably Edward Martin of Morriston), Thomas Sheasby junior was engaged as resident engineer, with Evan and David Hopkin as the contractors. Work began early in 1810. A considerable change in control took place soon afterwards. The Homfrays had long ago sold their shares, and Richard Hill had left the Committee in 1809. To partner the Wilkins interest, there now joined the Committee John and George Scale of the Aberdare works, Francis Tappenden of Aber-nant, F. W. Bowzer of Bowzer, Overton and Oliver, who had taken over Hirwaun from the Bacons about 1806, and Joseph Bailey, who may have had local colliery interests. With some changes this group of local industrialists ran the canal for ten years. In August 1811 Sheasby resigned and went as clerk and engineer to the Severn & Wye company, and George Overton took over from him.

The canal was opened about mid-August 1812. It was 6¾ miles long with two locks at Cwm-bach and Dyffryn and a stop-lock at the junction, and took craft of the same size as those on the Glamorganshire. A tramroad connexion from Canal Head had been built about 1811 to join the Glynneath–Hirwaun–Aber-nant tramroad at Llwydcoed. A private branch from the Gadlys works later joined this at Trecynon, while another from the Aber-nant works to Canal Head was probably built after 1819, when they had been taken over by the owners of the Aberdare works. The cost at opening was about £26,220, which was raised by calling £120 a share, though some shareholders refused to pay the calls over £100, and received proportionately lower dividends.

By the time the canal was open the Hirwaun company of Bowzer, Overton & Oliver was in liquidation, and for some years the canal had little iron to carry. Some of what was made seems to have gone to the Neath Canal, apparently by road, for shipment at Neath or Swansea. Then in 1819 there came a change, when the March canal meeting reduced all canal tolls by half. It was the year in which William Crawshay and his son William Crawshay II, acquired the Hirwaun works. He and his henchman Thomas Charles now appear as shareholders, together with Dr Richard Griffiths the coalowner. They also joined the Committee, on which George Scale, J. B. Bruce and Rowland Fothergill represented other interests. In 1820 the canal company agreed with the two groups of proprietors, Crawshay & Son of Hirwaun and the Scales of Aberdare and Aber-nant, to keep their tolls at the same level for three years if the companies carried by their tramroad and canal all the iron they made which was intended for shipment at Cardiff or for sale at Merthyr or elsewhere (they reserved the right to ship also at Neath and Swansea).

By 1822 William Crawshay II had increased his shareholding from 25 to 55 of the 225 shares, and in 1823 the company agreed to raise the canal banks to provide greater depth so that boats could carry their full 25 tons, as part of a policy of holding out every inducement 'to the proprietors of the Iron Works to convey their Iron by this line to Port in preference to the Neath Valley'.[120] In 1823 this inter-company agreement was renewed for three years, and in 1825 it was resolved, 'the Canal being now in an efficient state for carrying down the increased Trade, that the Tramroads be now also put in a state of thorough repair . . .'.[121] Crawshay had now 89 shares.

Crawshay's efficiency did not, however, extend to coping with the company's clerks. In 1825 Watkin Powell, who had been clerk and superintendent since 1801, apparently at £75 p.a. and a house, was found to owe the company £93 15s. 0¾d., and was discharged. His successor, James Peirce, went in 1827, and we can guess why, for his replacement Samuel Ball was told: 'no horse to be kept, or sporting Dogs'.[122] Though forbidden to be sporting, in 1828 there was a suspicion that he was sometimes intoxicated. He may have been, but he did pocket some cash, and he too went. At last the company raised their chief servant's salary to £100 p.a., and Thomas Wayne began a period of respectability.

The traffic on the canal in 1828 was still only 59,525 tons. The management was good, though increasingly associated with members of the Crawshay family and their associate William Thompson, who took over many of the shares, and who ran the Aberdare works with Rowland Fothergill and George Scale. The trade in iron was not big enough, though the Crawshays had started further ironworks at Penderyn, and also iron and tinplate works at Trefforest, which used iron carried from Hirwaun. In 1835 the toll on iron ore and ironstone was reduced to ½d. a ton per mile, but in 1838 the total tonnage at 60,898 was almost the same as it had been ten years before.

In 1841, after two years of negotiation between Crawshay and Fothergill as the principal freighters on the canal, the company bought from Benjamin Hall, the assignee of the Aber-nant works estate when the Tappendens went bankrupt, the Rhigos—Aber-nant portion of the old Glynneath–Aber-nant tramroad, part of which formed the connexion between the Hirwaun—Penderyn section of the company's tramroad and the Llwydcoed section. The money was raised by loan, and the Hirwaun–Rhigos section was then allowed to decay, since it was agreed that traffic should not pass that way.

A change was now coming to the canal: iron was being supplemented by the growing carriage of coal, as the great steam coal trade began in the Aberdare valley. 'The increasing Coal trade upon the Canal' was referred to in 1840,[123] and in 1842 Thomas Powell of Dyffryn was asking permission to carry coal from his famous colliery in containers in the boats. Sixteen steam coal pits were sunk in the valley between 1840 and 1853;[124] dividends rose, and in 1843 the swelling trade was helped by a 25 per cent reduction in the tolls on coal, iron, iron ore, ironstone, limestone, pitwood and quarry stone. Indeed, water to carry the trade was now getting short, and a pumping engine to raise water from the Cynon was put to work about 1846, the Glamorganshire company paying two-thirds of the cost, which was £4,143, because they would eventually get the water. By 1848 the tonnage had trebled in ten years to 159,653, and the dividends had equally improved.

Average of years ending 25 March	*Average dividend on £120 share* £	s.	d.
1814–18	1	12	0
1819–23	1	2	0
1824–28	1	14	0
1829–33	4	0	0
1834–38	5	4	0
1839–43*	7	5	0

Before then, however, a competitor had appeared in the valley. In July 1845 the Aberdare Railway had been incorporated 'from the Taff Vale Railway to a certain Tramroad leading from the Hirwain Iron Works to the Aberdare Canal . . .', with Sir Josiah J. Guest and Crawshay Bailey among its directors. It was opened in May 1846 and leased in perpetuity from the beginning of 1847 to the Taff Vale Railway.† This competition caused an immediate drop in the average dividends on the canal to £5 6s. per £120 share for the period 1844–8, and £5 9s. for 1849–53, in spite of which the canal toll on coal was increased 5 per cent in 1848.

Another railway was interested in the steam coal traffic. The Vale of Neath had reached Aberdare from Neath in 1851. In 1847 and again in 1850 it had considered buying portions of the canal company's tramroads, notably those from the end of their Aberdare branch to Canal Head, and from Hirwaun to Penderyn. Unofficial enquiries told them that the Aberdare company wanted to get rid of the liability for their maintenance, but, when approached, Crawshay as the principal proprietor did not think the canal company would benefit, and the proposal dropped.[125]

A junction between the railway at Aberdare and Canal Head was favoured by the railway company, to get Crawshay's downwards traffic and also to seek coal shipments from Dyffryn and the collieries below Aberdare for carriage to Swansea and Neath. In

* Omitting 1842, not known.

† For the Taff Vale's part in the development of the Aberdare valley, see D. S. M. Barrie: *The Taff Vale Railway*, 2nd ed., 1950.

November 1851 Brunel was ordered to 'have erected in the Aberdare Station Yard convenience for the transfer of Coal and other Materials from (or to) the Trams used on the Canal Tramroad to (or from) the Waggons on the Vale of Neath line . . .'.[126] This seems to have been done, though in June 1853 the railway line itself was extended for ½ mile to Canal Head.[127] However, Brunel did not, as he had been ordered, provide interchange apparatus there between boat and truck, and there were complaints of limited accommodation for loading coal trucks from the canal, so that the railway company ordered work to be carried on round the clock till permanent apparatus should be installed.[128] The interchange proved unsatisfactory, however, owing to the 'serious cost of transit and material damage to the Coal arising from the present mode of boating the Coal to the Canal Head and unloading it in the Trucks being found in practice so great as must of necessity prevent the continuance of the trade by such means'.[129] Therefore an extension railway, the Aberdare Valley, was promoted from Canal Head to Middle Dyffryn colliery, and opened in November 1856. It was leased to the Vale of Neath and became their property in 1864.

The competition from the first line that had been opened, the Aberdare, had for a time caused an economy drive in the running of the canal, which reached a severe point in August 1849 when it was ordered 'that Beer to the Workmen be discontinued in future except in the most extreme contingency'.[130]

Thenceforward, however, in spite of two railways in the valley, the output of the collieries was such that the canal entered its most prosperous period, the tonnage rising from 159,653 in 1848 to 216,704 in 1858, receipts from £3,778 to £4,352, and dividends to a maximum of £10 per £120 share for the years ending 25 March 1857–9. In 1864 a decline began, coinciding with the extension of the Aberdare Valley line to join the Taff Vale Extension of the Newport, Abergavenny & Hereford Railway at Quakers' Yard, which provided the valley with a double set of competing rails. By 1868 the tonnage had fallen to 93,542, the receipts proportionately less to £2,857. Traffic held this level for twenty years, the tonnage for 1888 being 102,805, but the receipts only £750.

However, in 1875, a bad year because of the stoppage of the Aberdare works and a strike, a canal meeting agreed that 'the trade on the Canal is so bad that the Company may be compelled to shut it up or sell it . . .',[131] and in 1883 the shareholders accepted the terms offered by Lord Bute as a consequential of his purchase of the Glamorganshire. He took over in 1885, becoming chairman. In 1888 the conversion of the greater part of the canal to a railway was agreed upon, but not pursued. In 1898 it was reported that difficulty was being experienced in working it because of subsidence, and in any case its traffic had now fallen to only 6,794 tons, none of it coal or iron. The waterway was closed in November 1900.[132]

The company's later dividend record had been as follows:

Average of years ending 25 March	*Average dividend on £120 share*		
	£	s.	d.
1854–58	8	4	0
1859–63	9	4	0
1864–68	6	2	0
1869–73	6	8	0
1874–78		10	0
1879–83	1	11	0

The tramroad from Aberdare through Hirwaun to Penderyn remained open and working, though that from Hirwaun towards Rhigos had been disused since the early 40's and that from Llwydcoed to Aber-nant for some time, part of it having been converted to a railway. By the Pontypridd Waterworks & Tramroad Act of 1908 the water company were authorized on payment of tolls to use the tramroad from Penderyn to Hirwaun with locomotives, and presumably at this time it was relaid with rails. The site was sold in 1944 to Roads Reconstruction (1934) Ltd., who had for many years rented it.

The canal itself and the rest of the tramroad were sold in 1923 to the Urban District Councils of Aberdare and Mountain Ash, most of the property going to Aberdare, the sale being confirmed by the Aberdare Canal Act of 1924. The site was thereupon used for road widening, and very few traces of the canal now exist. The company itself went into voluntary liquidation in 1955.

CHAPTER VII

The Monmouthshire Canal and its Tramroad Connexions

IN 1791 the population of Newport was 750, and 247 vessels with a registered tonnage of 12,349 had cleared the port.[1] Towards the end of the year a newspaper reported[2] that a canal was projected from Newport to Pontnewynydd, with a branch from Crindai farm to Crumlin, at an estimated cost of £108,477 including a number of tramroads, of which £51,000 had been subscribed at the first meeting. The annual (presumably net) revenue from tonnage was put at £10,421. By the end of February 1792 it was reported that the whole £108,000 had been subscribed, 'and half as much again ready to be advanced if necessary'.[3] 'At that period but one or two insignificant works existed near the town; and for want of better conveyance, their iron . . . was conveyed upon the backs of mules to Newport, and from one works to another.'[4]

The Act[5] was passed in June 1792. It authorized a capital of £120,000 in £100 shares, and £60,000 more if necessary, and presumably because the big subscribers were mainly local or Bristol ironmasters, colliery proprietors, businessmen and owners of land likely to be used for industrial development, it was enacted that no one shareholder could subscribe for more than 100 shares unless some remained not taken up, and that after five years no shareholder could have more than ten votes at a meeting. The principal subscribers were Josiah Wedgwood (£7,000), Sir Charles Morgan (£5,200), the Duke of Beaufort (£4,700), Thomas Hill* (£4,500), Harford & Co.† and James Harford (£4,500 and £3,000), John

* Thomas Hill with two partners leased the site of Blaenavon ironworks in 1789.

† Harford, Partridge & Co. of Melingriffith works near Cardiff. They became partners with Jeremiah Homfray in Ebbw Vale from 1791, and unsuccessfully with Thomas Hill as Hill, Harford & Co. in 1792 at Nant-y-glo.

Bowsher (£4,100), William Esdaile (£3,600), and Dr Richard Griffiths* (£3,400).

Of these, Bowsher and the Harfords represented the Bristol interest, Bowsher especially that of the coal importers. The Duke and Sir Charles Morgan were mainly landowners, Hill and the Harfords ironmasters, Dr Griffiths and Wedgwood colliery owners, and Esdaile a London banker. Later, there were to be difficulties over such people's double interest as industrialists and as canal owners. One instance occurs in 1800 when the canal company were thinking of seeking an Act to increase tolls, and a meeting was called by the 'Freighters and Proprietors of Mineral Estates' on the canal to consider what should be done about the proposal: of the eight signatories five were connected with the canal, including Harford & Co. and Edward Kendall.† There were other instances later.

The Act authorized a canal from the tideway of the Usk just below Newport bridge to Pontnewynydd,‡ with a branch from Crindai (Malpas) to Crumlin. From Pontnewynydd 'railways, waggonways or stoneroads' were projected to Blaenavon, to Trosnant with a branch to Blaendare, and from the Crumlin branch to Beaufort (Ebbw Vale) with a branch to Sirhowy, and another from Aberbeeg to Nant-y-glo. It was considered that these canals and railways would 'open an easy and commodious Communication into divers Iron Works, Lime Stone Quarries, Woods of Timber Trees, and Collieries in the Neighbourhood of Pontnewydd§ and Crumlin Bridge . . . and with large and extensive Tracts of Land abounding in Iron and Coal . . .'.[6] Other tramroads could be built to any ironworks, quarry or coalmine within 8 miles of the canal or its authorized tramroads, owners being empowered to do so if the canal company did not, but to charge a maximum toll of 5d. a ton per mile. Anyone could make a canal cut up to 2 miles long if the landowner agreed.

As built, the main line was 11 miles long, with one lock (Town) of 12 ft. rise below the junction at Crindai (Malpas), and then 41 locks to Pontnewynydd with a rise of 435 ft., and 3 short tunnels,

* Builder of the Doctor's Canal (see p. 117).

† Lessee of the Beaufort ironworks, and for a short time after 1800 a partner in the Clydach works till they were let on sub-lease to Frere & Cooke. Prominent in canal affairs, and several times Chairman, though a small shareholder. He died in 1807. Beaufort was bought by J. & C. Bailey in 1833 from Kendall & Co.

‡ Not to be confused with Pontnewydd just below Pontymoile near Pontypool. The original end of the canal was about 600 yards beyond the village of Pontnewynydd.

§ Pontnewynydd is probably meant.

two at Newport and one at Cwmbrân. The branch was 11 miles long from Crindai, rising 358 ft. by 32 locks to Crumlin. The main flights of locks on the main line were the 11 locks above Pontymoile (Pont-y-moel), five at Pontnewydd, ten at Cwmbrân and ten at Tŷ-coch; those on the branch were the five at Allt-yr-ynn, fourteen at Cefn (Rogerstone), and seven at Aber-carn. The first boats ordered were 62 ft. 6 in. by 8 ft. 10 in.,[7] but the size later became standardized at about 64 ft. 9 in. by 9 ft. 2 in.,[8] carrying 25–28 tons when fully loaded.[9]

The tolls authorized were 5d. on iron and merchandise, 2½d. a ton on ironstone, iron ore, coal and limestone, and 1½d. on roadstone and agricultural produce, the Commissioners* being given power to reduce tolls within stated limits when a dividend greater than 10 per cent could be paid.

Thomas Dadford junior, one of the contractor-engineers of the Glamorganshire Canal, and the engineer of the Leominster Canal, both then under construction, was made engineer. He was to give three-quarters of his time to the work, and was not to work elsewhere except on the Leominster, and 'during the continuance of his employment he is not to have any concern in any Contract for cutting'.[10] Labourers were sought as far away as Cardiganshire and Carmarthenshire, and work began. In 1793 shares were said to be selling at a premium of £450; then with the many bank failures of that year, they fell back.[11] In October, when money was beginning to get tight, only 1,080 shares out of 1,200 had been subscribed, and the remainder was offered to the shareholders in the proportion of one for every nine held,† while defaulters on calls were admonished. In this year the Brecknock & Abergavenny Canal was authorized to extend the eastern branch of the Monmouthshire from Pontymoile to Brecon.

The Crumlin–Aber-carn section was opened about March 1794: by October 4½ miles of this branch were navigable, and 3½ miles of the Pontnewynydd line. The cutting was proving troublesome; it was for instance reported of the Pontnewynydd line that 'This part of the Canal has been very expensive in Cutting through Rocks, Puddling and Lineing so as to make it watertight.'[12]

Sixteen months later, in February 1796,[13] the main line from Pontnewynydd to the basin at Newport became navigable, though some work remained to be done, and 14 boats were at work. The

* For the function of commissioners, see my *British Canals*, 3rd ed., 1966, p. 45.

† This led to shares being split into ninths. In January 1794 shareholders were asked to buy or sell fractions so that they held whole shares.

Crumlin line was complete except for 1½ miles between Rogerstone and Allt-yr-ynn which was still building, and so were the Blaenavon, Trosnant, Blaendare, Beaufort and Rassa* tramroads, but not the Nant-y-glo, in spite of an urgent request from Hill, Harford & Co.† These tramroads were laid as edge-railways to a gauge of 3 ft. 4 in., with rails 4 ft. long, 3 in. deep, and 2½ in. thick, narrowing to 2 in. on the top, mortised and tenoned into each other, and fastened at the joints to iron, later wooden, sleepers, themselves carried on a wooden block at each end. The horse trams had grooved wheels about 3½ in. wide straddling the rails, and carried about 2 tons.

Expenses had proved heavy. The company had already called more than £100 on each share, and because in February the bank refused further advances, additional calls were made on the share holders to bring the share capital up to the authorized maximum of £180,000. At this time the canal as it approached Newport passed through a short tunnel, a ½ mile farther on fell by Town Lock near Mill Street, then almost immediately passed through a second tunnel about 140 yds. long under the main road, and ended in a basin beside the river just short of Town pill. The tide came up to the main road bridge, and below the pill there was plenty of room for good river wharves to take sea-going ships. It seems to have been proposed in 1796 that the canal should be extended downwards for 1½ miles from the pill,[14] but as William Kemeys, one of the landowners affected, was hostile, an authorizing Act[15] was passed in 1797, after some quarrelling because certain proprietors thought that Sir Charles Morgan, whose river wharves served the existing basin, and some of whose family's land was needed for any extension, was trying to influence the Bill for personal reasons.[16]

The Act authorized £34,600 and £10,730 more if necessary, to be raised rateably from shareholders above the previously authorized capital of £180,000.‡ As regards the extension, the Act gave permission to extend 1½ miles, since 'there may not, in the Course of Time, be a sufficient Space . . . on the North Side of the Pill at Newport . . .'.[17] Meanwhile, however, Kemeys had in September 1796 given permission for the canal to be extended past the Town pill to his land, beyond which lay that of John Jones and

* The Rassa tramroad linked Beaufort to Sirhowy.

† Relations with the Brecknock & Abergavenny Company were still friendly, and the Monmouthshire Company probably thought that Nant-y-glo would be served by way of that company's tramroads from Gilwern (see p. 135).

‡ This caused a levy of one-sixth upon each share.

Sir Charles Morgan. On 16 October 1797 the shareholders decided to extend for about 350 yards past Town pill on a stone aqueduct strengthened with piles to Kemeys's land at Friars Fields, and the work was completed by October 1798. Tramroads were provided for the short distances between the canal wharves and those on the river where ships could lie.[18]

Meanwhile the Crumlin line had been completed, and in April 1799 it was resolved 'that this Assembly are of Opinion and do hereby declare the Canal finished'.[19] For the year ending 9 September 1799 the canal carried 44,528 tons, of which 29,000 was coal and 12,000 iron,[20] and by March 1802 the company felt sufficiently established to have the committee room in the canal office at Newport painted a French grey colour, and to order for it 'a Decent Carpet, Two Mahogany Tables, Two Dozen Chairs and Two Fine Screens'.[21]

Though the Nant-y-glo tramroad had not been built, the committee had already been empowered[22] to build any tramroad branch asked for if a clear 7½ per cent on cost was guaranteed, plus the expense of repairs. As a result the company agreed to make a tramroad to Wedgwood & Kendall's Llanhilleth (Blaen-y-cwm) collieries from the Pontnewynydd line at a cost not exceeding £2,000, the partners to repair and pay £100 p.a. in lieu of tolls, and to Sir Robert Salusbury's Llanhilleth collieries for not more than £1,000, he also to pay £100 p.a. and keep in repair.[23] This latter line was double-track, and came down an incline at Argoed to the Beaufort tramroad a little above Crumlin. In 1819 the company took over the plane and dismantled it. On the other line the Llanhilleth Coal company took over all except the portion below the plane.[24]

In 1799 Benjamin Outram, the best-known tramroad engineer of the time, was called in to survey the company's lines. He reported early in 1800, and recommended the substitution of plateways for edge-railways, the arguments being that: 'The labour of one horse on a railway of this kind* being equal to the labour of four horses on the best Railways that have been constructed on the plan of those belonging to the Monmouthshire Canal Company; and on these improved roads, the saving in repairs of roads and wagons is as great as the saving in expense of conveyance. . . . The sooner the Canal and Railways are made perfect, the earlier and more extensively will trade be established. . . .'[25] Plateways were worked with several waggons behind a horse, but the edge-railway practice of a single horse for each waggon is confirmed by

* A plateway.

Coxe in his *Monmouthshire*.[26] Again, the heavy breakages caused to the cast-iron edge-rails are clear from the canal records. Therefore the company accepted Outram's recommendations, and beginning in 1803, the Beaufort and probably the Trosnant lines were converted to plateways of Outram's standard 4 ft. 2 in. gauge. That to Blaenavon, however, remained an edge-railway for many years. It was probably converted about 1829 when the Trosnant tramroad was extended upwards to meet it (see p. 144). I have no date for the conversion of the Rassa. The Blaendare line (which went out of use about 1818) seems never to have been converted. After conversion the permitted waggon loading was raised from about 2 tons to 56 cwt. in 1811 and 61 cwt. in 1828.

The opening of the canal increased the company's concern with Newport, whose population had in 1801 risen to 1,135, as a port. Their first trouble was with the duty on coal carried coastwise by sea which had been re-enacted in 1787.[27] One of the objects of the canal had been to ship coal to Bristol, places on the Severn, and across to Somerset, and when promoting their enterprise the proprietors had relied upon the existing custom of shipping coal from Newport duty-free to points eastwards of the Holms, the islands that lie in the Bristol Channel a little west of Newport.[28] However, the custom was questioned, probably at the suggestion of rivals, and three test shipments up Severn were in fact seized.

Fortunately for the company, its Bill of 1797 was going through the House, and into it, at the suggestion of their London solicitor, Edmund Estcourt, a clause was inserted (section 29) which specifically exempted from duty coal from Newport carried eastwards of the Holms,[29] and was passed before the coal exporters of the Forest of Dean and west Wales realized what had happened.

By section 50 of the further Monmouthshire Canal Act of 1802 this exemption was extended to coal intended for the port of Bridgwater, even though for navigational reasons it passed westwards of the Holms. The same Act empowered the company to pay bounties on coal exported by sea, which meant that to other destinations they could if they wished offset some of the duty by a compensating bounty. By 1810 this had become 1s. a ton paid to the shipper, and 6d. to the captain of the vessel as gratuity: of the 1s. 6d., 3d. was paid by the canal company and 1s. 3d. by the coal exporters. In 1811 the bounties were taken over by the canal company, who financed them by an increase of canal toll on coal of ½d. a ton per mile.

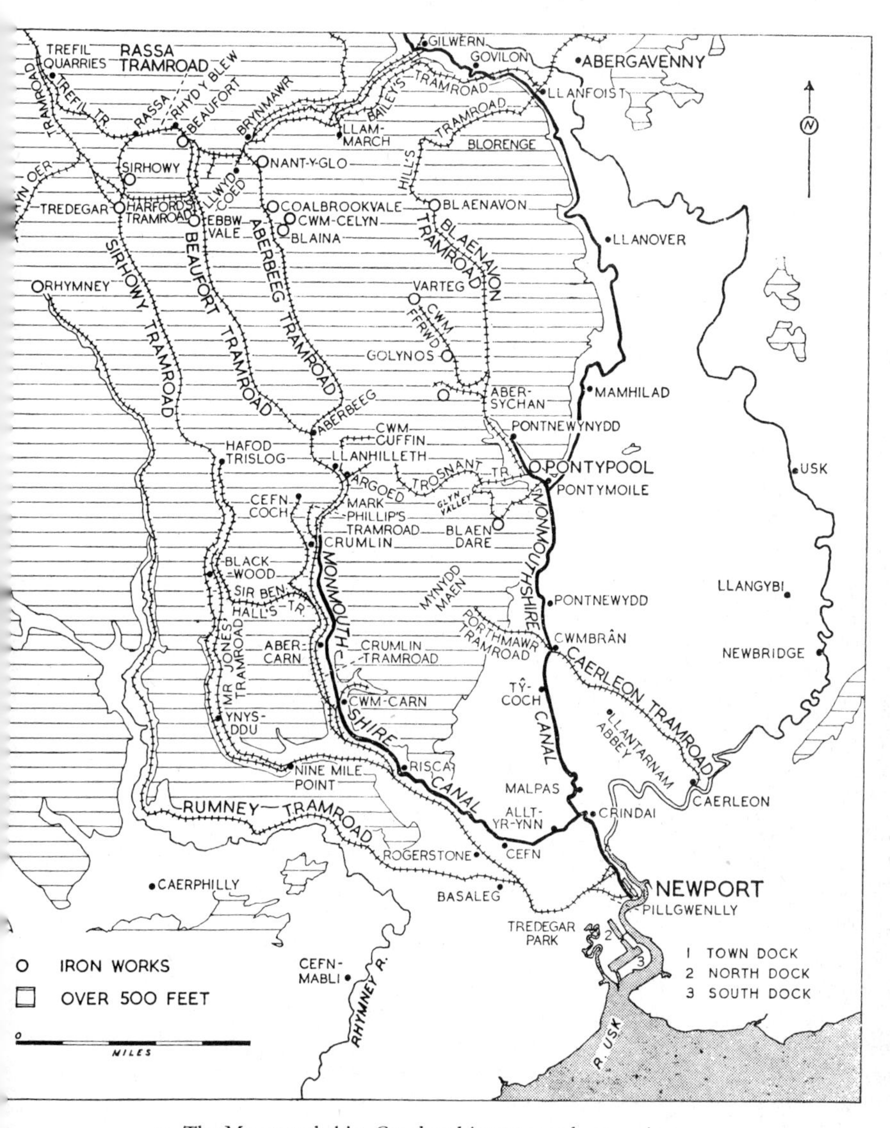

7. The Monmouthshire Canal and its tramroad connexions

By 1810 we can see the immense effect of these measures upon the coal trade of the Bristol Channel. The freedom from the coal duty of 5s. 4d. a ton enjoyed by Monmouthshire coal exported to Bridgwater and eastwards, combined with the bounty of 1s. 6d. a ton on that going westwards, had increased the tonnage exported from Newport as follows:

	tons		*tons*
1797	6,939	1804	64,393
1798	9,715	1805	73,823
1799	18,375	1806	89,129
1800	32,277	1807	109,648
1801	29,981	1808	132,316
1802	38,813	1809	148,019
1803	36,219		

Most of these shipments went eastwards of the Holms. In 1809, 41,703 tons were carried to Bridgwater and up the Parrett and Tone Rivers;* 55,556 tons to Bristol and up the Avon towards, but not to, Bath; 16,169 tons to the port of Gloucester, which included Framilode for the Stroudwater Canal;† and 6,949 tons to Chepstow. Of the balance 27,632 tons aided by the bounty went coastwise westwards of the Holms, quantities of over 2,000 tons going to Ilfracombe, Bideford, Barnstaple, Dartmouth and Exeter; and 21,155 tons to Ireland. Broadly, Newport coal was dominant eastwards of the Holms; but it only constituted a small part of the supply to the Westcountry west of Bridgwater, which drew its requirements mainly from Neath and Swansea. Newport did not supply culm, which paid only 1s. 9d. duty: Swansea shipped 9,407 tons, and 2,410 went from Neath.[30]

The Monmouthshire company's competitors in Wales and even more in the Forest of Dean kept up a battle against the exemption in Parliament and outside which caused many a nasty moment to the committee and the shareholders. In May 1817, for instance, the printed Report to the shareholders said: 'The general Assembly . . . wish to impress on the minds of the Proprietors at large, a due sense of the danger they have lately escaped, and of the extreme necessity that exists for the continued vigilence of the Company and its Committee, and for the increased exertions and activity of

* See my *The Canals of Southern England* for the canal and river system supplied through Bridgwater.

† For the canal system served from Framilode, see the map on pp. 136–7 of my *The Canals of Southern England*.

every individual Proprietor, in order to avert the destructive effects of the renewed attempt in Parliament, of certain Proprietors of Collieries in the Forest of Dean....'[31] An act lowering the duties was passed in 1817, and renewed in 1820, 1822 and 1824. The duties were finally abolished in 1831, by which time Newport coal could hold its own against increasing exports from elsewhere.

The company's other principal concern with Newport was to get it recognized as a head port for customs purposes, so that masters of vessels would no longer have to go to Cardiff to clear out for the Irish and foreign trade. Though their first request to the Board of Customs was made in 1799, it was not until 1822 that they achieved their object. In this year 5,565 vessels sailed from Newport, against 243 in 1795.[32] So much had the port grown.

Let us return to canal affairs. The Act of 1802[33] showed that £224,385 out of the £225,300 previously authorized had been raised, £213,700 of which had been divided into £100 shares and the rest obtained by an extra call of £5 per share. Power was now given to raise another £50,000 and once again to reduce the nominal value of the shares to £100 by separating and consolidating the odd amounts. This was done in 1808.

The main provision of the Act was for the construction of the Sirhowy tramroad, with the Penydarren perhaps the best known of all those built in Wales. In 1800, Richard Fothergill and Matthew Monkhouse, who with two partners owned the existing Sirhowy ironworks, joined with Samuel Homfray of Penydarren, William Thompson and William Forman to start the Tredegar works below Sirhowy, on land leased from Sir Charles Morgan. A tramroad 2½ miles long, the Rassa, owned by the Monmouthshire Canal company, connecting Sirhowy with the Beaufort works at Ebbw Vale, had been completed in 1794. From Beaufort the Monmouthshire company's tramroad ran down to Crumlin, while from the Rassa line at Rhyd-y-blew a branch led to the main line of the Brecknock & Abergavenny company's tramroad to their canal at Gilwern, but in this case there was no connexion yet to Newport because the canal between Gilwern and Pontymoile had not yet been built.

Morgan's original lease of 20 March 1800[34] to the partners included powers to make a tramroad from the works down the Sirhowy valley to the canal, which they shortly afterwards began to build. The canal committee did not like this development, and seem to have made a draft agreement[35] with Homfray and his partners themselves to build a tramroad from the canal at Risca to the Tredegar works 'according to the plans of Benjamin Outram, of Butterley . . .', and to agree to through tonnage rates to the Tredegar wharf at Newport. The shareholders' meeting of 18 December 1800, however, did not approve the agreement, but decided to seek an Act with 'powers to agree with Messrs. Homfray & Co. with regard to their intended new Tram Road and to regulate the respective rates of Tonnage on the New intended Tram Road and the present Canal as well as to prevent any New Collateral Cuts or Roads'.[36] This last remark may have referred to the Sirhowy ironworks company, which had recently built its own tramroad parallel to part of the Rassa line. This agreement was to include an undertaking that Homfray & Co. should not carry iron 'from any works already established and which have heretofore been carried on the Monmouthshire Canal except Sirhowy on a less Tonnage than shall be taken on the Monmouthshire Canal and Rail Roads for the time being'.[37]

A subsequent meeting of the two parties produced the agreement of 6 February 1801:[38] this, with some changes, formed the basis of the Act of 1802. This Act[39] provided that the tramroad should now run all the way from Sirhowy works to Newport. The section from the end of the projected canal extension at Pillgwenlly for 9 miles towards Tredegar was to be made by the canal company, less one mile through Tredegar Park near Newport (the Park Mile) to be made by Sir Charles Morgan, and also a branch from this line at Risca to the company's existing tramroad at Crumlin.* The remaining 15 miles of the tramroad from Nine Mile Point to Sirhowy through Tredegar was to be built as a public line by the Sirhowy Tramroad Company, incorporated by the Act with a capital of £30,000 and power to raise £15,000 more, and comprising the five Tredegar partners. The Act also provided for the building of a carriage road alongside the tramroad.

The Sirhowy tramroad was surveyed[40] by David Davies and built as a 4 ft. 2 in. gauge plateway by John Hodgkinson, who had formerly worked with Outram and was an experienced tramroad engineer. It was probably opened in May 1805,[41] though work was afterwards done on it, and because the canal extension had not then been built, it ran along the line of the present Ebenezer Terrace to end at the basin in Friars Fields. The canal company's portion was single track, and cost about £30,000, while the partners also spent £30,000, and Sir Charles Morgan £4,000.[42] The

* This line was not made till 1828.

normal downwards load was 10 tons. Many quarrels between the two companies followed, and one gets the impression that the tramroad was little used until a new agreement was made in November 1810. By it[43] the canal company agreed to complete the line to Pillgwenlly, and to take over one mile of the Sirhowy company's line in exchange for an annual payment of £110. The Sirhowy company agreed to finish their portion of the carriage road,* but released the canal company from making theirs. The Monmouthshire also agreed to make passing places on their tramroad, but in fact they doubled the track instead. It was probably this double-track line that W. L. Meredith[44] says was opened for public use on or about 11 August 1811. By this time the cost of the tramroad to the canal company had risen to over £40,000. The branch to Pillgwenlly was built in 1806, though later its line was altered, and about 1831 a third termination in Newport, at Jack's pill, was provided by a private branch built by John Jones, which ran along George Street, with another line along Grenville Street. The main engineering feature on the tramroad was a viaduct, now demolished, across the valley at Risca, 40–50 feet high and with 36 arches.

The line was a profitable one. The tolls charged enabled good dividends, 30 per cent at one time,[45] to be paid to the Sirhowy company's shareholders. We need perhaps only notice two incidents in its early history. The first was John Kingson's enterprise in the summer of 1822 in putting on a passenger vehicle from Tredegar to Newport, and a year later building a special 'Caravan' at a cost of £70.[46] The second was more important. After Harfords of Ebbw Vale bought the Sirhowy works in 1818, they made a tramroad and tunnel to carry iron from Sirhowy to be rolled at Ebbw Vale, which then went down the Brecknock & Abergavenny Canal company's tramroad to Gilwern. Harfords had, however, acquired an interest in the Sirhowy Tramroad company, which offered them a cut rate. From about 1832, therefore, Harfords sent down the Sirhowy line all the iron that had been smelted at Sirhowy and manufactured at Ebbw Vale, and also that smelted at Ebbw Vale (which was not separable, as all the manufacturing was done at Ebbw Vale). This the canal company held to be contrary to the agreement of 1801 mentioned above, which had been confirmed by the Act of 1802. They therefore brought an action

* The Sirhowy Company's portion of the carriage road was not made till about 1825, nor was the canal company's extra mile of tramroad taken over for many years.

against the Sirhowy concern, which was in the end dropped in favour of an agreement reached in 1838, under which the Sirhowy company repaid £1,250 in tolls to the Monmouthshire.

By the end of 1804 the basin at Friars Fields was becoming congested, for the company ordered that boats must be unloaded within 24 hours except on Sundays, and must move above Town lock to moor. The original extension plan made by John Hodgkinson in 1804 provided for a ½ mile extension and for doing away with Town lock and the tunnel. The extension authorized in the Act was, however, approved by the shareholders in 1805, after Hodgkinson had reverted to Dadford's line of 1796,[47] but nothing was done. In 1807 Hodgkinson's plan was altered to keep the lock and the tunnel, and to extend 'upon the plan of a gradual Elevation of the Canal below the Lock'.[48] The work was then done probably in 1808. The sides and bottom of the extension were, it is said, walled, Jack's pill culverted, and the river piled to enable wharves to be formed.[49] In January 1818 it was decided on the suggestion of the Tredegar Wharf company at Pillgwenlly to build a lock at the end of the extension with money advanced by the Wharf company, the advance to be repaid from the tolls of vessels passing through it. This Potter Street lock was the end of the company's canal, and the point from which the mileposts measure distance. Below it, the Wharf company were given permission to build their own extension with an arm extending nearly to the river at Pillgwenlly, and later at least two more private cuts were made between the canal and the river. The Tredegar Wharf company had been formed in 1807 by Sir Charles Morgan, Samuel Homfray, Richard Fothergill and Rowley Lascelles. It established wharves at Pillgwenlly, and also, by laying out Commercial Street, provided the basis for a spread of the town of Newport from Westgate parallel with the canal to Pillgwenlly.

From 1802 to 1806 the company was short of cash. At the end of 1802 they had offered the Treasurership to a London banking firm in exchange for a loan of £10,000 but the offer was not accepted, and a year later it was transferred to Buckle, Williams & Co., of Chepstow, who did provide finance. In 1805 and 1806, when trade was bad and it was difficult to get money from the freighters, the dividends were paid in debentures bearing interest at 5 per cent, and not in cash except to the smallest shareholders, and the balance of unissued shares was sold. By November 1806 the company had an issued share capital of £228,600 in £100 shares, and £43,526 of prior charges. At that time £270,028 had been spent on the works. Four years later the issued capital was £240,900, and in 1816 the company could say that it had expended 'upwards of £300,000' on the canal and tramroads.[50]

Before 1807 the receipts of the company are not known, though an average profit of £7,679 was returned for 1800–3, and a profit of £1,176 for the bad year of 1806. Before that date also the dividends had been irregular. For the period from 1807 to 1846 the following are the main statistics available, averaged in five-year periods.

Year	*Receipts from tolls* £	*Tons carried (coal and iron)*	*Dividends per cent* £	s.	d.
1807–11	23,516		4	16	0
1812–16	31,898		6	18	0
1817–21	32,463		8	14	0
1822–26	36,906		9	10	0
1827–31	42,795	563,086	11	8	0
1832–36	36,887	601,543	9	18	0
1837–41	40,973	676,561	10	0	0
1842–46	43,201	816,905	9	8	0

	Coal			*Iron*		
	Tonnage	*Receipts* £	*Average Receipts per ton** d.	*Tonnage*	*Receipts* £	*Average Receipts per ton** d.
1807–11				26,368†		
1812–16				41,666†		
1817–21				45,176†		
1822–26				68,780†		
1827–31						
1832–36	480,074	21,456	10·2	121,468	11,996	23·7
1837–41	523,293	20,738	9·5	153,268	14,416	22·6
1842–46	629,311	21,898	8·4	187,594	15,900	20·3

Compared with the two great traffics of coal and iron, the other exports of tinplate and firebricks were less important. As the ironworks outgrew local supplies, iron ore was imported from Lancashire, Cumberland and Cornwall, and as the towns increased in size, so did the quantities of imported agricultural produce from

* These figures are not, of course, exactly comparable without knowing the distances the tonnage was carried, but they show the trend.

† These figures from H. Scrivenor, *History of the Iron Trade*, 1854: all others from Monmouthshire Canal records.

the Westcountry and Ireland, and of timber, much of it from Riga. Danzig and Memel, that were carried up the canal and tramroads,

The financial history of the canal began with the period of establishment up to about 1811. Then came consolidation, when high tolls were charged, and shareholders began to get a good return for their money. Then in 1819, when some of the canal's best customers had, as we shall see (on p. 167), found a cheaper route by way of the Brecknock & Abergavenny Canal, came the first substantial toll reduction, that on iron from 5d. to 3½d. a mile per ton. In that year, according to Scrivenor's figures which are compiled on a different basis from those later available from the company's records, the tonnage of iron carried was 37,709¾. Five years later, in 1824, it was 76,320½; five years later again, in 1829, it was 116,531½. The notable increases of the decade were in the output of the Ebbw Vale, Varteg, Tredegar and Nant-y-glo works,* and these were helped by the building of new tramroads.

In the late '20's when these tramroads were built, such capital improvements by canal companies were difficult to finance, because of the efforts of Lord Shaftesbury, Chairman of the House of Lords Standing Committee, to get what he considered obnoxious clauses in early Canal Acts repealed as the price of new Bills. The Monmouthshire would not agree,[51] and therefore it had to raise capital from its remaining borrowing powers and from revenue. Rapidly improving trade enabled the company to do so, though expenditure on the Aberbeeg (Nant-y-glo) tramroad had deliberately to be spread out.

The financial position of the company, and its attitude to the iron masters, was at this time much affected by the competition of the Brecknock & Abergavenny Canal. This had been promoted (see p. 160) with every encouragement from the Monmouthshire who, when they bound themselves to pay the Brecknock & Abergavenny £3,000 to join them at Pontymoile, had agreed a charges clause,[52] and later permitted its insertion into the Brecknock & Abergavenny's Act as the vital section 108:

'. . . and the said Company of Proprietors of the Monmouthshire Canal Company, shall not take or demand, for any Coals, Goods, Merchandize, or other Things which shall pass or be navigated . . . upon the said Monmouthshire Canal, to or from the said Brecknock and Abergavenny Canal, any higher or greater Rate of Tonnage than shall, for the Time being, be taken by the said Company of Proprietors of the Brecknock and Abergavenny Canal Navigation for any Coals, Goods, Merchandize, or other

* For figures for each, see Scrivenor, op. cit.

Things passing or to be navigated on the said Brecknock and Abergavenny Canal, but never exceeding the Rate of Tonnage taken for the Time being, by the said Company of Proprietors of the Monmouthshire Canal Company.'

The opening of the canal extension brought this clause into operation, and so encouraged the building of tramroads to it from iron works served only by Monmouthshire lines (see p. 166). The owners of works dependent upon the Brecknock & Abergavenny, such as Edward Frere of Clydach, saw that greater competition would follow, and persuaded the canal shareholders to promote a Bill in Parliament in 1813 to annul the 8-mile clause of their Act, which empowered mine and ironworks owners to build tramroads of that length to the canal should the company not do so. The Bill was, however, defeated.[53]

The Nant-y-glo and Clydach companies had for some years been using the Brecknock & Abergavenny Canal at 3d. per ton per mile for their iron, when early in 1817 Harford & Co. of Ebbw Vale and Kendall & Bevan of Beaufort suggested to the Brecknock & Abergavenny company that if they would reduce their toll on iron from 3d. to 2d., they also would put all their iron on to the Brecknock & Abergavenny instead of using the Monmouthshire company's tramroad to Crumlin and then its canal to Newport. As the Monmouthshire company was still charging 5d. a ton, and as Section 108 quoted above in the view of the iron companies would compel the Monmouthshire company to charge 2d. also for iron coming on to their canal from the Brecknock & Abergavenny, Harfords and Kendalls hoped to reduce their tonnage bills considerably. Instead of using 5½ miles of Monmouthshire tramroad and 11 miles of Monmouthshire canal to Malpas at 5d., totalling 82½d. per ton, they would use 5 miles of Brecknock & Abergavenny tramroad, 14½ miles of Brecknock & Abergavenny canal, and 7 miles of Monmouthshire canal at 2d., totalling 53d. The two iron companies therefore told the Brecknock & Abergavenny that they estimated the increased revenue to the canal company at £800 p.a., and Harfords offered to build a tramroad to join the Brecknock & Abergavenny's tramroad near Beaufort. In spite of a protest from the Monmouthshire company, the Brecknock & Abergavenny agreed to the toll reduction,[54] and Harfords at once began to carry iron by horseback to the tramroad at Beaufort until their own line could be built.[55]

In June the Monmouthshire company notified Harfords that they would charge the full 5d. toll,[56] but later in the year tried to mitigate their attitude by offering free upwards carriage of goods to collieries and ironworks paying the full rate,[57] a concession not of great value. The ironmasters holding firm, the Monmouthshire brought an action against Kendall & Bevan 'who have deserted the Monmouthshire line of Road and Canal for the Brecon line to compel the payment of the tonnages due to this Company according to the rates fixed by the Monmouthshire Canal Act. . .'.[58] They relied, presumably, on the omission of the word 'Iron' from section 108, and were supported by the advice of two counsel and Sir Samuel Romilly.

The law's delays began. Hoping to mollify the ironmasters, the company in 1819 reduced their general iron toll from 5d. to 3½d.,* but the ironmasters using the Brecknock & Abergavenny line refused to be mollified. More, they were busy boating down iron while running up large unpaid accounts for tolls, till the Monmouthshire company was forced in 1821 to ask for the undisputed 2d. on account pending settlement of the case. Finally in June 1821, the verdict was given against the Monmouthshire company, who thereupon had to refund £3,185 they had overcharged in the past, and to carry iron from the Brecknock & Abergavenny Canal at 2d. In addition to Kendalls and Harfords, the Baileys of Nant-y-glo, Edward Frere & Co. of Clydach, and Thomas Hill of Blaenavon and Garnddyrys had been using the Brecknock & Abergavenny line, and in this same year the Brecknock & Abergavenny made an agreement with Hill for exclusive carriage that in 1853 was extended indefinitely. From 1821 we must regard the two canals as being in strong competition, and set the forthcoming construction of the Nant-y-glo and Crumlin tramroads by the Monmouthshire company against those built to the Brecknock & Abergavenny line by Hill and the Baileys, and against the Brecknock & Abergavenny's reduction of their toll on iron to 1½d. in 1828 and 1d. in 1830, so compelling the Monmouthshire to do likewise on iron boated off the Brecknock & Abergavenny Canal. In 1831, Beaufort, Nant-y-glo, Blaenavon and Blaina works were reported to be using the Brecknock & Abergavenny.[59]

This competition, and that which Newport coal had to meet in its export markets, did not affect the rising prosperity of the Monmouthshire company, though its tendency was to limit the amount of further rise that would take place. In December 1824

* It may be that the toll was reduced to 3d. at this time, and subsequently raised again to 3½d.

the coal toll was reduced from 2½d. to 2⅜d., and in May 1828 that on iron was reduced from 3½d. to 3d. and on coal to 1½d., the company no longer paying the bounty. In 1831 the committee were anxious to make another reduction in the toll on coal, but it did not seem to them likely that the proposition would get the necessary votes at a shareholders' meeting, presumably because of a fear of lower dividends. A Special Meeting in March 1830 therefore agreed to a motion that after paying for maintenance and improvements and a dividend of 12 per cent, the balance each year should be returned to the freighters in proportion to the tolls they had paid, as was done on the Glamorganshire Canal, and distributions were made for 1830, 1832 and 1833, the last two after the reserved dividend had been reduced to 10 per cent.

The fact remained that the Monmouthshire Canal and tramroads were expensive. In 1829, for instance, the toll on iron on the Monmouthshire was 3d. (except for cargoes off the Brecknock & Abergavenny): on the Brecknock & Abergavenny it was 1½d. and on the Glamorganshire 1¼d., and the Sirhowy tramroad seems also to have been cheaper. In 1833 this differential was estimated by the committee to be diverting one-third of the iron they ought to be carrying, and it remained a potent incentive to build competing tramroads and later railways. In 1830 the toll on coal on the Monmouthshire was 1½d., and on the Glamorganshire ½d.[60] At the end of 1833 the coal toll was reduced to 1¼d., and that on iron to 2½d.

It will be remembered that a tramroad to Nant-y-glo from the Beaufort line at Aberbeeg had been one of the original proposals of the canal's promoters. Owing to the unsettled early history of Nant-y-glo ironworks it had not been built, and subsequently the works had been served by a connecting tramroad to the Brecknock & Abergavenny company's line, completed in 1814. Soon after Crawshay Bailey had joined his brother Joseph at the works, and during the great lawsuit, another (Bailey's Tramroad, see p. 166) was built from Nant-y-glo to Govilon to connect both with the Brecknock & Abergavenny and with the Llanvihangel tramroad. In December 1823 the Monmouthshire company decided to build a line from Aberbeeg to the iron furnaces of George Brewer & Co. at Coalbrookvale. In July 1824, however, after an application had been received from the Baileys, the company decided to continue it past Coalbrookvale to Nant-y-glo on the Parliamentary line to connect with Bailey's Tramroad, and to apply for an Act authorizing an extra capital of £50,000 to pay for it and other lines. This was the Bill that was withdrawn before Lord Shaftesbury's frowns. Building began late in 1824 with William Wells as engineer and went on rather slowly because of financial stringency. By subsequent agreement it was constructed by the canal company only from Aberbeeg to Coalbrookvale, and was finished about the middle of 1828 at a cost of some £8,500. The extension to Nant-y-glo was built by the Baileys.

At the end of 1823 William Wells had also been asked to survey a tramroad to connect the Beaufort tramroad at Crumlin to the Sirhowy tramroad at Risca,[61] so providing through tramroad communication all the way from Beaufort and Ebbw Vale, and later Nant-y-glo, to Newport without trans-shipment and relieving the hard-pressed Crumlin line of canal with its frequent water shortage.[62] The object was also to pacify the ironmasters by enabling them to ship their iron quickly and without transfer from tramroad waggon to canal boat, and to give Benjamin Hall better facilities for carriage from his big collieries at Aber-carn, by providing a junction between his private tramroad* and the new line a mile above Risca. The line was laid up the west side of the valley opposite to the canal; the first mile from Risca to Hall's junction was finished about mid-1827, and the whole line in early 1829. Its length was 6⅜ miles, and cost about £12,150.

The topmost length of the Pontnewynydd branch of the canal from that place to the junction below the eleventh lock with the Brecknock & Abergavenny Canal at Pontymoile was difficult to supply with sufficient water. As early as 1810 the Trosnant tramroad had been extended from Pontypool beside the canal to Pontymoile to enable cargoes to be transferred below the locks, and in September 1825 John Hodgkinson was asked to survey for a tramroad to extend the Blaenavon line from Pontnewynydd to a junction with the Trosnant tramroad at Pontypool. This line was begun after some delay, and completed about June 1829 at a cost of about £2,140, more trans-shipment wharves being provided just below and at the junction with the Brecknock & Abergavenny. The upper canal was, however, still used for navigation. Its abandonment was authorized under the Acts of 1845 and 1848, but the Pontnewynydd–Pontypool section was not closed till 1849, or that from Pontypool to Pontymoile till 1853.[63] In that year and 1854 the site was taken mainly for conversion to a railway. An

* (See p. 146.) In the middle of 1829 the canal company feared that Hall might try to extend it up Ebbw Vale, and offered Capel Leigh, through whose land it would have to be taken, £300 p.a. for twenty years to refuse to allow it.

application in 1830 from three firms for a tramroad onwards from Pontymoile to Newport 'in aid of the Canal' was turned down on the grounds that the company had no power to build it: in fact, presumably because the company at that time thought the canal could carry the trade.[64] Lastly a company's tramroad from the Blaenavon line to the collieries at Cwm Ffrwd (1¼ miles) was begun in 1836, finished in 1837, and soon afterwards extended to the ironworks at Varteg. It cost rather over £3,000. This seems to have replaced an earlier private tramroad to Varteg, built about 1819, and transferred to the canal company in 1828. About 1839 the Blaenavon line itself was doubled, and soon afterwards that to Beaufort.

In September 1829[65] Samuel Homfray of the Sirhowy tramroad wrote to the canal company 'recommending the introduction and patronage of Locomotive Engines[66] on the Sirhowy Tram Road and stating that the only thing required is an alteration in the partings* and to make a few more communications between the two roads . . .'. The canal company agreed to make these alterations on its part of the Sirhowy line, and the first locomotive started to run on 17 December 1829. In May 1830 the company ordered heavier tramplates, presumably because of the locomotives, and in August resolved that the engines should be fitted with springs to lessen tramplate breakages. A year later breakages were still heavy in spite of the springs, but the clerk was ordered to offer locomotives 'every accommodation'.[67] They were working through to Newport by November 1831, trains being limited to a maximum speed of 5 m.p.h.

At this point it may be useful to list the tramroads in use in 1839 which were connected to the Monmouthshire Canal properties,[68] before railway development begins.

A. Tramroads belonging to the Canal Company

(*a*) *Beaufort* (9½ miles). Crumlin to Ebbw Vale and Beaufort ironworks.

(*b*) *Rassa* (2½ miles). Beaufort ironworks to Rhyd-y-blew, Trevil Machine (Rassa),† and Sirhowy ironworks.

(*c*) *Aberbeeg* (5½ miles). Aberbeeg on the Beaufort tramroad to Blaina and Coalbrookvale (continued by private tramroad to Nant-y-glo to connect with Bailey's Tramroad).

(*d*) *Crumlin* (6 miles). Crumlin to the canal at Risca.

* Points.

† For the Trevil tramroad see p. 158.

(*e*) *Sirhowy* (8 miles). Nine Mile Point to Newport and Pillgwenlly (except for the Park Mile), with a branch to the canal at Risca.

(*f*) *Blaenavon* (5 miles). Blaenavon to Pontnewynydd.

(*g*) *Cwm Ffrwd* (1½ miles). A branch from the Blaenavon tramroad to Varteg.

(*h*) *Pontypool* (2 miles). Pontnewynydd to a junction with the Trosnant tramroad near Pontypool.

(*i*) *Trosnant* (1 mile). Trosnant to Pontymoile; branch to Blaendare furnaces, a private branch to Blaen-y-cwm colliery, and one connecting Trosnant and Blaendare.

Other important tramroads

(*a*) *Rumney*. From Basaleg on the M.C.C.'s portion of the Sirhowy tramroad past Caerphilly to the Rhymney or Bute ironworks. Act 1825, open 1836 (69).*

(*b*) *Sirhowy*. Nine Mile Point past Tredegar to Sirhowy.

(*c*) *Sir Benjamin Hall's*, or the *Llanover*, or the *Aber-carn*. (i) from the Crumlin tramroad near Cross Keys above Risca through a tunnel and up the Sirhowy valley to Hafod Trislog colliery, opened 1814 with a branch to Cwm-carn. (ii) from Abergwydden canal basin just above Aber-carn up the valley to Cefn Coch colliery.

(*d*) *Cwm Cuffin* (*Llanhilleth*). From Crumlin up the valley and to the east to a colliery, this line being crossed by another down to the Crumlin tramroad.

(*e*) *Mark Phillip's*. A short line to Crumlin.

(*f*) *Abersychan*. Abersychan ironworks (built 1827) to the Blaenavon tramroad.

(*g*) *Mr Jones's* or *Penllwyn*. Nine Mile Point, junction with Monmouthshire Canal company's portion of Sirhowy tramroad, to Blackwood. Nine Mile Point–Ynys-ddu vested in Sirhowy Tramroad Co., 1824; rest then called *Llanarth* tramroad.

(*h*) *Porthmawr*. From a colliery at Mynydd Maen to the canal at Half Way House.

(*i*) *Caerleon*. From Caerleon to the canal at Half Way House.

(*j*) *Harford's*.(70) From a junction with the Sirhowy tramroad through tunnel to opposite Ebbw Vale furnaces, then south to Ebbw Vale Rolling Mills.

In Newport itself the steadily increasing traffic passing down the canals and tramroads was all shipped from the river wharves that lay between Newport bridge and Pillgwenlly. As early as

* Conversion into railway authorized by Act of 1861; vested in Brecon & Merthyr Railway 1863.

March 1830 the canal company had noted the Marquess of Bute's application for what became his Act of that year (see p. 104) for a dock at Cardiff, 'by which the Interests of this concern and of the Port of Newport may be seriously affected'.[71] It was clearly experiencing pressure upon the available wharf accommodation, for in May of the same year a new by-law prohibited boats remaining longer than 24 hours in Newport basin except on Sundays. In October 1830 a dock was suggested in the local newspaper, and in 1831 a committee was appointed to consider it.[72]

At the beginning of 1831 the local agents for Lloyds, C. H. Stonehouse, issued a broadside[73] which pointed out that Newport suffered from having no Port Authority to control the berthing of vessels or the throwing of ballast into the river. A public meeting was then held, and a committee set up; this suggested an Act should be sought granting powers to levy a toll on shipping and with the proceeds to provide a simple controlling body. This the canal company supported. However, the proposal then expanded into one for a floating dock also, and this again the canal company agreed to support.

The Newport Dock Act was passed in 1835. It provided for Commissioners for the Port, two out of 36 being nominated by the canal company, and for building a dock. This was the Old or Town Dock (now filled in), opened in 1842, and extended in 1858. The Dock company had among its founders Richard Blakemore and Sir Charles Morgan, both prominent in canal affairs, Samuel Homfray of Tredegar and the Sirhowy tramroad, and the Harfords of Ebbw Vale. The canal company subscribed at various times for £20,000 worth of shares in the original dock, and later for another £20,000 worth in the extension, and also built a tramroad from the dock alongside the canal to the tunnel. In terms of monetary return, the dock was not a profitable investment. The accommodation it offered supplemented, but did not replace, the river wharves: in 1843 the shipments of coal from the wharves were 528,075 tons, and from the dock 34,255 tons: twenty years later, in 1863, they were 549,003 tons from the wharves and 191,445 tons from the dock.[74]

These same increasing traffics on the canals and tramroads also led to proposals for locomotive railways. A line from Newport to Pontypool had been discussed as early as 1830,[75] when a survey was made. Again, in November 1833 the canal committee was empowered to oppose a line projected by Joseph Bailey from Abergavenny by Usk and Caerleon to Newport to connect with

J. J. Guest's proposed Cambrian, Gloucester & London Railway. Both the estimate of £100,000 for this line and the proposed tolls were very low.[76] At the same meeting, probably not by coincidence, the company reduced tolls on iron (and tinplate) from 3d. to 2½d., and on coal from 1½d. to 1¼d., in the latter case withdrawing some drawbacks at the same time.* Then, his object perhaps achieved, Joseph Bailey told the company's clerk in January 1834 that his plan was being withdrawn. In November 1836 Parliamentary notices were again given for a railway from Newport to Pontypool and Abergavenny, which caused the canal company to call in the engineer William Cubitt to report on the canal and tramroad between Pontymoile and Pontnewynydd. He recommended improved water supplies to the canal, and these were provided.

In May 1840 an idea that was to revolutionize the old canal company was put before the shareholders, when Summers Harford gave notice that he wanted them 'to substitute Rails for the present Tram plates on this Company's Roads, and that he will be prepared with information of the cost per Mile of the substitution and the saving of annual expence . . .'.[77] Wrought-iron rails were proposed, and the committee was empowered to obtain a report as to which tramroads could beneficially be converted to railways. This report was made by E. S. Barber,† and after seeing it, the committee decided not to recommend any action. However, in 1842 the company sent a party to the north of England to study tramroads there, and on its return agreed to the regular substitution of wrought iron for cast iron, to use tramplates 16 ft. long, and if necessary to substitute wooden sleepers for stone ones.

Events were now to move quickly, encouraged by the opening of Newport Dock in 1842. In November the canal committee heard about a proposed railway from Newport to Nant-y-glo, and at once ordered their own engineer to check the survey for the line. This single line was to run from Newport Dock by Pontypool to Nant-y-glo, Coalbrookvale and Blaina, at an estimated cost of £240,000. It was projected with two inclined planes and a 2,420-yd. tunnel by the engineers, John Hodgkinson and Thomas E.

* In November 1835 new drawbacks on coal carried at least 10 miles on the company's lines and shipped to Bristol were granted; in March 1839 these were extended to certain French ports, and in May to many English ports from Exeter along the south coast to London, to some Irish ports, and more in France. In November 1841 they were granted also on coke, and extended to a long list of ports, including some in Africa, Canada, the United States, South America, and Asia Minor.

† From February 1846 to August 1847 engineer to the canal company.

Marsh. The prospectus of 1 October 1842 said that: 'The Inconvenience and expense to the Freighters of the present defective means of Communication by canals and tram-roads, are so well known, that no vindication or apology for the present undertaking is required from its promoters.'[78] The scheme was soon extended to a double line at a cost of £275,000, and offered rates of 1½d. for iron and 1¼d. for coal, including freight. Initial support came from the Cwm Celyn & Blaina, and the Pentwyn (Abersychan) & Golynos ironworks. A meeting was held at Newport on 12 January 1843 at which a provisional committee was formed.[79] Before that, however, its provisional Chairman, R. J. Blewitt of Llantarnam Abbey, in a private letter to the canal clerk,[80] disclaimed any hostility to the Monmouthshire company. He said that the line had the object of opening new fields of minerals, and that it had been laid out to interfere as little as possible with the canal and its tramroads. 'That a railroad between Newport and the Pontypool Iron district is desirable, even some of your Committee do I know admit,' he added, and went on to suggest that when it had been built the line might be leased to the canal company, which could then sell the Pontypool line of their canal to the Brecknock & Abergavenny.

In May 1843 the canal committee decided to recommend the shareholders to seek an Act to empower them to convert the company's tramroads to railways, to become a carrying company, to make a new railway from Pontnewynydd to Newport 'whenever the state of the trade shall require it, and it shall be deemed expedient', and to reborrow the debt at lower interest.[81] It was estimated, very optimistically, that the cost of conversion of the tramroads and of building the new railway was not likely to exceed £90,000. Crawshay Bailey then set off with two others to see 'Stevenson' (either George or Robert Stephenson), and meanwhile the canal shareholders reduced the toll on iron to 2d. and that on coal to 1d., presumably the better to discourage competitors.

The intended Bill was postponed from 1843 to August 1844, when the company decided to go ahead, and ordered their new engineer, Thomas E. Marsh, who had recently surveyed the Nant-y-glo railway, to survey their own Pontypool–Newport line. A deputation then went to see the Board of Trade, who were favourably inclined, but meanwhile independent notices had been issued for a railway from Newport by Pontypool to Nant-y-glo, with a branch to Blaenavon, by a group acting in concert with the promoters of the proposed Newport, Abergavenny & Hereford Railway. This scheme the canal company decided to oppose. The Newport & Nant-y-glo promoters were the nucleus of the group, which now also included Crawshay Bailey of Nant-y-glo, and men from Blaenavon, Ebbw Vale and Sirhowy. They called themselves the Monmouthshire Railway company, and their proposed capital was £320,000.[82] We must remember here that Nant-y-glo, Blaenavon, Ebbw Vale and Sirhowy were the principal works whose iron went by way of the Brecknock & Abergavenny Canal or the Sirhowy tramroad.[83] In a paper for the Board of Trade in 1844, Blewitt said that the canal company had reduced its tolls 'under the wholesome terror of threatened competition', and of that company's proposed railway:

'The traders justly regard this proceeding of the Canal Company as an avowed determination to attempt to perpetuate for all time an oppressive and odious monopoly.'[84]

Two months later, in January 1845, a meeting of landowners and freighters under the chairmanship of Sir Charles Morgan, also chairman of the canal company, was held on the 18th. At this meeting Sir Benjamin Hall* moved and Richard Blakemore† seconded the proposal that the railway promoters should abandon their Bill, and that the Monmouthshire company should proceed with theirs, by which they would take powers to build a railway and to make branches, to become carriers of goods and passengers, and to shut both canal lines. They also suggested maximum rates, including waggons and haulage, of 2d. for iron and 1¼d. for coal after three years, against the present 2d. and 1d. for tolls alone. One must again remember here that the Monmouthshire Canal was expensive compared with the Glamorganshire, where the current tolls were a fraction under 1d. for iron and ½d. for coal, and that the ironmasters and colliery owners constantly pressed for reductions.

The canal company agreed to all the recommendations, and so apparently did the railway promoters. A Bill was prepared, which

* Hall was the grandson of Dr Benjamin Hall, Chancellor of the Diocese of Llandaff, and son of Benjamin Hall, Richard Crawshay's son-in-law, and both committeemen in their time of the Glamorganshire Canal. Sir Benjamin was a big colliery owner round Aber-carn: he was also the original of 'Big Ben'.

† Richard Blakemore had been the principal partner in the Melingriffith and Pentyrch works on the Glamorganshire Canal, and the principal thorn in the side of the Glamorganshire company. He was also concerned with the Harfords of Ebbw Vale. He is said to have retired in 1838, but after that date took a prominent part in the affairs of both the Glamorganshire and Monmouthshire Canals.

went through many changes, but in May, while it was before the House, the canal company was asked to sell its whole undertaking to the railway promoters, the Monmouthshire Railway company. It agreed to do so as soon as its Bill was through—this was obtained at the end of July—and in September settled the price as £481,800 (i.e. £200 per share), and repayment of the company's debt of £46,837. In October the railway company issued a prospectus showing a capital of £1m.[85] and in August 1846 got its Act. This prospectus, compared with that of 1844, showed less support among the ironmasters. Samuel Homfray of Tredegar was there, with representatives of Varteg, Beaufort and Coalbrookvale, but Nant-y-glo, Ebbw Vale, Sirhowy, Blaenavon, Cwm Celyn & Blaina, and Golynos were unrepresented. The railway company failed to complete the purchase by the agreed date of the end of 1846, and forfeited its £20,000 deposit to the canal company, which then turned back to building its own newly authorized railway. The reason for the failure to complete was the large proportion of canal shareholders who wanted to be paid out in cash (1,378¾ shares out of 2,409) rather than in shares or debentures of the railway company.[86]

The 1845 Act of the canal company[87] authorized a railway from Newport (Pentonville) to Pontymoile with branches, one from Pentonville to Newport Dock, and another from Pontymoile to Pontnewynydd, and gave power to abandon the canal only above Pontymoile. There were powers to improve the company's tramroads, and also the Sirhowy and Park Mile lines; for locomotives to travel at not more than 10 m.p.h.; to buy or rent private canals or tramroads connecting with the company's lines, and to carry passengers, animals and goods on canals, tramroads, and railways. Lastly, after three years no higher tolls* were to be charged on the existing canals and tramroads than were by the Act authorized for the new railway: 1½d. for iron until 1850 and then 1d., ¾d. for coal and then ½d. The capital of the company was increased by £119,100 above the existing £240,900, the new shares to be equal to the old; the debt, now £41,837, could also be increased to £120,000.

The prospects for the company must have looked bright. The canal and its tramroads had a reasonably prosperous past behind them, and the future was promising, for in this year of 1846 Newport shipped 130,000 tons more coal than Cardiff, in spite of the Taff Vale Railway, and the canal with its tramroads handled the

* Excluding waggons and carriage.

remarkable figures of 648,171 tons of coal and 219,199 tons of iron.

Relaying the tramroads with stronger tramplates suitable for locomotives was going on: by May 1846 thirty miles had been done, and 21¾ miles remained still to do. The need was urgent, for the locomotives weighed 13 tons. A writer of 1847 said:

'Since the introduction of locomotives on your roads the number of accidents from the bursting of the boilers, the breaking of engine and carriage axles, and other misadventures, outstrip those of all the railways in the kingdom.'[88]

Driving a Monmouthshire tramroad engine must have been quite a hazardous occupation. While the enterprise had been under a contract of sale, however, it had not been possible to raise money to start building the railway, but in January 1847 a serious effort was made. It was decided to offer £100 shares at £140, proprietors to have the first chance to subscribe in proportion to their holdings. But the railway mania was over, and in March it was found that only 203½ shares out of 803 offered had been taken up at this price. The company then began again, and offered the shares at £100. This time the issue was successful, and in May it was reported that nearly all the shares had been allotted, that a first call had been made, and some money borrowed also. Contracts for the construction of the first 4 miles had also been let. By November, however, the cost both of land and of building the line was exceeding the estimates, and it was clear that the line could not be completed within the time limit of three years from 31 July 1845.

In August 1848, soon after the tolls had been reduced to 1½d. on iron and ¾d. on coal, an amending Act[89] was obtained to extend the completion time of the railway by two years, to prevent the company abandoning the Pontnewynydd–Pontymoile section of canal till not only the main line of railway, but the Newport Dock branch also, should be built, and to authorize the raising of £112,500 more in shares (which could be Preference) and £37,500 by borrowing (after half the shares had been paid-up and the whole subscribed). The further lessening of tolls was postponed till after 1858, and dividends were limited to 5 per cent for the same period. It was enacted that after 1 August 1849 only the company's locomotives should be used on its tramroads (except the Rassa, Cwm Ffrwd and Blaendare lines) and, lastly, that the undertaking should in future be called the Monmouthshire Railway & Canal Company.

Locomotives seem to have started regular work on the Western

Valleys lines* to Blaina in October 1849, but there had been trouble earlier than that owing to the weight of the engines on the plates, and much of the track had had to be relaid with the sleepers closer together. There was also difficulty in hauling the freighters' old rolling stock. The company now became carriers, and on 20 April 1850 horse-drawn traffic was prohibited on these lines, or from Newport to Basaleg. In the middle of these difficulties, the company decided to convert its tramroad from plates to rails by using a combination of both in six years from 1 August 1849, and by November 1850 had relaid 2¼ miles of the Western Valleys lines.

The Report of the shareholders of 20 November 1850 precipitated trouble, for there had been little progress on the Newport–Pontypool railway, only a small number of Preference shares had been taken up, and it was proposed to pass an Ordinary dividend. The chairman of the meeting was Crawshay Bailey. A motion was carried by the majority of the shareholders 'that the Account rendered by the Committee exhibits so alarming a condition of the Company's affairs and so pressing are the difficulties by which the concern is environed that it is expedient to appoint a Committee for the purpose of investigating the expenditure of the money raised under the late Acts of Parliament and the General Management of the Company',[90] and to suggest what should be done for the future.

By the next shareholders' meeting on 2 April 1851 the report had been printed and circulated, as had the answer of the directors. However, a resolution was carried: 'That it is expedient for the future management of this company, that the Committee be comprised exclusively of gentlemen not having any interest as freighters or traders in the line or otherwise that may be liable to come into competition with the interests of the Company.'[91] This view had been expressed by Richard Blakemore in the previous June when he had retired as chairman because he disapproved of recent appointments to the Committee.[92] As a result, in May only four of the old Committee were re-elected, including Sir Digby Mackworth, who became chairman. Sir Charles Morgan and Crawshay Bailey left it, and were soon joined by Richard Blakemore, who, though re-elected, changed his mind and resigned to form an opposition group with the other two.

A passenger service over the tramroads from Newport (Court-y-bella station) to Blaina was introduced in December 1850, but the line above Blaina and from Aberbeeg to Ebbw Vale and Beaufort

* Those running past Crumlin.

would not yet take locomotives, nor was that from Court-y-bella to Dock Street yet ready for passengers. Cash was now very short, and a special meeting in July 1851 postponed the payment of the dividend declared at the annual meeting in April. By November the situation was worse. Because the company had failed to complete its works in the time allowed by Parliament, it was now called upon (after having lost a lawsuit with the Blaenavon company) to 'pay the difference between the rates at which goods could be carried on the unfinished parts of the line, by the old means of conveyance, and those which would have been payable under the Act, had the line been completed and worked by the Company, with locomotive engines—a difference amounting, in some cases, to as much as 4s. 3½d. a ton per mile'.[93] A report made to this meeting by Robert Stephenson and G. P. Bidder referred to many difficulties, among them that of working locomotives on tramroads where the curves were too sharp, and the waggons would not follow the engine smoothly.

In March 1852 the committee suggested the lease of all the company's property to Brassey, Wright, the railway contractors 'largely engaged in working the traffic on the London and North Western, and other railways' and the Ebbw Vale Iron Company for 99 years, for the interest on the debt and Preference shares, 2½ per cent on the Ordinary for two years, and then 4 rising to 4¼ per cent. The committee said ruefully: 'The return secured by such an arrangement, undoubtedly makes a poor figure, when compared with the dividends of former years; but it is useless to look back to the state of things, under conditions to which we cannot now return.'[94] They went on: 'The cause of the depreciation of your property . . . arises from the fatal imprudence of accepting the Act of 1845, which reduced the Tolls to one-half their former amount, while it entailed upon the Company an expenditure largely increasing the amount of Share Capital among which the income was to be divided. . . .' At this time the Ordinary shares stood at 42, the Preference at 75. The Ebbw Vale company in February 1852 described its reasons for intervening as only 'to protect themselves against a system of management which has unhappily proved so detrimental to the export trade, the shipping, and general commercial interests of Newport; and, by destroying all confidence in the undertaking, has brought the company to its present ruinous condition'.[95] However, the proposal for a lease was not accepted by the shareholders.

In April 5¼ miles of line from Aberbeeg to Ebbw Vale was

opened for passenger traffic, and on 1 July the long-delayed Newport and Pontypool railway was at last opened for passengers only as a single line from Crane Street station, Pontypool, to Marshes Turnpike Gate, Newport, the company being unable to acquire the land for the extension to the docks, having lost its compulsory powers. On 4 August the Western Valleys line was extended from Court-y-bella to Dock Street station,* but there was no connexion between the Eastern and Western lines.

At the shareholders' meeting in May the opposition group of men whose products were not, to their minds, being efficiently carried returned to power, led by Sir Charles Morgan, Crawshay Bailey, Richard Blakemore and Thomas Protheroe, after they had accused the old committee of faint-heartedness and incompetence. In November they announced that they would seek power to stop up the canal in Newport, 'and to construct Lines of Railway in lieu thereof, so that all the Wharfs may be connected with the Western Valleys, the Pontypool, and the Hereford Railways, and the Traffic generally more economically carried on'.[96] They also reported that a new lock had been built and the canal altered in order to build a temporary station at the Marshes Foundry, and that a railway siding to connect with the Brecknock & Abergavenny had been provided near Pontymoile. They also paid a dividend of 4 per cent which, though perhaps financially unjustified, had the beneficial effect of revivifying the shareholders, encouraging new investors, and showing up the old committee.

In 1853, with the iron trade prosperous, and dividends rising to 6 per cent, it was announced that the Pontypool railway had been opened, but still only for passengers, right through to Mill Street,† Newport, on 9 March, and that a single line of combined rail and plate was being laid between Crumlin and Aberbeeg. A further capital of £200,000 was authorized in this year, and power granted to convert the tramroads to railways. In 1854 it seems that the ½ mile of canal below Canal Terrace, Newport, was closed and filled in;[97] a more extensive closure had not been authorized.

By June 1854 the Blaenavon-Pontypool line had been opened as a railway for mineral traffic,‡ and all the Western Valleys tramroads to Blaina and Ebbw Vale except the Rassa had been con-

* The station was just below the lower part of George Street, and beside Dock Street.

† Near High Street.

‡ It used the site of the canal between Pontnewynydd and Pontypool.

verted to combined rail and plate, and junctions made with the Rumney line and at Nine Mile Point.* In November the Eastern and Western lines were joined at Newport for locomotive use (there had been a connexion for horse-drawn traffic since 1853), and it must have been in this year that the Pontypool–Newport railway was at last opened for mineral traffic, nine years after its authorization in 1845.

In 1855, the year that old Richard Blakemore died at the age of eighty, a further Act gave power to raise £270,000 more. The line from Blaina to Nant-y-glo Gate was now being reconstructed. This, when completed, would lead to the output of the Nant-y-glo works being carried over 20 miles on the company's railways, instead of going to the Brecknock & Abergavenny Canal, and then only 9 miles on the Monmouthshire company's waterway. The section of railway onwards to Nant-y-glo itself was leased by the company from Bailey in 1858.

It will be convenient here to summarize the capital structure of the company in May 1857, when the railways were nearly complete, although the company still had three tram-engines, the last of which was to disappear from stock by 1861.

The authorized share capital was £825,000, of which £240,900 had been raised before 1845, £119,100 in that year, £112,500 under the Act of 1848, £149,074 under that of 1853, and £130,433 under that of 1855. The authorized loan capital was £275,000, of which £120,000 had been raised under the 1845 Act or before, £37,500 under the 1848 Act, and £50,000 under that of 1853. A total of £959,508 had therefore been spent on the company's undertakings, out of £1,100,000 authorized.

The company now suffered two limitations. In 1857 it had proposed to extend the Western Valleys line to Rhyd-y-blew, but this was dropped in 1859 when the Sirhowy Tramroad company presented a Bill, passed in 1860, to change their name to the Sirhowy Railway company and to convert their line to rails,† since it was seen that traffic from the Tredegar and Sirhowy works would move by that line and not by the Western Valleys. In 1860 also Crawshay Bailey, who had never allowed his influence in either the Monmouthshire or the Brecknock & Abergavenny company to lessen his preoccupation with the prosperity of the Nant-y-glo

* The Park Mile tramroad had been converted under the powers of the Monmouthshire Act of 1853.

† It gave powers to build an extension from Sirhowy to Nant-y-bwch, on the Merthyr, Tredegar & Abergavenny line.

works, and who was Chairman of the proposed Merthyr, Tredegar & Abergavenny Railway (see p. 172), helped to get the Act for that line, 'passing near the several Iron Works at Nant-y-glo, Beaufort, Ebbwvale, Sirhowy, and Tredegar'.[98] In this year also trams disappeared from the Western Valleys lines after 30 September.

In 1861 a further £125,000 of capital was authorized. In May an ordinary meeting agreed to lease the whole concern to the West Midland Railway* for a guaranteed 5½ per cent dividend (the Monmouthshire company had recently been declaring 5 per cent), the canals to be kept open. The West Midland Railway failed, however, to obtain authority to lease Newport Docks, in spite of support in Newport for control of the docks by a company with greater financial resources than the Dock Company. Finally, a special meeting of the Monmouthshire in September resolved, in spite of the guaranteed dividend offered being raised to 6 per cent, 'That this Company are not prepared to Lease their Line to the West Midland Company until they are better satisfied with the security offered.'[99] In 1862, much to the company's annoyance, the West Midland Railway got running powers over the Eastern Valleys line from near Pontymoile (Coed-y-gric) to Newport, powers which the L.N.W.R., who had recently leased the Merthyr, Tredegar & Abergavenny, already possessed.

In 1865 more capital was raised, one of its purposes being to buy the Brecknock & Abergavenny Canal in September. The Monmouthshire's own canals were by this time very little used, and yielded only £1,222 in tolls in 1864, a figure below the cost of maintenance. The amalgamation enabled the Monmouthshire to carry by rail some traffic that had formerly gone by the Brecknock & Abergavenny Canal and their own, thus causing a sharp fall in canal tolls on the combined canals, from £1,906 in 1868 when the tonnage carried was 57,000, to £738 in 1878, in which year the expenses for maintenance were £2,738.

Newport was about to develop quickly, for the North Dock of the Alexandra Dock company had been authorized in 1868, and opened in 1875, to be followed by the South Dock in 1898, and its extension in 1905. In 1871 the Monmouthshire company had sought a Bill once more to close the canal in Newport 'and construct on the site thereof, lines of Railway, as the latter appeared

* Formed in 1860 by vesting the Newport, Abergavenny & Hereford and Worcester & Hereford Railways in the Oxford, Worcester & Wolverhampton, which then changed its name to the West Midland.

to be needed for the accommodation of increasing traffic whereas the traffic on the Canal is very inconsiderable and will in all probability decrease'.[100]

The Bill, which had other objects also, was withdrawn. In 1874 the Sirhowy Railway directors began negotiations with the Monmouthshire company, but in 1875 sold their concern instead to the L.N.W.R. In that year the Monmouthshire made an agreement with the G.W.R., and accepted a guarantee. Once more, in 1879, there was a Bill before Parliament 'to enable the Company to close a portion of the Monmouthshire Canal, in the Borough of Newport, extending from the Newport Docks* to Llanarth Street Bridge', and this was passed in the same year, the section of canal concerned being closed from 1 October. It is said to have been disused for the preceding five years.[101] On 1 August 1880 the Monmouthshire company lost its independent existence, and amalgamated with the Great Western.[102]

Thenceforward there was very little traffic on the canals. The last market boat carrying miscellaneous goods on a regular service ran from Llanarth Street, Newport, on 9 January 1915, after which the crew joined up and went to France.[103] Previously there had been two boats a week to Crumlin, and one to Brecon.[104] The last cargoes were carried on the Crumlin line in 1930, and on the Pontymoile line in 1938.

By a Newport Corporation Act of 1930, power was given to close the section between Llanarth Street and the north side of High Street bridge. This was soon afterwards done. The tunnel was removed, and the canal now ends at Mill Street. The same Act authorized the Great Western Railway at any time to abandon the length between High Street bridge and a point ten yards east of the junction with the Crumlin branch. A short length of four chains at the top of this branch had been abandoned under a Great Western Act of 1909; the rest of the branch was closed by a British Transport Commission Act of 1949. In 1954 a further Commission Act authorized the closing of a section rather over 2¼ miles long through the new town of Cwm-brân, and another of 1962 abandoned the remainder to Jockey Bridge, Pontypool.

Trevil (Trefil) Tramroad

On 12 March 1793 Thomas Dadford junior had been ordered by the Monmouthshire company to survey for a tramroad from

* i.e. Canal Terrace.

Beaufort and Ebbw Vale furnaces and Sirhowy to 'a place called the Trevil'. He probably did so at once, for a first meeting was held on 30 May of the Trevil Rail Road Company.[105] This took its powers from the 8-mile clause of the Monmouthshire Canal Act. A sum of £5,000 was subscribed, work probably soon began, and the lines opened about 1797. There was a tramroad $2\frac{5}{8}$ miles long from the Trevil limestone quarries to a junction with the Rassa at Trevil Machine, and another from the Rassa at Rhyd-y-blew via Shop Row, Beaufort, to Pont-y-gof (Ebbw Vale), with isolated sections giving Trevil independent connexions to Sirhowy and Beaufort works. At Rhyd-y-blew the Trevil line joined the Brecknock & Abergavenny Canal company's tramroad (see p. 161). The Brecknock & Abergavenny company also applied for a connexion between their line and the Trevil's near Ebbw Vale, but this the latter refused.[106]

The prime movers in the Trevil line originally were probably Homfray, then a partner in Ebbw Vale, and Fothergill and Monkhouse of Sirhowy, though Daniel Williams of Beaufort was concerned. This would account for the powers given under the Sirhowy Tramroad Act of 1802, presumably to strengthen the legal position, and the offer for sale of shares in 1803,[107] which might have been held by Homfray's partners the Harfords of Ebbw Vale. These, however, are conjectures.

Later, Richard Thomas & Baldwin Ltd. took over part of the Trevil tramroad between Trevil Machine and the quarries, converted it into a railway, and joined it to the Sirhowy ironworks line to Ebbw Vale, which had also been converted. The line was abandoned in 1964.[108]

CHAPTER VIII

The Brecknock & Abergavenny Canal and its Tramroad Connexions

THE Act for the Monmouthshire Canal had been passed in June 1792. The originally proposed line for the Brecknock & Abergavenny,* however, given in a notice of August of that year,[1] offered no connexion. It was to run from the River Usk at Newbridge above Caerleon and four miles below the town of Usk, up the river valley past Llangybi and Abergavenny to Llanelly† and the Glangrwyney ironworks. In September it was decided to extend this line to Brecon.[2] It is probable that the committee of the Monmouthshire Canal then stepped in, and were behind a 'Meeting arranged for 15th Oct. to consider the best line for a collateral cut or canal from near Pont-y-Pool to or near Llangattock-Crickhowell, and by a cut or Rail-way to communicate with Abergavenny'.[3] They also offered the Brecknock & Abergavenny promoters £3,000 to join their canal instead of the Usk, and also the water to fill the long bottom level from the proposed junction at Pontymoile near Pontypool to Llangynidr that would result.[4] The day after the meeting Thomas Dadford junior, the engineer of the Monmouthshire, was ordered by that company 'with the Assistance of Mr. Cockshutt‡ to make a Plan and Estimate of the Expence of making a Canal from the most convenient place below Pontypool to the Town of Brecon' with tramroad connexions.[5]

Dadford then surveyed a line 32⅞ miles long from Pontymoile on the Monmouthshire Canal to Brecon, with three connecting tramroads, from Gilwern up the valley of the Clydach to Wain

* It was then called the Abergavenny Canal.
† Near Gilwern.
‡ A shareholder and solicitor of the Monmouthshire Canal Company.

Dew near Beaufort, from Abergavenny wharf (Llanfoist) to Abergavenny bridge, and from Gilwern to Glangrwyney.[6] His plans and estimates were considered in November 1792,[7] and a Bill sought, Dadford's expenses in attending the hearings early in 1793 being paid by the Monmouthshire company, as also was the legal bill in London and Edward Kendall's* expenses for attendance upon it.

An Act[8] was obtained in March of the same year, authorizing a capital of £100,000, and £50,000 in addition if required. It included the important section 108 (see p. 141) which limited the Monmouthshire company on interchange traffic to the same tolls that were charged by the Brecknock & Abergavenny proprietors.

On 16 May 1793 the first meeting of shareholders took place at the *Golden Lion*, Brecon. There were a few shareholders who were prominent in the Monmouthshire company—the Duke of Beaufort, the Hanburys of Pontypool, Sir Charles Morgan, and Sir Robert Salusbury—and also Richard Hill of Plymouth works and the two Homfrays, Samuel and Jeremiah, Jeremiah at that time being in partnership with the Harfords and Partridge at Ebbw Vale, and Samuel at Tredegar. But most were local people, including the Wilkinses of the Old Bank at Brecon, founded in 1778 by Walter and Jeffreys Wilkins, who had returned home with an Indian fortune, and who took an interest in many commercial enterprises, including every important canal in Wales except the Monmouthshire.[9] Walter Davies[10] in 1814 referred to the Brecknock & Abergavenny as 'the only one as yet in the district which originated with the consumers; being undertaken with the laudable view of lowering the price of coals, lime, etc.'. The meeting set up a two-county organization for the company because the capital had been equally subscribed from them both,[11] with joint clerks and joint treasurers from Breconshire and Monmouthshire, and eleven members each on the managing committee.†

The Canal Act gave power to the company to build tramroads up to 8 miles from the canal or, if they did not wish to do so, powers to owners of collieries and works to do so. Rather unusually, the Brecknock & Abergavenny Canal company began operations by building not its canal, but a tramroad from Gelli-felen collieries in the Clydach valley belonging to Edward Kendall of Beaufort down to Gilwern, and then by a bridge over the Usk

* Of Beaufort ironworks; chairman of the Monmouthshire company.

† After 1804 these joint arrangements were abandoned, a single clerk and treasurer, and a committee of twelve being substituted.

to Glangrwyney, where a forge worked pig-iron from Ebbw Vale. John Dadford was made engineer for the tramroad, which was probably completed about August 1794.[12] It was laid as an edge-railway with rails from Penydarren and sleepers partly of iron, but then changed to wood. Waggon loadings of 3 tons were reduced to 2 in 1799, probably because of rail breakages. The cost was £6,167 plus £900 for the bridge over the Usk.

In March 1794 it was resolved to extend the tramroad upwards from the tramroad on the north side of the valley opposite Gelli-felen to Bryn-mawr, with a branch to Llwydcoed colliery and one to Nant-y-glo, Philip Williams, for a short time the canal company's agent, to be the engineer. Soon afterwards the extension of the line was authorized from Bryn-mawr, first to Beaufort and then to Rhyd-y-blew to join the Trevil tramroad and also the Rassa line of the Monmouthshire. The branch to Rhyd-y-blew was open by June 1795, and that to Llwydcoed* by the end of that year. The branch to Nant-y-glo seems to have been built only as a stone road between mid-1795 and mid-1796. Between 1796 and 1811, when Joseph Bailey† and Matthew Wayne took them over, Nant-y-glo works were little used.

The tramroad from Rhyd-y-blew to Glangrwyney, 7¼ miles long,‡ was mainly used to carry pig-iron from Beaufort (Ebbw Vale) to the forge at Glangrwyney, and also coal. Beaufort works themselves were served by the Monmouthshire Canal tramroad, which carried away its remaining output. A separate line 1⅜ miles long was surveyed by Thomas Dadford and Hugh Henshall in 1794 from Llam-march 'Coal and Mine Works'[13] to the Clydach ironworks, and was seemingly opened in June 1795. The cost was £2,110, which was met by the canal company under an agreement with Frere, Cooke & Kendall, the owners, to pay 8 per cent on the cost and also for the repairs. It was doubled in 1798–9 at the firm's expense, and connected to the wharf at Gilwern in 1803. In 1806, when Frere, Cooke & Powell, as they then were, represented that it 'is not equal to the whole of their business',[14] they were allowed at their own expense to build a branch from the company's main line near Gelli-felen to their works. This was completed in October 1811, and in 1813 the canal company apparently took it over.

* The branch to Llwydcoed was disused by 1812.

† He was joined by Crawshay Bailey about 1820, when Matthew Wayne left the partnership.

‡ The tramroad bridge over the Usk was destroyed in February 1795 by a flood. It was not rebuilt, the ford being used instead.

The Llam-march line provided the works with coal and iron ore, but gave no outlet for their iron. In 1797, therefore, the Monmouthshire company allowed Frere, Cooke & Co. to use a quarter of the tolls payable to them to build a road from Clydach to Blaenavon, presumably so that they could have access to the head of the Blaenavon tramroad. It seems to have been built by April 1799, when a further allowance was made for its repair. In 1804 still another allowance was made in return for the firm's (now Frere & Powell) agreement that they would use the Blaenavon tramroad till the Brecknock & Abergavenny Canal joined the Monmouthshire. We must bear in mind that this did not happen till 1812. Until then, Clydach, Beaufort and later Nant-y-glo had to look to the Monmouthshire company's tramroads; Glangrwyney, which could not, seems to have closed down early in the new century. The track to it was in place in 1811, but by 1833 the company had agreed to its conversion to a parish road.

The Monmouthshire company had paid over their £3,000 in March 1794, and in October, seventeen months after the Brecknock & Abergavenny's first meeting, asked that company when it proposed to start cutting its canal, and were told 'as soon as the Rail Roads are completed and a proper Engineer can be procured'.[15] The Monmouthshire then ordered their own engineer, Thomas Dadford, to stake out the line. A year later they enquired again, and were told that cutting would begin 'as soon as the necessary preparations can be made'.[16] At the end of 1795 Thomas Dadford was engaged as engineer, on a part-time basis at first, and later whole-time, when his work with the Monmouthshire came to an end at Christmas 1798.

Construction seems to have begun early in 1797,* when a contract was let for the aqueduct and embankment at Gilwern, the latter with an arch through it for the tramroad to Glangrwyney. Cutting then proceeded upwards towards Brecon, and the 8½ miles from Gilwern to Llangynidr was probably opened in November 1797. A further section to near Tal-y-bont, completing 12 miles, was open by February 1799.[17]

By April 1799 it was clear to the proprietors that more capital would be needed to complete the canal, and it was decided to make extra calls on the existing shares. The remaining section of canal from Tal-y-bont to Brecon was opened on 24 December

* *The History of the County of Brecknock*, by Theophilus Jones, 1805, says that cutting of the canal commenced in April 1796. The minute books, however, do not mention cutting before 13 February 1797.

1800,[18] and is said to have reduced the price of coal there from between 1s. 2d. and 1s. per cwt. to 9d.[19] The main engineering features of this Gilwern–Brecon section of the canal are the big embankment and lofty single-arched aqueduct at Gilwern, the short tunnel at Tal-y-bont, and the fine four-arched aqueduct over the Usk below Brecon. All three were engineered by Thomas Dadford, using local contractors.

The cost so far had been £120,000 including the tramroads, on the 9½ miles of which some £30,000 had been spent.[20] Further payment of interest on calls was now stopped. In March 1802 it was decided to extend the canal downwards from Gilwern to Llanfoist, the intended site for Abergavenny wharf, Thomas Cartwright, who had replaced Dadford as engineer, to do the survey. At the same time a first dividend of £1 17s. 6d. per share was paid. By June 1803 £150 per share had been called, and the canal was for the time being carried no farther than the Blaenavon road short of Llanfoist, to which point it was completed on 14 January 1805, by which time some £129,500 had been spent.[21] Meanwhile, as the result of a report of 1799 by Benjamin Outram, the edge-railed tramroads were replaced by plateways. There matters rested while the company considered how to raise enough capital to finish their waterway.

One purpose of the canal had already been accomplished. As early as August 1795 the company had itself begun to trade in coal carried on its tramroads to 'Penybont, Aberclydach, and Llanelly end of Llangroyney bridge',[22] and a year later they agreed to buy 200 tons of coal a week for 21 years, after failing to buy a suitable colliery for themselves. This direct trading seems soon to have been handed over to the newly formed Brecon Boat Company, first mentioned in December 1796, and largely owned by canal shareholders, though independent. The chief participants were Jeffreys Wilkins, John Lloyd, John Peirce and John Powell the solicitor, all of Brecon. This company in 1801 leased a colliery at Clydach, and thenceforward supplied much of the coal needed by the town of Brecon and its neighbourhood, and also by the Hay tramroad (see p. 179). In 1820 another colliery was leased, and, describing the hey-day of the trade, John Lloyd[23] says that sixteen canal boats each carrying 21 tons were used in the carriage of this coal to Brecon. 'All the country-side came for their supply of coal, and in the late Autumn every farmer came and fetched his stock of Coal from the Brecon Boat Company's wharf. . . . In severe frosts . . . the Yard at Brecon was always well stocked for winter.' The Boat Company also owned limestone quarries, maintained limekilns, and supplied lime.

The rapidly growing ironworks made it essential that the company should accomplish its second purpose of completing its canal to a junction with the Monmouthshire, who steadily protested against its unfinished state, and even asked for compensation for non-completion because their original payment of £3,000 had been in consideration of the Brecknock & Abergavenny company undertaking to join them. When the latter replied unhelpfully, the Monmouthshire decided to seek counsel's opinion upon how to 'obtain satisfaction and redress'.[24] This probably stimulated the Brecknock & Abergavenny to action. Power to raise an additional £80,000 for the extension by loan or the creation of new £150 shares had been granted by an Act of 1804,[25] but £50,000 in cash was still needed. In 1809 Richard Crawshay agreed to lend £30,000 for 20 years at 5 per cent, with the option of converting to shares at £150, George Frere lent £8,100, and others smaller sums to make up the amount. We may guess that Crawshay's loan was related to the take-over in 1811 of the Nant-y-glo works by his nephew Joseph Bailey, since Nant-y-glo would need the canal for its transport.

William Crosley, who had been engineer of the Rochdale Canal, was engaged at £500 a year, the line was re-surveyed in consultation with Hodgkinson, and a cutting substituted for the proposed tunnel near Pontymoile. Work began upwards from the Monmouthshire Canal junction, and went smoothly except that the aqueduct at Pontymoile had to be pulled down and rebuilt, apparently to prevent scouring of the foundations. The wharves at Gilwern and Brecon were extended, and at last, on 7 February 1812:

'The Committee set out to view the Canal towards Pontymoile and at Mr. Waddington's Boat House in Lanover, met him, and embarked there on board his Boat, and proceeded in the same all the way from thence to, and through, the stop Lock at the Junction with the Monmouthshire Canal, being the first entrance from this Canal into that, amidst the aclamation of a very numerous body of the inhabitants as a token of their Joy at an Event so very beneficial to this Country.'[26]

The cost of the canal and its tramroads seems to have been something over £200,000. The opening of the extension improved the company's revenue from tolls from £5,365 in 1810–11 to £8,849 in 1813–14.

While the extension was being built, Bailey & Wayne of Nant-y-glo asked permission in 1811 to build a tramroad from their works to join the Brecknock & Abergavenny's tramroad. However, the canal company decided itself to build the line, one mile long, for £600, and to allow Bailey & Wayne's iron to travel free to the canal in exchange for that firm's undertaking to send all their iron by way of the Brecknock & Abergavenny instead of the Monmouthshire. The Nant-y-glo branch was reported completed in January 1814. The canal extension also encouraged the building of the Llanvihangel and Grosmont tramroads (see p. 174), while higher up the canal the Bryn-oer from Tal-y-bont (see p. 178) and the Hay line from Brecon (see p. 179) were also begun. Another tramroad that had been authorized by Parliament, from Mamhilad on the canal extension to the town of Usk, was never started.

Later, other important tramroads were built. In 1821 J. & C. Bailey of Nant-y-glo asked permission to take a line over the canal near Govilon for the shipment of coal and iron by canal and the Llanvihangel tramroad. This, usually known as Bailey's tramroad, was built about 1822[27] from Nant-y-glo by Bryn-mawr and down the south side of the Clydach valley to Govilon. Some years later the Baileys acquired a third tramroad to the canal, this time to carry coal from their mines; they took over a lease from the Brecon Boat Company of the Brecknock & Abergavenny's tramroad from the Darren Cilau limestone quarries to the canal at Llangattock, opened about 1816 at a cost of £3,000, bought the inclined planes at its head, and extended it through Bryn-mawr to join Bailey's tramroad. Finally, about 1825 Thomas Hill of Blaenavon built a line, originally suggested in 1817, from Blaenavon round the east side of Blorenge through two tunnels and down inclined planes* to join the canal wharf at Llanfoist and the Llanvihangel tramroad near Abergavenny bridge. Its main purpose was to carry iron from the Blaenavon company's forge at Garnddyrys,[28] in preference to using the Monmouthshire company's Blaenavon tramroad, but it seems likely that from 1835 onwards this traffic returned to the latter, which was doubled in 1839.

The canal company had paid a dividend of £1 per £150 share for 1806–7, rising to £3 for 1808–9 and the two following years. Dividends from 1811–12 to 1816–17 were then passed so that the money could be used to pay off debts in connexion with the completion of the canal, the building of the Llangattock tramroad,

* There were three inclined planes down Blorenge to the canal, and a fourth from the canal downwards.[30]

and the improvement of wharves. It was, however, clear that the company was not making the profits that had been expected, and in 1814 the shareholders asked the Committee 'to take into consideration and adopt some Plan for encouraging the carriage of all Coal, and other Articles Travelling along the Canal and Rail Roads belonging to this Company so as to encourage an additional supply and increase the revenue of this concern'.[29] The war was about to end, and for a time the iron trade was to be in difficulties. Their solution was sought along a number of lines.

First, agreements were entered into with ironmasters that iron ore could be imported free of toll if the finished products were carried on the canal (e.g. the agreement of 19 October 1815 with the Baileys of Nant-y-glo).

Second, drawbacks or concessions were given to encourage long hauls (e.g. iron coming down the Brecknock & Abergavenny's Clydach tramroad was carried free if it then travelled from Gilwern to Pontymoile on the canal).

Third, agreements were made with Harfords and Kendalls that in exchange for a toll reduction on iron from 3d. to 2d. in 1817, all the iron made at their works would be put on the Brecknock & Abergavenny Canal, and that the cost of any new tramroads made to carry this traffic by the ironmasters would be refunded should the tolls be subsequently raised. We saw (see p. 142) that this action by the Brecknock & Abergavenny company led to a lawsuit with the Monmouthshire which the latter lost in 1821.

These efforts raised the dividend from £2 per £150 share in 1817–18 (the first after dividends were resumed) to £4 in 1821–2, and the company's annual revenue from £8,534 in 1816–17 to £11,021 in 1818–19.[31] By the year ending 29 March 1823, however, the total revenue was down to £10,221, of which £9,602 was derived from tolls. This is a year in which we can get a picture of the whole system. The company's canal carried 86,944 tons, and the tramroads 27,024½ tons, as follows:

	Canal tonnage	*Canal tolls*			*Tramroad tonnage*	*Tramroad revenue*		
		£	s.	d.		£	s.	d.
Coal and coke	32,612¾	3,617	14	1	16,557¾	512	12	8
Iron	32,741¾	3,528	4	1	5,927½	232	1	8
Lime and limestone	14,748½	318	15	8	1,161¼	5	16	1
Merchandise	3,242¾	1,052	0	4	151¼	6	10	9
Other traffic	3,598¼	296	17	4	3,226¾	32	6	10
Total	86,944	8,812	18	6	27,024½	789	8	0

In April 1821 there was an economy drive including wage cuts, and further wage cuts in October 1822, due to poor trade. All the sixteen employees except the Agent had their wages reduced, the worst-hit being the molecatcher, whose pay came down from £23 5s. 6d. to £16 p.a. Better trade then began, the dividend rose to £5 in 1822–3, £7 in 1823–4, £8 in 1824–5, and a maximum of £9 in 1825–6* to 1827–8, and some wage cuts were restored.

Then came a bad blow. The Monmouthshire company extended its tramroad from Aberbeeg towards Nant-y-glo, and reduced its iron tolls, 'by which the conveyance of that Article from several Iron Works connected with the Brecknock & Abergavenny Canal will be much facilitated'.[32] The shareholders were told that the 'Freighters (have) declared their inability to continue their present line unless a proportionate reduction takes place . . .'.[33] Tolls on iron were therefore reduced from 2d. to 1½d. Two years later they were further reduced to 1d., after the committee had reported that the Monmouthshire company were offering a bonus to carriers.

By April 1833, when the dividend had been reduced from £9 in 1827–8 to £4 in 1832–3, the Brecknock & Abergavenny had had enough of competition. The shareholders resolved that 'it would be highly beneficial to the Interests of this Concern that a satisfactory arrangement should be entered into with the Monmouthshire Canal Company respecting the Rates of Tonnage to be charged on the two Canals & Roads on Goods and Merchandise conveyed from the one along the other whereby the injurious competitions which have hitherto existed may be removed and the Freighters at large placed upon an equitable footing in regard to the Rates of Tonnage & Charges of conveyance of their Produce to the Port of Shipment'.[34] The Committee were instructed 'to meet with a friendly feeling any disposition on the part of the Monmouthshire Canal Company for the attainment of this object'.

The Monmouthshire company were helped to such a disposition by their quarrel with Harfords of Ebbw Vale. The latter considered the Monmouthshire company's rates too high, and in October 1831 they gave notice to the Brecknock & Abergavenny to build, or let them build, a tramroad from Ebbw Vale to the canal at Llanddeti above Llangynidr. The canal company were at first inclined to make the line, but after legal consultations returned a delaying answer in October 1832. In April 1833 Har-

* One half-year's dividend in 1826 is not known, but is assumed to have been at the same rate.

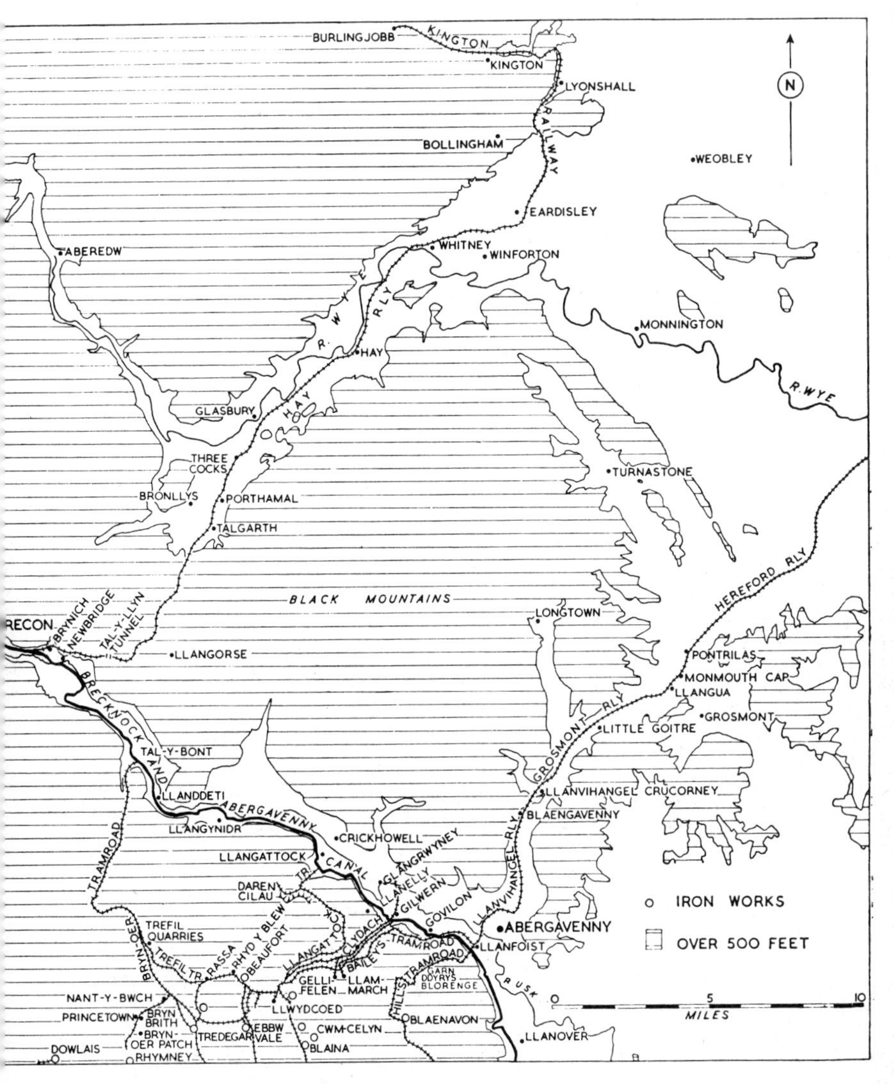

8. The Brecknock and Abergavenny Canal and its tramroad connexions

fords asked again for this line, now with a branch to Llangynidr, and also for a line from Ebbw Vale to Gilwern, which makes it clear that the company's original tramroad up the valley was little used at this time. In this same year the Bailey brothers bought Beaufort works and connected them by a new line to Nant-y-glo, so removing one possible source of traffic. The canal company agreed to make the first but not the second, and decided in July to start construction from the Ebbw Vale end, though nothing seems to have been done.

It was during these months of 1833 that meetings took place between representatives of the two canal companies to consider either a lease of the Brecknock & Abergavenny's tolls to the Monmouthshire, or a price-fixing agreement, but as there were legal obstacles to both these courses, amalgamation was considered on the basis of the Monmouthshire company guaranteeing £5 p.a. on Brecknock & Abergavenny shares, then £9 p.a. on their own shares, and then paying dividends *pari passu.* A meeting agreed on amalgamation, but the Brecknock & Abergavenny's committee, and subsequently its shareholders' meeting, refused to agree. This effort at unity was probably the result of Bailey influence, favouring Nant-y-glo as against Ebbw Vale. Joseph Bailey, already a director of the Glamorganshire Canal, joined the Monmouthshire committee in 1823, and that of the Brecknock & Abergavenny in 1826, where he was joined by Crawshay in 1829. The two brothers, together with the younger Joseph, held 110 shares in the latter in 1834, and exerted a concentrated influence that the company, accustomed to shareholdings widely spread in the Usk valley, had not known before. After the failure of amalgamation Joseph left the board of the Monmouthshire, and in 1837 for the first time became chairman of the Brecknock & Abergavenny. Thenceforward to the end of the canal's independent life the Baileys were powerful interests. These were again exerted on the Monmouthshire board also after Crawshay joined it in 1847.

Harfords' second move was to drive a tunnel through the mountain between the Ebbw and Sirhowy valleys. After they had lost their lawsuit with the Monmouthshire (see p. 137), Harfords returned to the Brecknock & Abergavenny company, but in spite of legal threats could not get them to make the line they had earlier asked for, presumably because the Brecknock & Abergavenny did not intend to fall out with the Monmouthshire. Harfords' final effort was in April 1839 to serve a notice on the Brecknock & Abergavenny to put its original tramroad from the

Rassa line to Gilwern* in repair, to which the committee replied that they would consider doing so if Harfords would carry a remunerative traffic on it for seven years. Otherwise they 'consider the Road to be utterly useless'.[35] At this Harfords gave up, and used the Sirhowy line at legal tolls.

The Brecknock & Abergavenny company's better understanding with the Monmouthshire had somewhat improved its dividend, from £4 in 1832–3 to £5 in 1833–4, 1834–5, and 1835–6, and thence for some years to £5 10s. per £150 share, till 1842–3 when it came down again to £5.

In the railway mania year of 1845 the company opposed the Monmouthshire's Newport–Pontypool railway. When the Act authorizing it was passed, the committee decided that it would be advisable to sell the canal. The Welsh Midland Railway, whose promoters had a passion for buying canals, and the Newport, Abergavenny & Hereford Railway companies made enquiries, and agreement was quickly reached with the former for a sale for £182,500, which, after deducting the remaining £37,700 of debt represented about £146 per £150 share. A 10 per cent deposit was paid, but in October 1846 the Welsh Midland company was dissolved, and the deposit was repaid, perhaps because Joseph Bailey had been its chairman.

In 1849 the canal company had a survey made to see if it were practicable to lay a single-line railway on the canal bank from Brecon to Pontypool, but no action followed. Instead, the company told the traders on the canal that they welcomed the use of steam tugs, though I do not know if any were used. In 1851 a projected Breconshire Railway from Abergavenny to Brecon asked if they could buy the canal, and were quoted £105,750 (£70 per share), but there was no result. In 1852 the Monmouthshire company tried to close part of their canal in Newport. This was prevented, as was a Bill for a line to Brecon from the Taff Vale extension of the Newport, Abergavenny & Hereford Railway. These events led the canal company in 1854 to decide itself to promote a railway from Abergavenny to Brecon. It was surveyed, but though the arguments against the future of the canal as a canal were strong, it was decided to take no action. Once again an agreement to sell was made, this time to McCormick, Brassey & Co., the railway contractors, for £122,000 in debentures and shares of a company they were promoting to make a line from Abergavenny to Brecon with a branch to Bryn-mawr, and then to lease

* In 1838 the tramplates beyond Gilwern to the Usk had been taken up as useless

it to the Newport, Abergavenny & Hereford Railway. Again the sale fell through. By this time the iron traffic on the canal had fallen away, for works like Nant-y-glo used the Monmouthshire company's railways as soon as they were open.

Then in 1858 two proposals appeared, each of which bore much upon the other. On the one hand, six of the committeemen of the canal company, headed by J. P. de Winton* the banker of Brecon, and including John Powell of Clydach ironworks, joined with others, including representatives of the Newport, Abergavenny & Hereford Railway, to promote the Breconshire Railway & Canal Co. The prospectus stated that:

'This Company is projected in conjunction with the Brecknock and Abergavenny Canal Company, and under the sanction of the Newport, Abergavenny and Hereford, the Oxford, Worcester and Wolverhampton, and the Worcester and Hereford Railway Companies,† for the purpose of applying to Parliament for powers to lease the Canal from Brecon to Pontypool, and to convert the portion between Brecon and Abergavenny and the Railroad to Bryn-mawr‡ into a Railway.'[36]

This proposal to provide Brecon with railway access seems also to have been influenced by the promotion late in 1857 of the Hereford, Hay and Brecon Railway, for shortly before the Breconshire prospectus appeared, a notice was published that: 'A line to supply Brecon with Railway Accommodation by the best and cheapest route will be immediately brought before the Public with an influential provisional Committee. In the meantime the supporters of Railway Communication in the district are requested not to pledge themselves to any particular project.'[37] The Breconshire company proposed to lease the canal and its tramroad for about £5,000 p.a. and to take over its debt, now £36,450, and had an agreement with the Brecon & Merthyr Railway§ that if authorized they would grant them running powers from Brecon to Tal-y-bont.

The second scheme was for the Merthyr, Tredegar & Abergavenny Railway, which was supported by Crawshay Bailey. This company proposed first to build the line from Abergavenny to Nant-y-bwch (with connexions to Tredegar and the Sirhowy

* A branch of the Wilkinses had changed their name to de Winton in 1839.

† These three railways in 1860 amalgamated to form the West Midland.

‡ Not Bailey's tramroad, but the canal company's old line.

§ Authorized in 1859. For the history of this line see D. S. M. Barrie: *The Brecon & Merthyr Railway*, 1957. J. P. de Winton was chairman of it as of the Breconshire project.

tramroad), absorbing Bailey's tramroad on the north side of the Clydach valley, and passing through Bryn-mawr.

Both schemes became Bills in 1859. That for the Breconshire was withdrawn, for lack of subscriptions and support from the canal shareholders,[38] and that for the Merthyr, Tredegar & Abergavenny Railway was passed. Construction began, and the line was opened to Bryn-mawr in 1862 and Nant-y-bwch in 1864, causing a heavy fall in canal traffic, so that in 1865 the Brecon Boat Company ceased to trade.[39] Meanwhile in 1862 the West Midland had brought in a Bill to lease the Merthyr, Tredegar & Abergavenny Railway and also the Sirhowy, and also to join the Brecon & Merthyr then under construction, but it was forestalled by the London and North Western Railway who agreed in November 1861 upon a lease to itself of the Merthyr, Tredegar & Abergavenny. This company was absorbed in 1866.

For many years it had been difficult to get enough canal shareholders together to elect a committee, or to take responsible decisions, while from 1855–6 onwards loss of trade brought the dividend down from £6 per £150 share in that year to £4 in 1858–9, to £2 10s. in 1860–1, and to 10s. in the following year. The iron trade had already been lost to the Monmouthshire's Eastern and Western Valleys lines, and the opening of the Merthyr, Tredegar and Abergavenny to Bryn-mawr in 1862, and the Brecon & Merthyr in 1863, removed much of the coal traffic.

In November 1862 there had been a heavy reduction in tolls, and in 1864 the company, having once more considered and rejected the idea of building a railway themselves, and in face of the Act of that year for a line from Abergavenny to Crickhowell, offered themselves to the Monmouthshire company for £61,200* (£25 per share on the remaining 990 shares of £150, and payment of the debt of £36,450), on condition that no part of the canal or its tramroads would be discontinued without Parliamentary sanction. The purchase date was 29 September 1865. One piece of property, the tramroad west of Bryn-mawr, was sold to J. & C. Bailey for £300, and was not included in the sale. When the G.W.R. later amalgamated with the Monmouthshire, it paid £72,025 in stock for the Brecknock & Abergavenny.

The purchase of the Brecknock & Abergavenny by the Monmouthshire was probably partly protective, to prevent its remaining trade and its line going to a rival. But a main reason was its water supply taken from the Usk at Brecon. The Newport Dock

* So the minute book. The Returns of 1898 to the Board of Trade give £61,861.

Company had in 1854 obtained power to divert water from the Monmouthshire Canal. In addition, the Monmouthshire had closed its reservoirs in the Glyn valley so that in 1854 the N. A. & H. R. extension from Pontypool to Taff Vale could be built along it. It therefore relied on the Brecknock & Abergavenny not only to supply the line downwards from Pontypool and Newport Dock, but also, after it had bought the company, for water for sale to works along the lines of canal. So heavy were these drawings that the Conservators of the River Usk, and others concerned, contemplated taking action in 1869 and again in 1899, when about 20m. gallons a day were being taken. However, the Great Western Railway somewhat restricted its takings, and no action resulted. By the turn of the century only about one boat a week passed over the whole canal, the market boat from Newport, and two or three worked on the upper part. The last toll taken on the Llangattock tramroad seems to have been in March 1911, and on the canal at Llangynidr in February 1933. This beautiful canal carries some pleasure craft, but is maintained mainly for water supply purposes.

Curiously enough, no railway parallel to the canal between Tal-y-bont and Abergavenny was ever built, the railway route between these points being a roundabout one by way of Dowlais Top.

The Llanvihangel, Grosmont and Hereford Tramroads

In September 1793[40] a notice was issued, probably by supporters of the Brecknock & Abergavenny Canal, for a branch canal from the Brecknock & Abergavenny at Llanfoist (Abergavenny) to Hereford, apparently with branch tramroads from Longtown and Turnastone. The route was surveyed by Dadford, whose plan and estimate were considered at a meeting at Grosmont in November,[41] at which they were 'unanimously rejected as injurious to the Landowners and without utility to the public in the county of Hereford'.[42]

In 1809 and 1810 tramroads were the thing. In 1809 the Severn & Wye (see p. 208) had been authorized; in April 1810 the Monmouth tramroad Bill had had its first reading; in July the first part of the Gloucester & Cheltenham tramroad had been opened, and in July also the first meeting had been held to promote the Hay tramroad.

On 26 September 1810 a meeting resolved that a tramroad from the canal near Abergavenny to Hereford would be beneficial, and a committee was appointed to promote it.[43] They issued a Parliamentary notice and got Dadford to make a survey. The main motive, the insufficient coal supply to Hereford by the River Wye, is clearly put by Walter Davies:

'At Hereford, a ton of the Forest of Dean coal sells for 32s.; Welsh coal, superior in quality, and owing to so great a distance of land carriage, sells for 45s. a ton; but by the railroad, it is supposed it might be afforded at 25s. a ton. On this line, by the customary land carriage, the turnpike tolls for five horses, amount to a sum nearly equivalent to the whole carriage of an equal quantity of coal by the railroad.'[44]

Hugh Powell, a committeeman of the canal company and sometime chairman, owned limestone quarries near Llanvihangel Crucorney, and evidently decided to proceed independently, for in October he asked the canal company to make a tramroad from near Llanfoist to Llanvihangel and his quarries. They refused.[45] Though the committee of the Abergavenny–Hereford proposal were empowered to consider his plans,[46] Powell and his friends went ahead to promote a Bill. The canal company, after brief thought of making a canal branch to Llanvihangel, agreed to certain restrictions upon their own powers to make parallel tramroads, or others near Abergavenny or Llanvihangel, and also to the tramroad company 'giving facilities to the continuation of the same towards Hereford'.[47]

William Crosley surveyed the line,[48] and in May 1811 an Act[49] was passed to authorize the tramroad company to raise £20,000, and £15,000 more if needed, to build a line 7¾ miles long from Govilon by Llanfoist and Abergavenny to Llanvihangel.*

Meanwhile the remainder of the Hereford project went ahead. In March 1811 the newspaper reported that: 'We understand it is fully resolved to bring the projected Abergavenny and Hereford Tramroad to Pontrilas . . . and it is hoped that it will be continued to this city.'[50] In the same month an agreement was approved with the Llanvihangel company[51] by which the latter would extend their line to Lower Goitre† to join that proposed. Money was then sought; in September a notice was issued for a tramroad from Llanvihangel to Hereford,[52] and in October it was reported that £28,050 had been subscribed out of the £30,000 said to be

* The official titles of the Llanvihangel, Grosmont and Hereford companies all described them as 'railway' companies.

† I presume Little Goitre.

needed, and that Hodgkinson had been given the job of building it.[53]

However, it proved too great a work for the times, and instead a shorter scheme, for the Grosmont tramroad for 5½ miles from Llanvihangel to Monmouth Cap, was proceeded with. Hodgkinson estimated this at £12,000,[54] and by the time the Act[55] was passed in May 1812, £10,900 had been subscribed.[56] The Act authorized a capital of £12,000, and £7,000 more if necessary, but even for this less ambitious scheme there was difficulty in getting a shareholders' meeting.[57]

The Llanvihangel tramroad was opened on 12 March 1814 when several waggons laden with coal, and preceded by colours and a band of music, went to Llanvihangel Court.*[58] It had been built from 'Abergavenny Wharf'† to Blaengavenny near the present Llanvihangel station.

In October 1817 there was a proposal by Messrs. Hill of the Blaenavon collieries to make a tramroad thence to cross the canal and join the Llanvihangel tramroad, to which the company raised no objection if compensation were paid, and in October 1818 an agreement was made with Hills for a bridge and embankment over the canal near Llanfoist church.

It was probably the prospect of this tramroad and perhaps talk of what later became Bailey's tramroad, that in early 1818 caused the Llanvihangel line to be extended through the village of Llanvihangel Crucorney to join the Grosmont.

Thomas Hill was a member of the Grosmont company's board. This concern, though authorized in 1812, did not get under way till the end of 1817; its line was finished early in 1819, for on 10 March it is referred to as complete to Llangua.‡[59] On the 24th a meeting was held at Hereford to consider an application for a Bill to extend it to Hereford,[60] and by early May £7,400 had been subscribed.[61] The Grosmont company then seems to have considered joining up with the Hereford subscribers, or alternatively extending its own line somewhat nearer Hereford.[62]

No action followed till a meeting in Hereford on 18 August 1825, which decided to seek an Act for a line from the Grosmont at Llangua to Wye Bridge, Hereford. Hodgkinson, helped by

* I think Pen-y-clawdd Court may be meant.

† I take this to have been the wharf by the Blaenavon road and just short of Govilon, built when the canal extension of 1805 was completed.

‡ Monmouth. The company also built a toll-road for 4 miles alongside its track.

David Davies as a surveyor, made an estimate of £24,383 14s., and by October a subscription of £25,000 had been closed, Thomas Hill of Blaenavon having put his name down for £1,000, and Richard Blakemore for a similar amount. The Act[63] was obtained in May 1826, and authorized a capital of £23,200 and £12,000 more if necessary, after some opposition from the barge-owners on the Wye, though shareholders in the towing path were among the subscribers.

By this time both Hill's tramroad from Blaenavon to Llanfoist and Bailey's tramroad to Govilon had met the Llanvihangel, and these must have much encouraged the completion of the Hereford line. It was opened on 21 September 1829, when 15 trams with coal from Blaenavon collieries and 18 from Pontypool, together with one loaded with grain, arrived at a wharf by Wye bridge.[64] The length was about 11¾ miles.

The Hereford tramroad must have cost at least £2,600 more than the authorized share capital of £23,200, itself less than Hodgkinson's original estimate,[65] and by 1833 there was a mortgage debt of £6,014. With its connecting lines, it was partly successful in easing the coal supply of Hereford; on the one hand, its opening caused the Severn & Wye company (see p. 208) to increase its toll drawback on coal carried on its tramroad to Bishop's Wood wharf, Lydbrook, 'with a hope that a proportionate reduction will be made in the selling price of Coal at Hereford . . .';[66] on the other, the tolls, which after 1835 were probably farmed out, rose from an average of about £800 p.a. to about £1,100, and then fell back to rather more than £800 for the next eight years, falling to £650 in 1846. The Llanvihangel line, however, seems to have earned more. These receipts and the price at which coal still had to be sold at Hereford probably encouraged the Herefordshire & Gloucestershire Canal proprietors (see p. 198) who were supporting the proposed extension of their canal from Ledbury to Hereford to think that they had nothing to fear from the tramroad, and that their Forest of Dean coal could undersell that from Monmouthshire.

In 1836 the tolls on the Hereford tramroad were reduced from 2½d. per ton per mile to 2d.[67] All mortgages except £800 had been paid off by 1846, and dividends of 2 per cent seem to have been declared from 1844. Then, on the first day of 1845, it was reported that the promoters of the Hereford Independent Railway (later the Newport, Abergavenny & Hereford, authorized in 1846 to build a line from the Monmouthshire Canal company's new Newport–

Pontypool railway to Hereford),[68] were proposing to buy the three tramroads between Hereford and Abergavenny.[69] This purchase was authorized by the railway company's 1846 Act, the prices being £19,460 for the Hereford, £16,250 for the Grosmont, and £21,750 for the Llanvihangel, the last, and therefore probably the others, being based on 25 years' purchase of the net annual income.

It had been intended that the purchases should be completed in April 1848,[70] but the railway had not the money. The purchase price was therefore paid in instalments. When about half had been transferred, the N. A. & H. company seem to have taken over the working of the three tramroads from 1 January 1850. Two purchases were completed on 31 July 1851, construction of the N. A. & H. began soon afterwards, and the three lines were finally closed on 1 May 1853.[71] Some of the tramroad track was used for the railway, which was opened from Hereford to Pontypool in January 1854.* The section of tramroad from Abergavenny to Govilon was used longer. It seems to have been converted to railway track after August 1857,[72] and then bought in 1862 under the powers of the Merthyr, Tredegar & Abergavenny Railway's Act of 1859, and partly used for the exchange sidings with the canal maintained by that railway at Govilon.

Bryn-oer Tramroad

The first suggestion for what later became an important tramroad branch of the Brecknock & Abergavenny Canal came as a notice from Benjamin Hall in the autumn of 1812, asking for a line from Trevil limestone quarries to the canal at Tal-y-bont. This was withdrawn, but in 1813 a new notice was put in by Samuel Church, a solicitor of Brecon apparently acting for Hall and supported by Penry Williams, for a tramroad 12 miles long from a colliery at Bryn-oer near Rhymney by way of the Trevil quarries to the canal at Tal-y-bont.

The colliery was rented from Benjamin Hall by Dixon & Overton, who agreed to lease the line. The canal company having refused to make it, for they would have preferred the traffic to come by way of their own tramroad down the Clydach valley, a small group of shareholders decided to build it as far as Trevil under the 8-mile clause, the continuation to Bryn-oer to be made by Hall as a public line.[73] A meeting was held at Brecon on 20 December 1813, and £6,300 was subscribed at it towards the estimated cost

* The former railway station of Tram Inn recalled the old tramroad.

of £12,000 including land.[74] By March 1814 £13,000 had been raised.

George Overton, builder of the Penydarren tramroad, and one of the lessees of the colliery, was engineer, the line being opened in May or June 1815.[75] Dixon & Overton then leased it for five years at 7 per cent on the £13,000 it had cost. At Trevil there was a connexion to the Rhymney Iron company's tramroad built by Hall.

Traffic was mainly lime, pitwood from Brecon towards the collieries, and coal the other way, much of it for trans-shipment to the canal, then again to the Hay and Kington tramroads. In 1832, for instance, Overton & Co. and Overton & Scroop were factors of coal and lime on the Hay tramroad.[76]

I do not know when the lease ended, but the tramroad's profits must have been affected by the opening of the Rumney tramroad in 1836, which gave Hall a more direct outlet to Newport for his production. By 1855 a dividend of only 2½ per cent was being paid. About that time estimates were obtained to convert the line for locomotives at a cost of £6,200, but this was not done. It was in 1860 provisionally sold to the proposed Sirhowy & Brecknockshire Railway company, which was supported by the Brecon & Merthyr,[77] but the Bill failed in 1861. Much of it was now in bad condition,[78] and the opening of the Rhymney Railway and of the Brecon & Merthyr (for the building of which it carried materials and equipment) took away most of its traffic. It ceased to be used by 1865.[79]

Hay Tramroad*

On 28 March 1793 the Act for the Brecknock & Abergavenny Canal was passed, and on 11 June a meeting was called to consider a plan and estimate by Dadford for a canal from the Brecknock & Abergavenny Canal near the intended Usk aqueduct to the River Wye at Whitney;[80] £47,000 was subscribed, and a notice was issued in September.[81] The proposal shows that the carriage of Forest coal up the Wye towards Hay in flood time was no longer considered a satisfactory method of supply.

This scheme died with so many others born in the canal mania. The opening of the Brecknock & Abergavenny Canal in 1800 from Gilwern to Brecon must have revived interest in the idea, and in 1805 a survey was made by Thomas Cartwright[82] for a tramroad

* The official title was the Hay Railway.

between Brecon and Hay. In August 1810 the canal company was asked by a group of promoters whether its engineer, William Crosley, might be borrowed for a tramroad survey from Brecon to Eardisley beyond Hay. They gladly agreed, and in December received a deputation from the promoters, both of whom were conveniently already on the canal committee. The latter 'Resolved that the Undertaking appears likely to be highly beneficial to this Concern . . .',[83] and early in the following year circulated its shareholders on the subject with enthusiasm.

The tramroad company had been promoted largely by people who were prominently connected with the canal. Of the 17 who called the first meeting on 26 July 1810,[84] 10 were shareholders of the Brecknock & Abergavenny or the Monmouthshire. Two more were shareholders in the Wye Towing Path, and probably represented coal consumers.

A public meeting on 18 January 1811 welcomed the scheme,[85] its purpose being to carry coal to the agricultural areas and bring back corn and other farm products, and in March the canal company waived its right to make the first 8 miles, and agreed not to build any competing line. The proposed tramroad was 22½ miles long via Bronllys to Hay and Parton Cross (Eardisley), and had a rise of 309 ft. Crosley estimated the cost at £41,100 for single track and £60,250 for double.[86]

By February £51,300 had been subscribed,[87] and in May an Act[88] was passed. During the summer John Hodgkinson was appointed engineer; his assistant, William Dunsford, later acted as resident engineer. Discussion took place upon the suitability of Crosley's route, and in 1812[89] a different line proposed by Hodgkinson was authorized, farther to the east, and with a rise of 154 ft. from Brecon and a length of 24⅛ miles. This ran by way of Tal-y-llyn and Talgarth with a tunnel 674 yds. long at Tal-y-llyn. A proposed branch to New Bridge (by the Brynich aqueduct over the Usk) to link the tramroad more directly to the Bryn-oer tramroad at Tal-y-bont was successfully opposed by the canal company and the Brecon Boat company. The Hay company proposed to build this branch without compulsory powers:[90] the Brecknock & Abergavenny company, however, thought that it was intending to make use of the 8-miles clause of the Brecknock & Abergavenny Act, and, worried by this proposal and that for the Bryn-oer tramroad, both of which had a tendency to reduce canal tolls, promoted a Bill to repeal the clause. The Bill was lost, but so was the branch.

The capital of the Hay company was £50,000 with authority to raise £15,000 more, Hodgkinson's estimate for the revised line being £52,743 18s.[91] The actual cost was £63,380. The line began at the public wharf at Brecon, and was opened to Hay on 7 May 1816,[92] and to Eardisley on 1 December 1818. It crossed the Wye on the wooden road bridge at Whitney, and there were wharves at Brecon, Tal-y-llyn, Talgarth, Glasbury, Hay, Clifford, Winforton and Eardisley. The gauge was 3 ft. 6 in., and most trams carried 1½ to 2 tons, though there were a few larger ones.

The need for such tramroads at a time of bad roads is indirectly shown in a paragraph from Walter Davies's *General View of the Agriculture and Domestic Economy of South Wales*, published in 1814:

'The Brecon canal reduced the price of coal in that town from 14d. to 9d. per cwt. This coal, carried from Brecon to Pen y Bont, on the Ithon, in Radnorshire, costs 2s. 6d. per cwt; the distance being 28 miles. Some go from this part of Radnorshire to the Clee Hill collieries, in Shropshire, the distance of 37 miles, for much worse fuel, owing to the badness of the roads to the Brecon canal.'

Little is known about the working of the tramroad, except that for the half-year ending 29 September 1839 the tonnage carried was 10,793, of which 9,270 was in coal and coke, and 1,124½ in lime and limestone. In 1832 the coal supplies were coming from three sources: along the Bryn-oer tramroad, from Llanelly wharf by the Brecon Boat company's craft, and from near Pontypool. The revenue averaged some £2,000 p.a. during the years 1831–42; there were no dividends until 1842, the net profit being used to reduce the debt, of which only £150 remained in July 1843. Afterwards small amounts seem to have been distributed.

In April 1854 the Hay company asked the Brecknock & Abergavenny for a drawback on coal carried on their tramroad, and offered reciprocal benefit. A Special Assembly of the canal shareholders was called to consider it, but no one came. This set-back must have had a connexion with the meeting held at Brecon on 31 July of the same year when a committee was formed to consider a Leominster, Hay & Brecon Railway, for probably many of them were, like the chairman Lord Hereford, connected with the Hay tramroad.[93] In September a subscription was opened, and in December a meeting of the Hay company was called to consider leasing their tolls to the railway company for two years.[94] However, there was not sufficient support for a Bill.[95]

In 1858 this was changed, when the Breconshire Railway & Canal company (see p. 172) was formed to turn the canal into a railway. Another company seeking an Act, the Brecon & Merthyr Railway, then made an agreement with the Breconshire for running powers over its Brecon–Tal-y-bont section. By the time the latter had got its Act in 1859, the former scheme had fallen through, and the Brecon & Merthyr was left without access to Brecon. Meanwhile another company authorized in 1859, the Hereford, Hay & Brecon Railway, was negotiating to buy the tramroad, though its authorized route from Three Cocks to Brecon lay to the north of it. This purchase would have excluded both the Brecon & Merthyr and another interested company, the Mid-Wales, from Brecon. The Brecon & Merthyr therefore promoted its own line towards Hay, while groups of the Hay shareholders supported one side or the other. Eventually in 1860 the tramroad was sold to the Hereford, Hay & Brecon Railway, seemingly for £10,201 in shares and cash, and was vested in it, but parts were made transferable to the Brecon & Merthyr and the Mid-Wales, and these transfers were later made.[96]

Kington Tramroad*

We have seen that the Hay tramroad was opened to Hay in May 1816, and to Eardisley in December 1818. Early in 1818 it was proposed to extend this tramroad by that of another company based on Kington from Eardisley through Lyonshall and Kington to limestone quarries at Burlingjobb, near the Stanner station on the New Radnor line. This route was preferred by Hodgkinson to an earlier proposal from Whitney bridge via Bollingham. The estimate was £16,400. An Act[97] was passed in June, authorizing £18,000 in capital, and £5,000 more if necessary. The line, 12⅛ miles long in all, was begun in the autumn of the same year with John Hodgkinson as engineer and William Hazeldine of Shrewsbury and Morris Sayce of Kington as contractors. On 1 May 1820 it was opened to the Floodgates at Kington,[98] and celebrated by a dinner at the *King's Head* at three o'clock. It was soon afterwards completed to Burlingjobb.[99] Apart from the lime business, the tramroad served the small iron foundry of Richard Meredith at Kington. This received coal, iron and sand, and sent away castings. In 1828 John Meredith junior, who was a tramroad shareholder, owned 92 single and 4 double trams.[100]

In the early '30's the fortunes of the company, which up to then seem to have been low, took a turn for the better. Some dividends

* The official title was the Kington Railway.

of 2 per cent were paid in this decade and the next, and one of 3½ per cent.[101] However, the opening of the Leominster & Kington Railway in 1857 seems to have taken most of its traffic, and it was almost disused when the Kington & Eardisley Railway promoters agreed in December 1861 to buy the tramroad for £45 cash for each £100 share. Part was used for the Kington & Eardisley line, but the remainder, from Sunset Wharf near Kington to Burlingjobb, was kept at work until the Kington to New Radnor extension railway was opened in 1875.[102]

CHAPTER IX

The Waterways of Herefordshire and the Forest of Dean

IN the pre-railway period four means were sought, besides the tramroad lines from Gilwern to Hereford and from Brecon to Hay and Kington described in the previous chapter, to bring coal and manufactures to Herefordshire, and take away its produce. The River Wye to Hereford, Hay and above was the first, together with its tributary the Lugg to Leominster. Then the creation of Stourport as a canal centre for the Midlands led to the planning and partial construction of a canal thence through Leominster to Kington. Very soon afterwards the promotion of the Gloucester & Berkeley Canal* and the increased traffic of the Severn led to the building of the Herefordshire & Gloucestershire Canal from Gloucester to Ledbury, afterwards continued to Hereford. Lastly, the Severn & Wye tramroad was constructed to improve the export of Forest of Dean coal both up the Wye towards Hereford, and from shipping places on the Severn, with the Lydney Canal as a part of the project.

Rivers Wye and Lugg

The Wye† was to some extent navigable long before the early seventeenth century, when a Commission of Sewers was appointed to remove nuisances on it which hindered navigation and fishing. In 1622 Gloucestershire, Herefordshire, Monmouthshire and Hereford city petitioned that it be not obstructed in its work, but the main obstructions were the weirs held by the king, and it does

* See my *The Canals of Southern England*, pp. 182 et seq.

† For information on the history of the Wye Navigation see Mr I. Cohen's paper on *The Non-Tidal Wye and its Navigation*, in the *Transactions* of the Woolhope Naturalists' Field Club for 1956.

not appear that the Commission did anything to remove them, though the king had refused protection to other weir owners. In 1641 there were seven of these weirs supplying power to mills and forges, which obstructed 'all goodnesse that should come from Monmouth to Hereford by water',[1] and ten years later the position was the same. The boats used at this time to Hereford were small flat-bottomed craft drawing 16 in. of water and carrying 4 tons.[2]

About the time of the Commonwealth improvements were proposed by installing flash-locks* at the weirs and deepening the channel at a cost of about £340. There were many arguments for and against.[3] In 1662 Sir William Sandys, who had made the Warwickshire Avon navigable, was appointed[4] to make navigable the Rivers Wye and Lugg for goods and passengers,† being joined with his cousin Henry Sandys and his grand-nephew Windsor Sandys. He took over the sum of £1,300 which had already been raised for this purpose in the county.[5] There is no certain information about what he did. The statement that he built pound-locks[6] can hardly be true; it seems more likely that he built a number of weirs and flash-locks. By 1695 the river was more or less back in its natural state, except that the Earl of Kent built a flash-lock at New Weir (Symonds Yat), where he had ironworks. The preamble to the Act of 1736 says that Sandys did nothing to the Lugg, and work on the Wye was done 'very slightly'.

In 1695 another Act[7] was passed, which set up a body of men who were to improve the two rivers by means of a rate levied on Herefordshire. This body included many powerful local notabilities, among them the Hon. Paul Foley, M.P. for Hereford, and it was said that Foley as a forge owner was trying to get power to destroy the weir that supplied the rival forge of the Earl of Kent.[8] The Act established a perhaps not very impartial commission to value the weirs, which the trustees were empowered to remove. They could raise up to £4,526 13s. 1d. a year till 1700, with the Commission's approval, and could also borrow £16,000. By 1727 £18,000 had been raised in Herefordshire, some of which was in hand.[9] About thirteen weirs had been removed, though the flash-lock at New Weir remained, and certain works had also been carried out on the Lugg, but were soon afterwards destroyed by floods.[10]

This work on the Wye, though it removed one kind of obstruc-

* See my *British Canals*, 3rd ed., 1966, p. 16.
† Passenger boats from Bristol to Hereford were envisaged.

tion, produced another, for the demolition of the weirs 'occasioned great Shoals and other Inconveniences whereby the Navigation of the said River is much obstructed'.[11] A further Act was passed in 1727,[12] which provided for the spending of what was left of the £18,000, and for the continuance of the trustees. Further weirs were now apparently bought up but not destroyed, their rents being used for the purposes of the navigation.[13]

Yarranton[14] and others say that the Wye was navigable to Monmouth in 1695–6, before the trustees began work. After the Act of 1727 it seems that it was navigable at least to Hereford and the Lugg to Leominster,[15] and that coal from the Forest of Dean wharves was carried upwards past Welsh Bicknor to villages on the Lugg.[16] There must also have been a general trade, for Defoe described Chepstow as 'the sea port for all the towns seated on the Wye and Lug, where their commerce seems to center'.[17]

Early in the eighteenth century some money was raised by subscription to improve the navigation of the Lugg. A 'contest' then arose about this money,[18] and soon afterwards, in 1723, the Corporation of Leominster wrote to local people to 'desire their interest in perfecting the navigation of the Lug',[19] and in 1748 they paid a subscription themselves.[20] It was probably now that one Chinn built half-locks.* In 1756 the river was sufficiently passable for the seven bells of the church to be taken down the river to be re-cast, though this passage seems to have been exceptional.[21] A wharf at Lugg Mills was in use in 1826, and there was probably intermittent navigation during the first part of the nineteenth century on the lower river. Three of the half-locks were reported still in existence in 1906.[22]

The Wye in the eighteenth century seems to have been moderately used. There were many village quays, and wharves at Hereford, and trows were built at several places. In 1777 the downwards traffic included 9,000 tons of corn and meal, and 2,000 tons of cider.[23] 'To the city of Hereford, and its vicinity, it is of service, as coal and other heavy articles are brought there from the Forest of Dean and Bristol. It also enables the inhabitants to send cyder, bark, timber, etc., back by the same conveyance to the Severn . . .', John Clark wrote in his *General View of the Agriculture of the County of Hereford*, published in 1794. An aspect of its usefulness was noted by the ubiquitous Gilpin, who had himself rowed down part of the river in 1770, and described the scene at Lydbrook:

'At Lidbrooke is a large wharf, where coals are shipped for

* Single-gates, equivalent to flash-locks.

Hereford, and other places. . . . A road runs diagonally along the bank; and horses, and carts appear passing to the small vessels, which lie against the wharf, to receive their burdens. . . . The contrast of all this business, the engines used in lading, and unlading, together with the solemnity of the scene, produce all together a picturesque assemblage.'[24]

In 1789 the Herefordshire & Gloucestershire Canal (see p. 198) was being promoted, and the trustees of the river employed Robert Whitworth to survey it.[25] They do not seem to have opposed the canal, especially if coal were to be found plentifully near Newent, but to have regarded both it and an improved river as useful. Whitworth appears to have recommended canalization of part of the river and a canal paralleling the rest, and to have put forward two plans, costing respectively £27,000 and £48,000.[26] From 1790 to 1796 there was talk of a Bill to enable the river to be improved, though the canal promoters criticized Whitworth's proposals as likely to cause floods and alter the river's course.

When it was clear about 1800 that the Herefordshire & Gloucestershire Canal would get no farther towards Hereford than Ledbury in the foreseeable future, there was a movement towards improving the Wye, mainly by building a towpath, while the promotion at the same time of what later became the Severn & Wye tramroad promised better supplies of coal to be carried. The trade was there if facilities could be provided; a newspaper of 1804 referred to 'The Scarcity of Men to navigate the Barges, and the exorbitant Wages demanded by the few remaining on the river (which require) that some measure should speedily be adopted to remedy so great an evil'.[27] The scarcity meant, I think, was not in men to man the barges, but to tow them. Archdeacon Coxe, in *An Historical Tour through Monmouthshire*, written at the turn of the century, says: 'From Lidbrook large quantities of coal are sent to Ross and Hereford; and we passed several barges towed by ten or eleven men, which by great exertions are drawn to Hereford in two days.' In 1805 Jessop made a survey, and notice of a Bill was given,[28] but the matter did not become active till 1808, nor was an Act obtained[29] till 1809. It incorporated a company to build a horse towing path for the 37 miles from Hereford to Lydbrook, to take tolls, and to maintain ferries where it crossed the river five times. A capital of £6,000 was authorized, and £3,000 more if necessary. The Act named 33 subscribers who with the trustees appointed by previous Acts were to become one body.

The evidence given in connexion with this Act by Thomas

Bird, former solicitor to the Wye Trustees and now clerk to the newly formed company, said that Hereford, Ross and the greater part of the county were supplied with Dean Forest coal by barges on the river drawn by men, the supply of whom was uncertain; 10,000 tons of coal moved to Hereford each year by river and 3,000 tons of other goods, while another 4,000 tons of lime and other traffic was landed along its course. He considered that these figures would be greatly increased if the towing path improved the navigation and the river took some of the land traffic. Barges held about 10 tons, and the cost of hauling to Hereford was £6 1s. 6d. a barge, which with a towpath ought to be reduced by 15s. The estimated income of the towing path company was £1,312 10s., and expenses £1,106 2s.

Calls were made rapidly, and the newspaper of 23 January 1811 contained the announcement: 'Two barges belonging to Mr. Crompton, of Hereford, completed the voyage from Lidbrook by the new Towing Path, two horses being used for each barge.'[30] The Severn & Wye tramroad from the collieries to the Wye at Bishop's Wood was probably not opened, however, till early in 1813, when a more easily transported supply of coal became available. Some calls seem to have been in arrears, but in spite of that a first dividend of £2 per £50 share was paid in mid-1814.[31] The work was probably done under the supervision of James Cranston of Hereford.[32] The cost appears to have been only £5,000, for it was said that the works were completed for 20 per cent less than the estimate,[33] in which case the £50 shares were presumably only £40 paid up.

The tolls were quickly farmed out,[34] and by 1815 10 per cent was being paid.[35] A good rate of dividend was thereafter maintained, for in 1833 an advertisement offering shares for sale said that averaged over the previous nineteen years the dividends had been upwards of 8 per cent on each share.[36]

Some bow-hauling by men above Lydbrook seems still to have gone on, perhaps at flood-times. In 1825 a notice was given to extend the towing path downwards from Lydbrook to Walwar's Oak in Tidenham parish,[37] but nothing was done, and in 1847 the newspaper quoted a description of an occasion when, a little above Brockweir, 32 men were seen on one barge, harnessed 8 at a time to a rope by a chest-band, the strain being so great that sometimes the men had to go down on hands and feet and cling to stones to get sufficient grip.[38] Steam towing was also considered, and the Wye Steam Boat company was formed in 1825.[39] It built a tug which was successfully tested, but difficulties being found in providing suitable barges,[10] she was sold.

Below Hereford there are occasional glimpses of the nineteenth-century traffic, mainly coal upwards and timber down, with lime to the country wharves, slates, bark[41] and groceries as subsidiary cargoes. Traffic depended on the depth of water in the river: it was mostly during the winter, and sometimes during July and August, depending upon the rainfall in mid-Wales. At other times much went by road. Barges had increased in size, for in 1826 two of 25 and 32 tons were offered for sale. About 1835 regular passenger and pleasure boat trips were put on between Ross, Monmouth and Chepstow, and ran for a year or two; a similar service was started in 1855 from Ross to Goodrich, and in 1859 was running also to Monmouth, Tintern and Chepstow.

Above Hereford, itself 69 miles from the Severn, the river seems to have been navigable in some degree when there was enough water, and therefore especially in the winter. A modern author says that at some time after 1674 it was navigable from Aberedw Castle, a little above Hay, for small barges,[42] and a source of 1794 described it as 'in floods navigable six miles above Hay'.[43] The Carriers' Account Book[44] shows that there was traffic from Hay about 1825; this had probably existed earlier, and it also lasted for some time later, but probably only in timber, and only downwards, once the Hay tramroad had been opened. It was said in 1906[45] that the river had been navigable above Hereford within living memory, craft being hauled up the rapids at Monnington rocks by ropes and pulleys.

The coal trade up the Wye to Hereford benefited by the Severn & Wye tramroad, much less so by the Monmouth tramroad's river wharves at Redbrook, but it must have been hit by the opening of that to Hereford in 1829, and still more when the Herefordshire & Gloucestershire Canal reached the city in 1845. It had been a struggle to get there, and there had been times from 1834 onwards when they had thought of joining the Wye near Rotherwas.[46]

There is little information about the towing path company after the opening of the Hereford tramroad and later the canal, but in May 1853 a dividend of 35s. per share was declared. This was stated to be the largest for some years, and the report adds that there would have been more trade on the river if more coal had been available from the Forest.[47] The previous twelve months had been the last of the Hereford tramroad, while the Newport, Abergavenny & Hereford Railway was not yet open, so I think

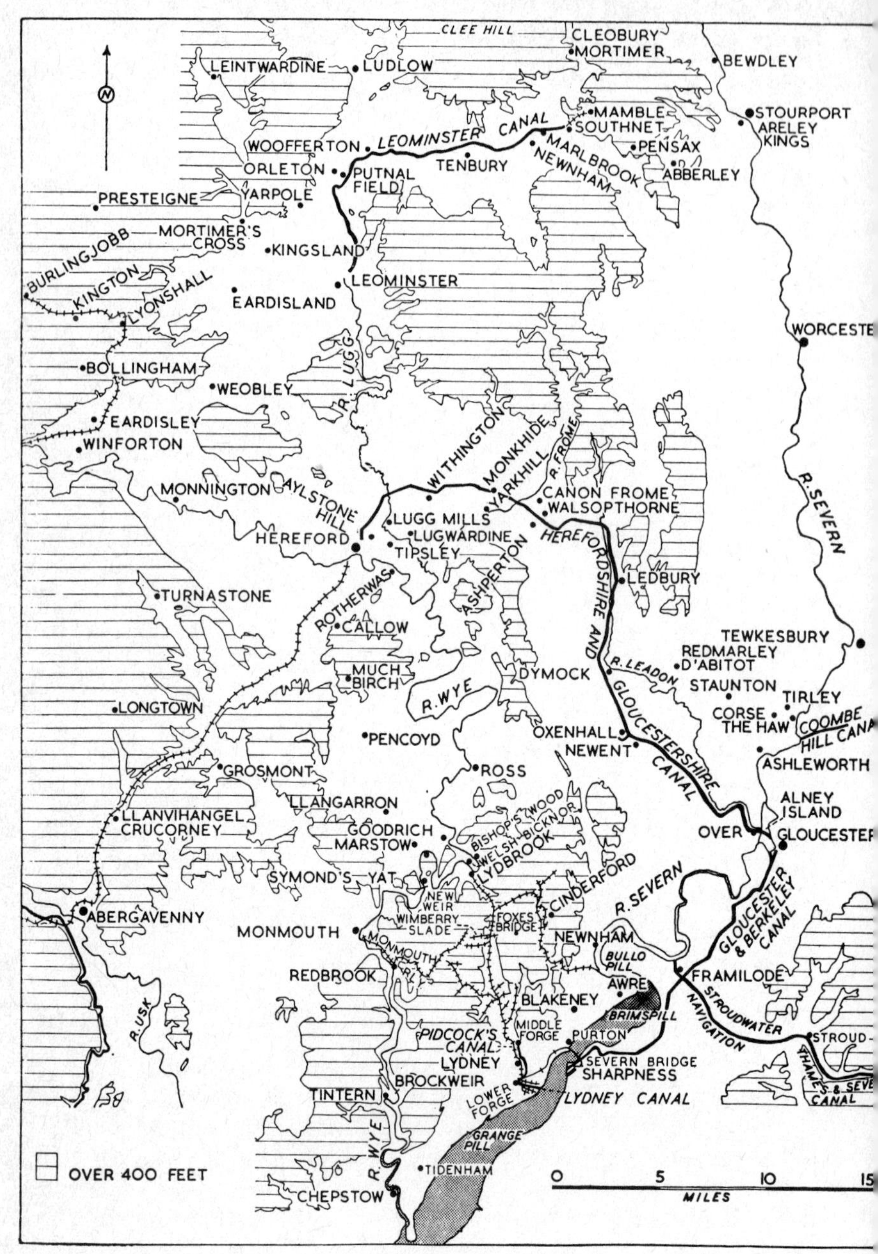

9. The waterways of Herefordshire and the Forest of Dean

the dividend represents a lessening of competition from the tramroad, the principal coal supplier.

Trade by river to Hereford ended soon after the opening of the Newport, Abergavenny & Hereford Railway in January 1854, and the Hereford, Ross & Gloucester Railway in June 1855, after which the towpath company was dissolved,[48] though the Act of 1859 for the Hereford, Hay & Brecon Railway imposed precautions for the protection of craft, including navigation warning lights in perpetuity at the river crossing near Hay 'for the Navigation and Safe Guidance of Vessels'. At the coal supplying end, the inclined plane on the Severn & Wye tramroad bringing it down to Lydbrook for shipment there was still in use in 1852, though traffic was fairly light, but was disused in 1856. It is said that a little coal brought by road was shipped from Lydbrook wharf to Symonds Yat till about 1890.[49] Soon after the Wye Valley Railway was opened in 1876, the highest point of navigation became Brockweir, and later, owing to silting, Tintern.

Leominster Canal

The first proposal to join Herefordshire to the upper Severn by water seems to have been for a canal from Bridgnorth through Corvedale to Leintwardine on the upper Teme, which would presumably then have been made navigable downwards. After the opening of the Staffordshire & Worcestershire Canal in 1772, which connected the Severn at Stourport with the collieries and industry of the Midlands, Robert Whitworth in 1777[50] suggested a canal from Hereford by Leominster and Pensax to Stourport to join it (this, he said, could be connected to the former proposal by a canal link between Woofferton and Ludlow), as well as one from Hereford to Ledbury and Gloucester.

After meetings from July 1789 onwards at Leominster and Tenbury, a survey of the country between Leominster and Stourport was decided upon. One optimist described the line as through level country with good water supply, needing few locks and a short tunnel at Abberley (Pensax), and thought the cost would be about £1,000 a mile.[51]

Thomas Dadford junior made the survey and estimate in time for a meeting in December. The length would be 31 miles, with tunnels at Putnal Field (330 yds.), Southnet (Sousnant) (1,254 yds.) and Pensax (3,850 yds.). The cost would be £83,000 and receipts £4,300 p.a.[52] A meeting in January 1790 decided to proceed in spite of this unattractive financial picture, and £18,000 was subscribed.[53]

In April a meeting at Kington asked for a survey thence to Leominster to join the proposed canal.[54] As a result the two schemes were amalgamated, and a canal 46 miles long was proposed, with lockage rising 48 ft. from Kington and then falling 496 ft. to the Severn.[55] The purposes envisaged were to carry stone, lime, iron ore and agricultural produce to the Severn,[56] to bring back coal thence and also from Sir Walter Blount's mines at Mamble and that at Pensax, and to supply with merchandise the small towns of Kington, Presteigne, Leominster, Ludlow, Tenbury and Cleobury Mortimer on or near its line.[57]

Dadford's plans and estimates for this very speculative agricultural canal through difficult country were approved in January 1791,[58] and an Act[59] was passed in the same year, authorizing a capital of £150,000, and £40,000 more if necessary. In July 1791 it was reported that subscriptions went on with spirit, and soon afterwards construction began with Dadford as engineer. It was the time of the canal mania, when many other local canals were also being talked of. A map of May 1791[60] shows one proposed from Hereford by Weobley, Eardisland and Kingsland to Leintwardine, and another to the same place from Hereford by Leominster and Kingsland. Again, discussion in 1792 upon what became the Montgomeryshire Canal* produced a suggestion that it be linked with the Leominster,[61] which in turn caused the editor of the Hereford newspaper to propose that the Herefordshire & Gloucestershire Canal should also be linked to Leominster.[62] The last idea was not then taken up, but Dadford surveyed a line from the Montgomeryshire to the Leominster Canal by Montgomery, Bishop's Castle and Ludlow, but its cost, as that of a shortened scheme from the Leominster Canal to Bishop's Castle via Ludlow, was too great, and the plans were dropped at the end of 1793.[63]

Meanwhile the Leominster Canal was opened during 1794 from above Marlbrook near Mamble to Woofferton beyond Tenbury and the nearest point to Ludlow, and in October a local newspaper[64] reported that 'Monday se'nnight the first boat's loading of coal upon the Leominster Canal, which was from Sir Walter Blount's mines, arrived at Tenbury, and by his order was distributed among the poor of that place. Ringing of bells, firing of cannon, roasting of sheep, etc., manifested the joy of the numerous spectators who were drawn together on this happy event. Six

* From Newtown in Montgomeryshire to Carreghofa to join the Ellesmere Canal.

more boats passed on and went over the grand aqueduct to Woofferton wharf, three miles from Ludlow, where there were similar rejoicings.' The opening date appears to have been 20 October, according to a shorter announcement in the *Glocester Journal* of 3 November.

By the end of 1795 cutting had been completed from the Kimbolton road near Leominster to Woofferton to join the portion already built to Marlbrook, the Southnet tunnel had been finished, a little cutting done beyond it towards Stourport, and the foundation of the aqueduct over the Lugg at Kingsland and some cutting near it* had been started. A total of £79,000 had been spent, and £11,000 was owed as well. In this year, however, a part of the as yet unused Southnet tunnel fell in, and in December John Rennie was therefore summoned by the anxious proprietors. He was highly critical of Dadford's work,† and estimated that £20,000 more would be needed to complete what had already been built from Southnet to Leominster, and £135,937 to finish the rest.[65]

The proprietors were resilient enough to get a second Act[66] in April 1796 authorizing them to raise another £180,000. In July it was announced that 'the tunnel at Putnal Field, which has long baffled the skill of the miners, is now happily finished',[67] and in December that: 'The Leominster Canal . . . is now completely open, from Sir Walter Blount's coal-works at Mamble‡ to the town of Leominster . . . 14 barges laden with coal, having arrived at Leominster the first day that the navigation was opened, the coal was sold to the inhabitants at 15s. per ton. A former 1/6 per cwt. is now 9d. or delivered at own house, at 10d.'[68] The canal was now 18½ miles long, Southnet tunnel having been left isolated and unrepaired. On the 1st of the following June a ceremonial cut was made at the spot where the canal was to join the Severn,[69] perhaps as a sales device to seek further subscriptions. But the money ran out and work stopped: so far, £68,582 had been raised in shares, and £25,000 was owed. The canal was of some use for carrying coal for domestic use and lime-burning, though the Mamble pits were not prolific; it seems to have been thought also that the completed section of canal would be used, together with

* The work near Kingsland may have been done later. For a description of this work, and for other information on the canal, Mr I. Cohen's paper on *The Leominster–Stourport Canal* in the *Transactions* of the Woolhope Naturalists' Field Club for 1955–7 should be consulted.

† In July 1792 Dadford had been appointed engineer of the Monmouthshire Canal, and after that he had given at most a quarter of his time to the Leominster.

‡ Actually from Wharf House, Marlbrook.

the road, to make a through route from Stourport and Hereford, hops going to Stourport on their way to Worcester being exchanged for wool.[70]

In 1801 there was a proposal to raise additional money by calls on existing shareholders to finish the canal, and to charge a special tonnage rate on 'every loaded Boat or Barge passing out of or into the river Severn from the Bason intended to be formed near Stourport Bridge'.[71] Then in 1803 John Hodgkinson suggested that tramroads were much cheaper than canals, and could be built from the end of the canal at Leominster to Kington, and from Southnet tunnel to Stourport, for £35,000, to which £50,000 or £60,000 must be added to pay off debts, rebuild Southnet tunnel, and put the canal into proper shape.[72] His proposals were accepted, and a third Act was passed in August 1803[73] to authorize these tramroads, and to raise £50,000 by additional calls on the shares and up to £40,000 on mortgage.

The company had especially in mind the tramroad from Southnet to Stourport. The Act put this section under the semi-independent control of a separate committee largely made up of members of the management committee of the Staffordshire & Worcestershire Canal, together with Sir William Blount the colliery owner of Mamble. At the time the Act was passed these must have been willing to subscribe the cost of the tramroad, about £15,000. A 10 per cent call was made in March, and another in July 1804. Then there seems to have been an upset in the company, for both the Clerk and Treasurer were changed, and a new call notice announced that: 'This is to be considered as the First Call.'[74] Since one of the Select Committee for the tramroad named in the 1803 Act, Coleman, was the dispossessed Treasurer, the upset may have meant the defeat of the Staffordshire & Worcestershire party. Two or three more calls were made,[75] but the shareholders put up only about £500, and no mortgages could be arranged. There was also a proposal in 1805[76] to open new coal and iron mines at Pensax, which it was hoped might help the canal. At least one such must have been opened, for a short tramroad appears to have been built from it to the road. It is possible also that what seem to be the remains of an unfinished tramroad from the Severn upwards past Areley Kings indicate that the tramroad authorized by the Act was in fact begun with the few hundreds subscribed.

At this time a local writer was excited by the beauty of the canal, and the prospects it opened for his district, and wrote:

'The whole line presents a romantic and picturesque appearance, sometimes gliding quietly through a level country, at other times hanging by the sides of hills; now hiding itself under ground, and now rolling its waves over subjected rivers; at length descending into the Severn . . . and thereby opening a communication with every part of the kingdom, and of the world.'[77]

In August 1810 there had been a proposal for a tramroad from the coal pits at Clee Hill to the canal.[78] In 1811[79] an important shareholder was induced to pay up his arrears of calls, and it was decided 'to continue the line of the canal from Leominster to Kingsland Field',* Thomas Perry of the Staffordshire & Worcestershire being a signatory of the notice. In 1812 both these ideas were incorporated in altered form in a larger scheme, of which notice for an Act was given.[80] This proposed a tramroad or canal from the Rea aqueduct to Worcester to join the Worcester & Birmingham Canal; a tramroad or canal from the existing canal near Olteton through Yarpole and Kingsland to the Lugg at Morimrer's Cross and thence to form a junction with the original line of canal 'as far as shall be considered practicable and useful'; a tramroad from the canal near Tenbury to the Clee Hill collieries; and a tramroad to 'the mines of coal, limestone, ironstone and other minerals' by way of Mamble, Pensax and Abberley.

Except for talks with the Staffordshire & Worcestershire, nothing was done, and in 1820 proposals for extension beyond Leominster were made obsolete by the opening of the Kington tramroad (see p. 182), along which North Herefordshire was supplied with coal from the canal wharf at Brecon.

At the turn of the year 1824 discussions on reorganization and extension began again, and as a result in 1826 yet another Act[81] was passed to authorize £60,000 worth of preference shares. A call of 1 per cent was made to pay for it, but the Act failed to achieve anything against the rooted disinclination of the local people to part with their money. The tramroad idea blossomed once again in November 1833[82] with a proposal for a line from Stourport to the Rea aqueduct and Sir Edward Blount's colliery, and also from Leominster to Eardisley (where it would have met the Hay tramroad), a total of 28 miles at an estimated cost of £61,000. In January 1834 this became a scheme also to buy the canal 'which has not sufficient water for any considerable traffic, and to let out the water and lay a tram road on the base of the present line to prevent the inconvenience, delay and damage in loading and unloading goods'.[83] If the canal could not be bought

* It may have been at this time that the work at Kingsland was done.

on equitable terms, then the tramroad should be continued past it at an extra cost of £40,000. It appears that this project was put forward by a group separate from the canal company, that the destination of the tramroad was Kington, and that the estimated cost was £65,000 for the new tramroads, plus £40,000 if necessary for the line by-passing the canal. The group seems to have had a Leominster and a Stourport committee.

The canal company now smartly called a meeting of their own at Leominster about the end of January 'to take into consideration a projected line of tram-road from the Aquaduct at Newnham* to connect the Leominster Canal with the River Severn at Stourport bridge etc.'[84] and on 27 February John U. Raistrick was asked by them to survey this section. After his report early in August, the Leominster company got in touch with the Staffordshire & Worcestershire, who told Raistrick, now their engineer, to look also at the plans of the independent group, and see if 'such a Railway as the Brecon and Hay Railroad cannot be made at a Expense of £1,200 a mile exclusive of . . . land'.[85] In March 1835 he produced his recommendations, his cheapest line costing £44,394, not counting the cost of converting the canal itself to a tramroad.[86] Nothing more was heard of the idea.

In 1837 Stephen Ballard of the Herefordshire & Gloucestershire Canal, then considering its extension from Ledbury to Hereford, was told to survey the Lugg to show the practicability of a junction with the Leominster Canal. In 1838 it seems that the Leominster company offered to help in making the Lugg navigable to Leominster,[87] but the Herefordshire & Gloucestershire, while willing to keep the idea in mind for future development, were too committed to the Hereford extension to spare any money for the Lugg.

In a few years bigger things were afoot, for railways were coming into Herefordshire, and nostalgia must have prompted the publication in 1845[88] of a a poem by Thomas Parker of Kington written in 1785.

> . . . If Navigation here were brought to thrive,
> 'Twould make the town and country more alive,
> A cut from hence to Stourport would be found
> Of greatest service to the country round:
> All kinds of business then would brisker grow,
> And trade and commerce round us gaily flow.
> Arise ye friends, ye patriots of the town,

* The Rea aqueduct.

And make your active public spirit known;
For this affair (if rightly understood)
Cements the private with the public good;
I wish with my whole heart to see it done,
Let every friend to commerce help it on.

In June 1845 a sub-committee of the proposed Shrewsbury & Hereford Railway (incorporated 1846) was appointed to get into touch with the Leominster company.[89] Apparently nothing resulted from the contact, for when in November a meeting was held in Leominster with Sir Edward Blount in the Chair, to consider the sale of the canal and the price, it decided that £20,000 should be asked from the Welsh Midland Railway for the canal to form part of their line, and a committee was appointed to effect the sale.[90] In February 1846, however, the Shrewsbury & Hereford offered to buy the canal for £12,000 if they got their Act,[91] and this was agreed by the canal company in July.[92] The purchase figure represented £16 per £100 share, on which no dividend had ever been paid. On 23 February 1847 the railway committee reported to a special meeting of the shareholders that they 'have entered into an arrangement with the Proprietors of the Leominster Canal Navigation for the purchase of that Canal; a part of which will be made available in the construction of the line, and the remainder held with a view to future objects; . . . the possession of this Canal will effect a considerable saving in the construction of the line . . .'.[93] The price was still £12,000, with 160 acres of land, and the meeting accepted the canal company's undisturbed possession of this for over 40 years as a satisfactory title.

An Act[94] was passed in the same year to authorize the sale of the canal which 'is of little Use for the purposes for which the same is intended, and by the Construction of the said proposed Railway the Utility thereof will be further diminished, and it is probable that the Proprietors thereof will be no longer able to maintain the same'.[95] The canal bed was not, however, used for the Shrewsbury & Hereford line between Leominster and Woofferton, nor did the company then buy the canal: it is likely that a questionable title to land was one of the reasons. After the railway had been built, however, the possibility of an extension to and beyond Tenbury was discussed in 1852 (probably the phrase 'future objects' in 1847 referred to the same proposal), and the railway company agreed to the purchase after pressure from the canal company's solicitors. No action followed until in 1855 a canal deputation visited the railway committee 'urgently pressing the purchase should be completed'.[96] Getting no satisfactory answer, the canal company filed a Bill in Chancery to compel the Shrewsbury & Hereford Railway to carry out its agreement to buy the canal, and to pay interest on the £12,000 from 1 January 1847. The Bill was dismissed on the technicality that two railway Directors had not signed the agreement as the Railway's Act required, and after the Vice-Chancellor had said of the railway company: 'There never was a more shocking case of dishonesty if they succeed in escaping, but it may be so.'[97] Maybe because of these remarks the railway company then decided to buy, and the canal company to sell, for the original price of £12,000 without interest. The conveyance was dated 25 March 1858.

The Shrewsbury & Hereford Railway at first considered keeping open that part of the canal from Woofferton to Marlbrook which did not compete with its own line, but on 24 November 1857 their officer reported 'that he had communicated with the Agent of Sir Edward Blount and had ascertained that no increase of traffic could be obtained on that portion of the Canal between Sousnat and Woofferton, and that the profit to be derived therefrom would not defray the expense of maintaining the Canal'.[98] The Leominster–Woofferton section was formally closed in June 1858,[99] and the whole was drained in 1859.[100] In 1860 some of the land was sold for £548 to the Tenbury Railway,[101] which built its line over part of the bed.

Herefordshire & Gloucestershire Canal

On 27 December 1774 a meeting was held at Ledbury to advocate a canal to the Severn, 'having been for many Years much wished for by People of every Degree'.[102] This idea may have been known to Robert Whitworth, when, at the request of a group of gentlemen in Herefordshire, he reported in 1777 on various ways of connecting Hereford by water with the Severn, including a canal by Ledbury to Gloucester.[103]

The idea of a Hereford–Gloucester canal was revived in 1789. A survey was made by Richard Hall, and a line proposed from the Severn at The Haw above Gloucester by Tirley, Corse, Staunton and Redmarley d'Abitot to Dymock, then to Ashperton, and so to Hereford by way of Yarkhill, Lugwardine and Tupsley.[104] In March 1790 it was decided[105] to seek a Bill. The engineer was to be Josiah Clowes,* and there were to be joint solicitors and treasurers from Gloucester and Hereford. In April, presumably after a re-survey, Clowes reported upon a canal from Hereford by Ledbury to Gloucester with a branch to Newent.[106] He proposed a narrow canal taking boats 70 ft. by 8 ft., to carry 35 tons and drawing 3 ft. 6 in., at a cost of just under £70,000.

At this point some of the canal promoters seem to have preferred making the Wye more easily navigable to building a new waterway, for a meeting in May of the canal committee ruled out the practicability of building locks on the river, while a pamphlet was issued drawing attention to the uncertain navigation of the Wye and explaining that even if it were improved, trade towards Bristol would be helped, and not that towards Gloucester and the north. It proposed that the collieries near Newent should be restarted, and that Staffordshire and Forest of Dean coal should be carried upwards, together with limestone to Ledbury and farm produce downwards. A trade of 17,203 tons a year to and from Hereford, yielding £6,573 7s. 11d., and of 16,000 tons to and from Ledbury, yielding £3,008 6s. 8d., was looked for.[107]

After some delay an organizing committee was appointed in January 1791 and a first call made. Later in the month it was learned that additional veins of coal had been discovered at Newent,[108] and this encouraged a decision to go ahead. There was little opposition, and the Act[109] was obtained in April. The canal line was to follow the River Leadon to Ledbury, and then pass by Canon Frome and Withington to Hereford. A 1,320-yard tunnel was projected at Walsopthorne (then Wazzington), and one of 440 yds. under Aylstone Hill just outside Hereford. A branch left the main line near the junction of the Ell Brook with the Leadon, and ran to Newent. At the Gloucester end the line crossed the western branch of the Severn by an aqueduct at Over, and ran across Alney Island, under the Causeway, into the eastern branch of the river opposite Gloucester. As projected the canal was 35½ miles long, with a 3-mile branch, the distance from Gloucester to Ledbury being 18 miles.

The Act authorized a share capital of £75,000, with power to raise £30,000 more. There was from the beginning an impression of lukewarmness about the project. At the first shareholders' meeting it was agreed that Clowes—and also Whitworth if he were

* He had previously worked on the Chester Canal, and had been for a short time its engineer, and had later helped Robert Whitworth to build the Thames & Severn Canal.

available—should estimate for a canal 'on a reduced Scale'.[110] It took nine adjournments to get a second together, and thereafter it was seldom that a meeting was held without previous adjournments. Whitworth was too busy to come, and nothing happened during the summer except some brick-making, and the raising of the capital, which was fully subscribed by August.[111] In September Hugh Henshall* was asked to re-survey the line, which he did at once. He now suggested that the draught of the boats to be used should be increased from 3½ ft. to 4½ ft., so enlarging their capacity but needing a more deeply excavated canal, and also proposed that the main line should be carried along the proposed Newent branch and then through a tunnel at Oxenhall to join the original line again near Dymock, so eliminating the branch.

In 1793 an Act[112] was passed to authorize the variation of the line at Oxenhall, and some other smaller changes. It was now announced that 'the undertaking . . . will be set about with spirit . . .',[113] and cutting began on the line to Newent, and at Oxenhall and Walsopthorne tunnels, and preparations were made to build the Severn aqueduct at Over. The local landowners at once protested that their property might be injured by floods caused by the aqueduct obstructing the river and also causing ice-blockages. In June, therefore, Clowes recommended that instead of an aqueduct the canal should cross the Severn on the level, and run across Alney Island to Gloucester a little below the Westgate bridge. Here John Carne's cutting machine was set to work, with the inventor as contractor, to cut the canal level with low-water mark in the river.† This portion of the canal between the two branches of the Severn was reported nearly finished in October 1794, and in November negotiations were begun with Gloucester Corporation to buy land for a basin and wharves between 'the Canal as cut and the Causeway'.[114] In June 1795 Whitworth, now engineer because Clowes had died early in the year, was told to hurry on with its completion, and to plan a drawbridge to allow 'the largest Vessels carrying Bark'[115] to enter the basin. It is not clear whether the basin was ever built—probably not—or the Alney section of canal used. It silted up badly because mud got carried into it with the tide, and in June 1797 Whitworth recommended a dam across the river at Over to prevent the silt getting

* James Brindley's brother-in-law, the engineer who completed the Trent & Mersey Canal.

† On 16 December 1793 it was reported that Carne's machine had removed 1,007 cu. yds. of earth in seven days, using eleven men and four horses.

in. This naturally raised even more opposition than had the original proposal for an aqueduct. After protest meetings in Gloucester and Tewkesbury, some fishermen and watermen seem to have had the company indicted in July 1799, and in February 1800 the partly built dam was in consequence ordered to be removed. Thenceforward the cut was given up, and the canal ended at Over, whence boats worked to Gloucester round by the upper or lower Partings.

Let us return to the main canal. As with so many others at the end of the canal mania, the shareholders were slow in paying their calls; in the autumn of 1793 the canal committee said firmly that 'As the Committee can neither make advantageous contracts nor expedite the works unless regularly supplied with cash, it is expected that payment will be punctual.'[116] Early in 1794 serious work began on the Oxenhall tunnel (for which gin wheels were bought from the works now completed at Sapperton)* and some on that at Walsopthorne. In April the committee, which had been directing searches for coal near Newent, decided to lease ground and sink a shaft near Oxenhall, the coal from which could be 'for the use of the Compy in the making of Bricks, burning Lime, etc.',[117] and also for sale. An agreement with the landowner was signed in November.

A portion of canal was open by July 1794, and by December £44,297 had been spent. By now the coal pit was yielding small coal, and another was to be sunk. These collieries were in January 1796 leased to Mr. Richard Perkins, part of the agreement with him being that a short branch canal should be made to them. This, sometimes called the Oxenhall, sometimes the Kilcot, branch, was completed in November 1796. It left the main line on the east side of Oxenhall church and circled round it for about ¼ mile. The pits themselves were probably below White House, to the west of the village, the coal being taken to the end of the branch by cart.†

The line from Over to Newent and Oxenhall was opened about the end of October 1795, when a newspaper report says: 'The Herefordshire and Gloucestershire Canal is now navigable from Gloucester to Oxenhall; and on Saturday a barge arrived at the former place with coals, and also the Newent Trader with goods, both from Newent.'[118] So little trade offered that the company put on three boats of its own to be run regularly, traffic or not,

* On the Thames & Severn Canal. See my *The Canals of Southern England.*

† This branch was probably disused by 1800.

but had to report after some months that one of the causes of the small trade carried on was 'the difficulty to induce tradesmen and farmers to adopt a mode of carrying different to that to which they have become accustomed'.[119] Another reason was probably unreliability due to water shortage, for in spite of the newspaper statement quoted, another in August 1796 says that: 'The Hereford and Gloucester Canal is now completely navigable from the Severn to Newent.'[120] In February 1797, 'it appearing absolutely necessary that every possible effort should be made to create a Tonnage upon the Canal',[121] the company began trading in coal generally, and also decided to build two limekilns.

By November the whole capital of £75,000 had been spent, while the next year 1796 saw much trouble from water in cutting the 2,192-yard Oxenhall tunnel, to cope with which two steam-engines had to be installed. By November only 1,400 yards had been cut, and 'Great has been the delay and expence . . . in the progress of the Tunnel . . . from the immense quantity of Water . . . which has several times filled pits already only half sunk, and driven the workmen entirely from their labour. . . .'[122] By October 1797 £101,397 had been spent, of which the tunnel had taken about £28,000, and the company was in serious financial trouble. It struggled on, and at last, having raised from its shareholders the whole of the authorized capital that should have taken the waterway to Hereford:

'The Herefordshire and Gloucestershire Canal from Glocester to Ledbury is completed; the opening of this navigation took place on the 30th. of March [1798], when several of the proprietors and gentlemen of the Committee, embarked at the junction of the coal branch near Newent. . . . They passed through the Tunnel at Oxenhall . . . in the space of 52 minutes. . . . Both ends of the tunnel, as well as the banks of the canal, were lined with spectators, who hailed the boats with reiterated acclamations. It is supposed that upwards of 2000 persons were present on their arrival at Ledbury, (about 9 miles) which they reached in 4 hours. A dinner was provided on the occasion, at the George Inn, where the greatest conviviality prevailed, and many appropriate toasts were drunk. . . . Coals of the first quality are now delivered at the wharf, close to Ledbury, at 13s. 6d. whereas the former price was 24s. per ton.'[123]

By early 1800 this canal, 16 miles long, with 13 locks, which had cost over £100,000, had yielded £500 in gross receipts for the four months January to April, and 'little appears to be doing at the collieries'.[124] Because the canal had not reached the Frome River beyond Ledbury, the top part was chronically short of water. It was a situation for which no one wished to take responsibility. For twelve years, therefore, from 23 July 1800 to 26 November 1812, not a single committee or general assembly meeting appears to have taken place. The canal was run by the superintendent and perhaps one man with great devotion, for when at last a meeting was held, there was £1,200 in the bank to the credit of the proprietors, and one Thomas Hatchett applied 'for some remuneration for attendance as Lock-keeper for thirteen years past'.[125] He was given £20, which seems little enough. Receipts had increased from £453 in 1804 to £1,061 in 1812.

Walker the engineer (probably Ralph) was called in to advise on increasing the water supply to the summit, and a little was got. There was talk of extending the canal upwards to obtain more, but the storage capacity of the top pound was increased instead, and a proper wharf and wharf house provided at Ledbury, a mile south of the town where the Ross road now crosses the railway.*

It was still difficult to induce the proprietors to take an interest in a canal which appeared unlikely ever to yield them a penny. No committee meeting was recorded in 1814–16 and 1821–5, and no general assembly in the years 1815–27. Then, in August 1827, the Committee appointed Stephen Ballard clerk, and he took his duties seriously. He says: 'On my first entering on the business of this Canal I was led to believe that there was no trade for a Canal, that even the short time in each year that it was navigable was sufficient for the trade, and that if there was ever so good a supply of water the trade would not be increased thereby.'[126] He soon decided this was not so, helped perhaps by the favourable atmosphere for canals produced locally by the opening of the Gloucester & Berkeley in the year in which he was appointed, and he seems to have been the active mover in what followed.

In 1828 a new committee was elected, new by-laws made, and a new schedule of tolls drawn up based on coal at 2d. per ton per mile. The basin at Ledbury was enlarged to make it more convenient and to increase its storage capacity, and a feeder was built from the Leadon. Discussion on a further water supply from the Frome, however, raised the possibility of extending the canal, so increasing both water and trade. In May 1828 Ballard was asked to report on an extension either to the end of the proposed summit

* The wharf house still stands.

level at Monkhide, or to Hereford. He did so, estimating the cost of continuing to Hereford at £52,960, and the extra annual receipts at £4,750. The latter turned out to be reasonably accurate; the former was not. He proposed to eliminate both the Walsopthorne and the Aylestone Hill tunnels by deep cuttings, and to vary the Parliamentary line. He was then sent off to look at some canals in the north, and in the course of the tour he was taken over the Liverpool & Manchester Railway, then building, by George Stephenson. This experience does not seem to have affected his faith in canals, though years later it was said, perhaps with truth, that the extension to Hereford was built in such a way that it could easily be converted into a railway. If so, it never was.

The shareholders agreed to go ahead with what money could be raised, and work began in 1830, though little was done except to buy land, and build a lock at Ledbury. In March 1834 it was decided to borrow £15,000 to cut to Walsopthorne and then drive a heading through the hill to get the Frome water, and a proposal to continue the canal when possible to join the Wye was circulated. However, counsel held that there was no power to raise the money, and an application to borrow £50,000 for the whole extension from the Exchequer Bill Loan Commissioners was refused till Parliamentary powers should have been obtained to vary the line. Such a varied line was surveyed in October 1834 by Ballard, but not adopted by the committee.[127] In May 1835 there was a meeting to consider applying for a Bill to raise £75,000 in shares, all profits to go to the new shareholders up to 5 per cent before the old benefited. The income of the finished portion was now stated to be £1,500 p.a., and that of the proposed extension was estimated at £5,638, mostly coal to Hereford and timber downwards. Applications for shares were invited, but nothing happened, though a Gloucester & Hereford Railway scheme was announced in 1836,[128] and dropped in 1837.[129] The canal company occupied itself with arguments with those who were proposing to improve the Severn, and discussions upon whether the canal should be carried to the Wye or direct to Hereford. In August Ballard's varied line for an extension was approved by the shareholders,[130] but Ralph Walker, who was then called in to make his own survey, supported the Parliamentary line and the tunnels. His report was accepted and Ballard's proposals to join the Wye rejected.

The enabling Act[131] was passed in May 1839, authorizing the raising of £45,000 in shares and £50,000 by mortgage, and a meeting in July[132] agreed that the capital should be sought in 7½ per cent Preference shares, on which 4 per cent would be paid during construction.* Immediately after the Act the committee reported 'the extreme apathy of those most interested in the completion of the Canal'.[133] They soon realized that money would have to be looked for, and resolved: 'That Agents be appointed at Worcester, London, Bristol, Leominster and other Towns, to obtain shares on a commission of 2s. 6d. per share.'[134] They were successful, for by October the Preference shares had been subscribed, and in December cutting began, with Stephen Ballard as engineer. Curiously enough, no one at the canal meetings is reported as having mentioned railways, though they must have been in the minds of the apathetic, except to say in 1841 that the canal was benefiting from the completion of the Birmingham & Gloucester Railway, and to suggest in 1843 that the Great Western should build a waterside station at Gloucester to make direct transhipment possible.

By April 1840, 500 men were at work.[135] Money was borrowed on mortgage, and in October 1842 the extension was open to Canon Frome, 7½ miles, at a cost of £65,738, more than Ballard's earlier estimate for the whole distance to Hereford. However, the canal at last had a reliable water supply. The tunnel at Walsopthorne had been shortened to 400 yds. by long approach cuttings with a maximum depth of 50 ft.

Regular fly-boats† now began to run from Gloucester, and on 11 January 1843 the *Hereford Journal* reported that:

'On Wednesday last the carriers Bunning and Gibson had their first boat load of goods to Canon Frome wharf. From that day may be dated the desertion of the River Wye as a navigation for the conveyance of foreign produce. The opening of the Berkeley Canal in 1827 and now the extension of the Hereford and Gloucester Canal to within 10 miles of Hereford have given facilities that will probably for ever supersede the Wye as a navigation for conveyance of Hereford goods. . . .'

On 26 February 1844 the canal was opened for a further 4½ miles to Withington,[136] which led to an 'abatement of Prejudice and increase of Interest with which . . . the Canal is looked upon in the Town of Ledbury, the City of Hereford, and the County generally . . .'.[137] By October 1844 twice-weekly boats were run-

* This was stopped in 1844, and thenceforward no Preference interest was paid till the railway lease.

† See my *British Canals*, 3rd ed., 1966, p. 164.

ning from Birmingham via the Worcester & Birmingham Canal,[138] and on 21 May 1845 water was let into the remaining section to Barr's Court basin, Hereford, including the Aylstone Hill tunnel of about 440 yards.

The extension had cost £141,436, and the whole 34 miles of the canal about £248,000. Of this total about £149,000 was in shares and £78,000 in mortgages and loan notes; the balance seems to have been taken from income. The extension was the last main line canal to be built in England outside the Birmingham area or Yorkshire.

The year of completion was the year also of the railway mania. Already in 1844 the proposal for a Gloucester–Hereford Railway had been revived,[139] but had been abandoned to the Great Western in December, a proposition that the canal company opposed in 1845. Indeed, on 10 May, a few days before their canal was opened, the committee asked some of its members 'to enter into such preliminary measures as might seem desirable with any Railway Company that might see the eligibility of treating with this Company for the purchase of the Canal'.[140] Two bids were got, one from the Herefordshire, Gloucestershire, South Wales & Worcester Railway, and one from the Welsh Midland, which wanted to convert the canal to a railway. The bid of the latter of £130,000* was accepted subject to the railway company getting its Act. It did not do so. Other negotiations took place, and in November 1846 the proposed Hereford & Gloucester Railway, promoted by the L.N.W.R., announced that it would apply for an Act authorizing it to buy the canal.[141] This caused the Staffordshire & Worcestershire Canal company to send a memorial to the Railway Commissioners and a petition to the House of Commons against it,[142] though the Hereford & Gloucester company itself said in a petition that in 1839 'the comparative merits of Canals and Railways for the conveyance of Goods were imperfectly understood and it was concluded that the extension of the Canal presented the greatest amount of advantage to the district. That since the opening of the last extension in 1845 the total Traffic on the Canal has been doubled but during the interval of its construction the prepossession in favour of Railway Transit has become so decided as to leave no expectation of any further increase'.[143] The purchase Bill was, however, lost in June 1847.[144]

As they were now on their own, the committee set out to in-

* So the canal company's records. The *Hereford Journal* for 5 November 1845 says £140,000 inclusive.

crease traffic, mainly by reciprocal toll agreements with the Staffordshire & Worcestershire and the Worcester & Birmingham Canal companies to enable Staffordshire coal to be carried cheaply to Hereford. The canal's trade has risen from an average annual income of £1,800 in the years before 1840 to one of £5,504 for those from 1845 to 1847, and the tonnage carried from 16,030 in 1838 to 43,080 in 1848. The company could just cover its mortgage and loan interest, which ran at about £3,750 p.a. against a net revenue of £3,885 in 1847.

In 1852, in exchange for withdrawing its opposition, the company negotiated an agreement with the proposed Worcester & Hereford Railway for the sale of the canal between Hereford and Ledbury, but this too fell through. Again the company went on its independent way, and in 1854 agreed with the Newport, Abergavenny & Hereford Railway, which had opened that year, for a cheap coal rate on the canal down to Newent and for a coal trans-shipment stage 'to transfer coal from the Railway trucks to the Canal boats . . .',[145] which was reported at the end of June 1855 to be ready. The Staffordshire coal trade up the canal to Hereford had been lost to the railway, which now brought Monmouthshire coal to be sent down the canal line.

Because the Worcester & Hereford project which had been authorized in 1853, began about 1858 to go forward seriously and there was no real hope of competing with it, the Company began about this time a policy of cutting the interest paid on their mortgages and loan notes, and then buying them up at reduced prices, so making sure that the prior charge holders got at any rate some of their money back. The line was completed in 1861.

They then opened negotiations with the Great Western and West Midland Railway companies, as supporters of a line from Gloucester through Ledbury that intended to convert the Oxenhall tunnel for railway use, and on 17 January 1862 signed an agreement with both companies (later to be maintained by the G.W.R. alone) for the lease of the canal for £5,000 a year, the waterway to be managed by a joint committee of railway and canal representatives till an Act was obtained.

The G.W.R. then delayed year after year to get an authorizing Act, till in 1869 representatives of the canal company in despair went to see Sir Daniel Gooch at Paddington. He 'consented to give the requisite Notice for that purpose, but . . . expressed his belief that the Great Western shareholders would not entertain the application, unless some abatement of the terms was agreed to by the Canal Committee . . .'.[146] The G.W.R. also said that they would abandon the agreement if Parliament struck out either the power to convert the canal to a railway or that to levy the maximum existing authorized tolls.

However, the Act went through without change, compensation being given to the Severn Commissioners for loss of tolls,[147] and by 20 October 1870 the Great Western Railway had taken over. The company had by 1871 repaid about £50,000 nominal of the debt, and thenceforward it remained in existence till nationalization only to distribute the G.W.R.'s yearly payment.

In 1873 two schemes were approved by Parliament, the Newent Railway from a junction with the G.W.R. at Over through Newent to Dymock, to join the second, the Ross & Ledbury Railway. Both companies were authorized to use the line of the canal. In 1876 the G.W.R. took over *de facto* control of both companies, when it was decided not to proceed with the Dymock–Ross portion. The rest was begun in 1880, and the section of canal from Ledbury to the Severn was closed to traffic on 30 June 1881,[148] though the southern half was used by railway contractors for nearly nine months after that. The railway from Over to Ledbury was opened on 27 July 1885.* These railways were absorbed by the G.W.R. in 1892.

The canal upwards from Ledbury to Hereford presumably became disused after 1882.

The Lydney Canal and Severn & Wye Tramroad: Pidcock's Canal

By 1800 several influences were at work in the Forest of Dean coalfield. This field had two potential markets, the one across the Severn, the other up the Wye. As we have seen, coal shipped at Newport did not have to pay the coastwise duty that was levied on shipments from the Forest of Dean down the Severn, and therefore had an advantage in the Bristol market. To the north, Staffordshire coal brought down the Staffordshire & Worcestershire or the Worcester & Birmingham canals and then down the Severn prevented a trade upwards. But across the Severn markets were opening. The old Stroudwater Navigation, completed in 1779, had been extended through to the Thames in 1789 when the

* John Masefield's poem, 'The Widow in the Bye Street', refers to the building of the railway on the canal. There was a canal warehouse at the bottom of Bye Street, Ledbury.

Thames & Severn Canal was opened. Forest coal could now move up the Stroud valley and on to Cirencester, Cricklade and the Thames valley, unaffected by the coastwise duty, since Lydney, Gloucester and Framilode (at the entrance of the Stroudwater Navigation) were all within the Port of Gloucester, and the duty did not apply to shipments within a single port. The opportunity was an incentive to the development both of the Forest collieries and of better transport facilities from the pits to Severnside.

To the west, it was clear that the Herefordshire & Gloucestershire Canal, which had reached Ledbury from Gloucester in March 1798, was unlikely to be extended to Hereford for many years, if ever. Therefore it was necessary to improve the carriage of coal to the wharves on the Wye and also the facilities of the river itself.

The impetus towards action seems to have come first from Hereford, frustrated in its hopes of a canal.[149] A meeting there in March 1800[150] planned to build a tramroad from the Forest collieries to Lydbrook, the shipping place on the Wye. By the next meeting on 5 January 1801, however,[151] supporters from Ross and Monmouth were present, and it was decided to ask Benjamin Outram to report upon 'the best Mode of opening a Communication, by means of Rail or Tram Roads, from the collieries in the Forest of Dean to the Rivers Wye and Severn'. In September, after Henry Price of Hereford had surveyed the line and Outram had reported, Parliamentary notices were issued for a tramroad from the Forest collieries to Lydbrook on the Wye and Lydney on the Severn,[152] and an estimate of £21,500 was approved in principle.[153]

A second group was also active, and issued a notice for a line from the collieries near Parkend and Lydney.[154] Maybe because of this activity and also because of the lukewarmness of the Gloucester supporters, discouraged by the failure at that time of the Gloucester & Berkeley Canal, the first group, at a meeting in November, decided to go ahead only with the Wye section of the tramroad, and by early 1802 £3,000 had been subscribed.[155] At this point there was a movement to extend the proposed line right on to Hereford. In September a notice was issued for such a line, 24 miles long, from the Wye opposite Lydbrook by Goodrich, Marstow, Llangarron, Pencoyd, Llanwarne, Much Birch and Callow to Hereford. It had been surveyed by Price. A long list of owners and occupiers of land through which it would pass opposed it,[156] and there the project ended. It was revived in 1804, but failed again in face of a hostile report from Lord Glenbirvie, Surveyor-General of H.M.'s Woods and Forests; instead men turned to the improvement of the Wye, and especially to the building of a horse towing path (see p. 187).

From 1806 onwards a number of causes worked to produce in 1808 a revival of the plan for tramroads to Lydbrook and Lydney from the Forest collieries. One was the projected tramroad from Gloucester to Cheltenham, proposed in 1806,[157] and authorized in 1809, which could be used by Forest coal to compete with the Staffordshire product carried on the Severn and the Coombe Hill Canal. Another was the building, begun without an Act, of the Bullo Pill tramroad from collieries near Cinderford to Bullo Pill on the Severn near Newnham. It was being talked of in mid-1807,[158] and was subsequently authorized in 1809 on the same day as the Severn & Wye.* A third was the appointment in 1806 of a more sympathetic Surveyor-General, Lord Robert Spencer. A fourth was, of course, the Wye towing path project itself.

The Bullo Pill and the Lydney & Lydbrook projects caused the Department of Woods & Forests, who administered the Forest for the Crown, to ask John Rennie to report on the development of transport there in the light of these two proposals. Rennie suggested a wet-dock or basin at Nass Point beyond Lydney, perhaps with a canal up to Lydney and a basin there, and a cut to the tail of the iron mills above the town. He estimated the cost of such a canal at £7,356 excluding land. He also proposed spheres of interest for the two groups of projectors and a boundary between them dividing those collieries conveniently served by Bullo Pill from those served by Lydney.[159] The report was made in February 1807, and this sensible piece of early transport planning became the basis of the Acts of 1809 for the two companies.

The Lydney & Lydbrook promoters, who had in 1806 again issued tramroad notices for the whole line, hoped that most of the coal and stone from the Forest, passing at the rate of about 100 tons a day by land carriage, would go by tramroad to the Wye. 'In return it is expected that part of the bark, timber, and corn, which annually descend the Wye . . . will cross the Forest, by means of the rail-road, into the river Severn, to avoid the tedious navigation of the Wye, particularly during the summer months.'[160] Whereas the Wye traffic might yield 30,000 tons a year, the main

* The Bullo Pill tramroad was a privately owned line from Bullo Pill to Cinderford Bridge, and public under this Act from Cinderford Bridge to Churchway. It later became a Great Western Railway branch.

object was the carriage of coal, stone, iron ore and lime to Lydney, at a hoped-for rate of 300 tons of coal and 100 tons of stone a day, or perhaps 120,000 tons a year.

After unsuccessful attempts in 1807 and 1808, the Lydney & Lydbrook company was authorized in June 1809,[161] with a capital of £35,000, and £20,000 more if necessary. The principal promoters were Edward and John Protheroe of Parkend and other collieries, who between them held 240 shares of £50, but the chairman, E. B. Clive, and a committeeman, Dr William Symonds, both of Hereford, were also promoters of the Wye Horse Towing Path.

Rennie's proposal for a canal at Lydney had not been followed. Instead the promoters intended to bring the tramroad down to the edge of Lydney Pill near Lower Forge, to build a basin and wharves there, and also a canal upwards from the basin to 'the Lower Storehouse' in Pidcock & Homfray's ironworks, presumably to connect with Pidcock's Canal.

Thomas Bathurst of Lydney Park on 8 April 1779 leased Lydney Furnace to David Tanner. The lease provided for the free use of Lydney pill, and gave permission to make a navigable canal.[162] This canal, about 1½ miles long from a basin by the pill up the valley to Middle Forge, seemingly with three locks just below the Forge, was probably built soon afterwards, and passed with the works to John Pidcock and George Homfray. When the Lydney Canal was built it joined Pidcock's Canal, and the latter is found on maps of the 1840's and on a Severn & Wye plan of 1877, but I have no information upon its use, though its appearance on G. Bradshaw's usually accurate canal map of 1830 indicates that it was then open. The Severn & Wye tramroad twice crossed it on drawbridges.

Astley Bowdler was appointed both clerk and engineer of the Severn & Wye company, a plateway was decided upon, and contractors were engaged. There were two main difficulties, to fill the subscription list and to agree with Charles Bathurst, who owned the land that was needed for wharves. Both were solved in time, but meanwhile the proprietors seem to have become a good deal more optimistic about their prospects. They therefore reverted in that year to Rennie's original plan for a canal, which would enable them to do without the shallow tidal Lydney pill, that could only take craft carrying 20–30 tons and drawing not more than 5 ft,[163] and obtained an Act[164] authorizing a small ship canal. It was to have a lock at the entrance leading into an outer harbour and another into the canal itself. A basin was to be built about 5½ furlongs up the cut, beyond which the canal was to continue for about ½ mile to its junction with Pidcock's.

Bowdler was told to draw up plans for the canal and basin, while the company, which by this Act had changed its name to the Severn & Wye Railway & Canal company, made a drive for money. It was now that a connexion was formed between the Severn & Wye and the Wilts & Berks Canal company. In this same year of 1810 the latter had opened its line throughout from Semington on the Kennet & Avon Canal, which in turn had access by the Somersetshire Coal Canal to the Somerset coalfield, to Abingdon on the Thames by way of Swindon. In 1810 also the Wilts & Berks had suggested to the Thames & Severn Canal company the building of a junction between the two canals. This junction was opened in 1819 and was known as the North Wilts; by it Forest coal could pass to the coal-consuming Vale of White Horse.* From 1810 onwards some of those connected with the Wilts & Berks Canal seem to have regarded the Severn & Wye as an alternative source of coal supply not under the control of the Somerset coalowners and the Somersetshire Coal Canal company, and to have formed an 'interest' within the Severn & Wye company. The first symptom of this interest was the purchase by William Whitworth, who engineered the Wilts & Berks and was a shareholder in it, of £1,000 worth of Severn & Wye shares. By 1812, when he was elected to the committee, he had colliery interests in the Forest also. Soon afterwards Joseph Priestley, first Clerk of the Wilts & Berks, and James Crowdy, who was also connected with it, became shareholders.

Bowdler was clearly not up to the job of building the canal, and in August 1810 he was dismissed, and Jessop† junior was appointed consulting engineer on William Whitworth's recommendation. It was he who drew up the plans for the canal and basins. In 1811 both the tramroad to Lydbrook and also the Wye towing path were opened, and Hereford could now get more reliable supplies of coal. In 1814 the tramroad, under powers of the Act of 1810, was extended a short distance from the top of the inclined plane at Lydbrook to a better wharf at Bishop's Wood, which became the permanent coal wharf till 1830, when it was closed and shipments were again made from Lydbrook wharf, though the tramroad to Bishop's Wood continued to be

* These canals are described in my *The Canals of Southern England*.
† Probably Josias Jessop.

used for coal traffic transferred there to road waggons for Ross and Hereford. In 1811 also the company felt that they must have a resident engineer, and Jessop was replaced by Thomas Sheasby junior, who had helped his father build the Swansea Canal and between 1799 and 1802 had been its engineer.

The proposed outer harbour was dispensed with, but work went on upon the remainder and on 16 March 1813: 'The Water was let into the Canal & Basin this Day and the Rail ways being in a state of work the undertaking may therefore be considered as completed.'[165] On the following day 'Five decorated boats with passengers entered with the flood tide. . . . The bed of the lock is parallel with low water in the river; height of tide in the lock was 23 feet and in the canal and basin 13 feet, which is enough to admit brigs of 300 tons. The canal and basin are 2000 yards in length. The railway from the basin to Lydbrook on the river Wye is 11 miles long, and with collateral branches in the Forest of Dean forms nearly 30 miles of railway.'[166] By this time the competing harbour of Bullo Pill, fed by its own tramroad, was already at work. The cost of the canal and basin seems to have been some £20,000. To begin with, ships were charged a ship duty according to tonnage for entering the canal, plus a toll of 3d. per ton on cargoes loaded.

Though its works were complete the company owed £10,000, its tramplate suppliers were threatening to sue, and it needed some working capital. The passing of the North Wilts Canal Act in July 1813* was an encouragement, and in a year the money had been raised, though new shares had to be offered at a heavy discount. The following years were spent in efforts to build up trade across the Severn and up the Thames & Severn† to the North Wilts and the Thames, drawbacks on tolls for cargoes consigned to distant places being usually matched by similar rebates given by the other canal companies. In the same way, the company tried to build up a trade in coal to Bristol and beyond, to and below Old Forge on the Wye, to Ashleworth, Tewkesbury and upwards on the Severn, and up the Herefordshire & Gloucestershire Canal to Ledbury.

At a general meeting in 1820, 'having taken into consideration

* The date 1812 given in *The Canals of Southern England* is a misprint.

† See the tonnage figures of coal passing up the Thames & Severn Canal from various sources during the first months of 1817 given in my *The Canals of Southern England*, p. 175. Of 9,481 tons of coal arriving during that period at Brimscombe Port, 3,844½ tons were from Lydney.

the increasing trade of the Port of Lydney, and the additional accommodation required for vessels . . .' it was decided to build an outer harbour as had been intended by the Act of 1810, to take larger vessels 'than can now reach the Basin from the occasional scarcity of Water in the Canal, and thus encouraging an increase of Trade to Ireland, and other places to the Westward'.[167] The estimated cost was £4,349, to be found from profits. Work began, but the contractor having got into difficulties, Sheasby took it on himself. It was finished in April 1821, and the engineer collected a gratuity of fifty guineas from his grateful employers. The outer harbour could now take craft up to 400 tons: the bigger ships used it, while the smaller entered the canal itself.

In 1827, after a quarrel within the company, the Forest colliery interests led by Edward Protheroe were replaced in control of the company by a Bristol group, which gave more emphasis to coal shipments thence and westwards. At this time about £100,000 had been spent on the tramroads and canal. Trade slowly improved, as the following figures for lock dues paid at the entrance of the canal show:

Years	*Average receipts from lock dues*
	£
1831–35	2,114
1836–40	3,158
1841–45	3,321

Many of the old drawbacks were cancelled, and shipments increased.

In 1826 the Bullo Pill tramroad, which was in a bad way financially, was taken over by a new company, the Forest of Dean Railway company, under Edward Protheroe's leadership. In 1832 the Severn & Wye combined with the Forest of Dean company to defeat a proposal first made in 1826 for a third (locomotive) tramroad in the Forest, leading down to Purton pill, though in doing so they made some unwise promises of transport development.

In 1839 the Severn & Wye company considered itself to be in need of better shipping facilities, and agreed to Sheasby's proposal that a branch line should be made for 3½ miles from Lydney basin to Grange pill, where a basin could be built to take larger vessels. In the same year the Forest of Dean company proposed a railway through Blakeney to Brimspill. This scheme led to a brisk exchange of letters between the companies. The Severn & Wye considered it incompatible with Rennie's division of 1807. Protheroe replied in a friendly way that he thought the tramroad companies had not carried out the promises they had made at the time of the Purton Bill, that tramroads were out of date and expensive, and that 'to enter into successful competition with the Coal proprietors of Wales we must have the advantage of the most improved Railway communication'.[168] Joseph Cookson of the Severn & Wye replied that if improvements were needed, it was a pity that the coalowners had not supported the Grange pill harbour, whereupon Protheroe wrote witheringly of people who came twice a year from Bristol to spend a few hours in the Forest, and attacked the 'miserable and expensive means of conveyance afforded' the coal proprietors 'and the petty system of vexation wantonly adopted towards them by your chief officer and regulator'.[169] That was Sheasby.

The Forest of Dean company sold itself to the new South Wales Railway in 1845 (though the purchase was not completed till 1850), after the Protheroes had in 1842 promoted a Dean Forest & Gloucester Railway, the purpose being to preserve the Stroud valley market for Forest coal, which was otherwise likely to be lost when the Bristol & Gloucester Railway was completed. The Bill was, however, thrown out in 1843,[170] though a new Gloucester & Dean Forest Railway was authorized in 1846, and built a connexion between the G.W.R. at Gloucester and the South Wales Railway near Awre. The Forest of Dean was converted to broad-gauge railway by the South Wales company and opened in 1854, but the Severn & Wye persisted in its old-fashioned ways; thenceforward things went less well, though in 1847 Sheasby, who, one fancies, had become an old man of the sea, resigned amid flattering remarks.

As he looked back, he would know that the possibility of attracting trade which would use the route across the Forest to and from the Wye had come to very little. In 1821 it had been proposed by the Lydney Trading Company, which carried much of this traffic, to put on a 'Pleasure Tram drawn by one Horse' on the through route, which was also to carry goods. Again in 1842 it had been reported that the company had a craft, the *Lydney Trader*, which carried goods from Bristol for shipment via Lydney to Ross in competition with other carriers working not up the Wye, but by way of Gloucester. A year later the Severn & Wye company offered a bonus of 8d. a ton on all traffic from Lydney basin to Bishop's Wood* and back; after that no more references to through carriage are recorded.

An Act was passed in 1856 for the Forest of Dean Central Railway from Foxes Bridge by Blakeney to Brimspill, on the general line of the Forest of Dean Railway's proposal of 1839, which had been revived in this new form from 1849 onwards. The line was partly opened in 1868, but the harbour at Brimspill was never completed, and traffic passed on to the South Wales Railway at Awre.

In 1847 the Severn & Wye made an agreement with the South Wales Railway for interchange arrangements at Lydney which were completed in 1851, and must to some extent have affected shipments from there. The company now began to talk of building a broad-gauge steam line, and of improving the harbour, but nothing was done on the former and little on the latter, though an Act was obtained in 1853. This Act enabled the company to buy the wharves and tolls at Lydney from the Bathurst family for £650 p.a., and this was done in September.

Again in 1861 the company decided to seek an Act to enlarge the harbour entrance and to deepen the inner basin, along lines recommended by Thomas Howard of the Bristol Dock company. The Bill was withdrawn in 1862, and the enlargement of the entrance was never subsequently carried out. By the mid-sixties combination rails and tramplates were being used on the lines, and some steam locomotives. In 1869 the line from the Great Western at Lydney upwards to Wimberry Junction was paralleled by one in broad-gauge, and in 1871 the branch from the G.W.R. to the harbour was laid broad. They were soon converted to standard.

In 1865 occurs the first mention in the company's records of the Severn Bridge scheme which was to occupy so much of its attention. This plan to connect the Forest by a bridge over the Severn to Sharpness Docks at the end of the Gloucester & Berkeley Canal meant that the improvement of Lydney harbour was not as important as it had been, though traffic increased enough in the '70's for some new work to have been done by 1875. The Severn Bridge company was incorporated in 1872, and in 1879 it amalgamated with the Severn & Wye as the Severn & Wye & Severn Bridge Railway Company. The bridge was opened in 1879, but the financial strain added to the general depression of the Forest industries had been too great, and in 1894 the concern

* The Lydney Trading Company had its own wharf at Wyelands near Bishop's Wood.

was taken over jointly by the Midland and Great Western Railways.

Even after the opening of the Severn Bridge, however, the Port of Lydney handled considerable traffic: in the years 1897–8, for instance, an average of 2,494 vessels a year loaded an average of 301,000 tons. In the present century the trade has fallen away, though it is still appreciable. The coal tips at the upper end of the basin were dismantled in 1927, after which that part went slowly out of use, and shipments took place from the lower end only. By 1965 all railway lines serving the harbour had been lifted.[171]

Cinderford Canal

A small private canal about 1¼ miles long was built from the dam pool at Broad Moor to the Cinderford ironworks by 1795, when the works were blown in. It was about 15 feet wide, took small boats, and probably had the double purpose of conveying water from the dam to supply a waterwheel powering the blast apparatus at the works, and of carrying coke made on the spot from coal mined in the small Broad Moor pits then working.

The works did not stay open long. They re-opened in 1829, but by then the Bullo Pill tramroad had been built, partly on the canal bed, and the waterwheel had been superseded.[172]

Conclusion

INCLUDING the Wye to Hereford and the Lugg to Lugg Bridge, there were at their fullest extent about 273 miles of navigable waterways within the area covered by this book, out of a total of some 4,100 miles in Great Britain.* Our group therefore accounted for less than 7 per cent of the total. The tonnage carried, if one makes no attempt to eliminate the same goods transported over more than one waterway, probably amounted to about 2,460,000 tons in 1845.† Of this total, the waterways outside South Wales and Monmouthshire, the Wye, the Leominster Canal, and the Herefordshire & Gloucestershire Canal, probably only accounted for about 75,000 tons in that year, against about 1,000,000 tons for the Monmouthshire and Brecknock & Abergavenny Canals, 410,000 for the Glamorganshire, 300,000 tons for the Swansea, and 300,000 for the Neath and the Tennant. For our area as a whole, therefore, rather less than 7 per cent of the waterways carried rather over 8 per cent of the probable total traffic of Great Britain carried at that time by inland waterways. For South Wales and Monmouthshire alone, less than 5 per cent of the total mileage carried about 8 per cent of the traffic.

If we exclude the Wye and the Lugg, which were virtually natural navigations except for a few half-locks and a towing path over part of the course, and leave a margin for error in estimating the cost of the smaller Welsh canals, then the 200 miles of artificial waterway described in this book cost at opening about £1,150,000.‡ Of this sum, £341,500 is attributable to the Herefordshire &

* The reader may be interested to compare the figures given in this chapter with those in the corresponding chapter in my *The Canals of Southern England*.

† I have excluded the tonnage on the Lydney Canal, which is more in the nature of a harbour.

‡ This sum excludes the cost of Port Tennant and of the Lydney Canal, but includes that of the floating harbour of the Glamorganshire Canal at Cardiff. I have tried to exclude the cost of tramroads.

Gloucestershire and Leominster Canals, leaving some £808,500 as the estimated cost at opening of the canals of South Wales and Monmouthshire.

The industrialists who largely financed the South Wales and Monmouthshire Canals made a cheap investment in the future. In addition to the benefit cheap transport gave them as manufacturers or colliery-owners, they had the advantage of good dividends: in 1845 the statutory 8 per cent on the Glamorganshire,* 5 per cent on the Aberdare, 17 per cent on the Neath, 15 per cent on the Swansea, 9½ per cent on the Monmouthshire and 4⅔ per cent on the Brecknock & Abergavenny. On the other hand, the Kidwelly & Llanelly, the Herefordshire & Gloucestershire and the Leominster paid nothing.

The day of the Wye, the Herefordshire & Gloucestershire and the Leominster was virtually over by the '50's, but the economic strength of the waterways in the industrial areas enabled them to hold their own into the '70's. By 1900, however, though most of the Welsh mileage remained, it was little used. The following figures for that year may be compared with those in Chapter I.

Date	*Ship Canal*	*Broad Canal*	*Narrow Canal*	*Tub-boat or Small Canal*	*River*	*Total*
	miles	miles	miles	miles	miles	miles
1900	2	5⅞	116	—	11⅞	135¾

To-day, of all the undertakings described in this book, only the Lydney Canal still carries commercial traffic. Some of the Welsh canals, the Monmouthshire, Brecknock & Abergavenny, Neath, Tennant and Swansea, are partially or wholly used to supply water for industrial and other users: much of the Glamorganshire has been piped for the same purpose. The Aberdare has been converted to a road, and the Kidwelly & Llanelly to a railway, some of which has been closed in its turn: the smaller ones are derelict. Outside Wales, part of the Herefordshire & Gloucestershire and of the Leominster were used for railway construction; the rest has long been disused, while the Wye, which has seen so many changes, bears now with fishermen and tourists, but no longer with coal barges upwards from the Forest, or timber downstream.

Yet the waterways are still there, open to the eyes and the feet of those who wish to walk beside their liquid history. From Newport to Brecon or Crumlin, from Giant's Grave to Glynneath or

* 5 per cent on a small amount of the company's capital.

Swansea to Ystradgynlais, from Burry Port or Kidwelly to Cwm-mawr, the towpaths still lie open, and the observant eye can trace the wharves, the tracks of tramroads and their inclined planes, the limekilns and ruined works that were once the foundations on which the Industrial Revolution was built. They are dead now, and at Pontypool, Ebbw Vale, Trefforest, Nantgarw, Margam, Velindre, Trostre, Llandarcy and many places else, newer works, served by newer transport systems, carry on what the waterways began. Yet

> Men are we, and must grieve when even the shade
> Of that which once was great is passed away.

NOTES

Notes to Chapter I

1. For much material on the Welsh coasting trade between 1600 and 1750, see T. S. Willan, *The English Coasting Trade*, 1600–1750. 1938.
2. For road development see D. E. Fraser, 'The Development of the Road System in Glamorgan up to 1844', thesis, University of Wales. 1940.
3. Samuel Lewis's *A Topographical History of Wales*, 1840, art. *Merthyr Tydfil*, gives Homfray the credit for having suggested the Glamorganshire Canal.
4. *Glocester Journal*, 12 February 1794.
5. Ibid., 29 February 1796.
6. For the general development of tramroads see Charles E. Lee, *The Evolution of Railways*, 1943, though there is no support in South Wales tramroad history for his contention that the plateway was designed to take ordinary road vehicles.
7. Clifford Davies, 'The Evolution of Industries and Settlements between Merthyr Tydfil and Abergavenny from 1740 to 1840', thesis, University of Wales. 1949. Map No. 25.
8. For a contemporary description see W. Coxe, *An Historical Tour in Monmouthshire*, 1801, p. 202.
9. *Observations of Benjamin Outram on the Brecknock & Abergavenny Canal and Railways*, 1 July 1799. Maybery Papers, National Library of Wales, Bundle 14.
10. George Overton, *A Description of the Faults or Dykes of the Mineral Basin of South Wales*, Part 1, 1825.
11. Monmouthshire County Records, personal account book.
12. Figures from H. Scrivenor, *History of the Iron Trade*, 1854, the Monmouthshire Canal records, and in the case of the first quoted, Clifford Davies, 'The Evolution of Industries', op. cit.
13. C. F. Cliffe, *The Book of South Wales*, etc., 1847, p. ix.
14. T. W. Booker, *Treatise on the Mineral Basin of Glamorgan*, 1834.
15. *Report from the Committee on the Petition of Owners of Col ieries in South Wales*, 7 June 1810.
16. T. W. Booker, *Treatise*, op. cit.
17. T. W. Booker, *A Speech . . . at the Annual Meeting of the Royal British Association . . .*, 1848.
18. Hunt's *Directory of South Wales*, 1848.
19. B.T.C. Historical Records, M.N.R.C. 8/150. 2 February 1830.

Notes to Chapter II

1. Rev. D. Daven Jones, *A History of Kidwelly*, 1908, p. 102.
2. 6 Geo III *c*. 55.
3. Ap Huw (Peter Williams), *Hanes Dyffryn Gwendraeth, gan Hanesydd y Cynoesau*, Llanelly, 1873.
4. J. Hopkin Morgan, MS., 'History of Llanelly', Llanelly Public Library.

5. Nevill, Druce Documents, National Library of Wales, Deeds, etc. No. 709, 20 November 1752.
6. J. Hopkin Morgan, 'Llanelly', op. cit., and see Nevill, Druce Documents, National Library of Wales, Deeds, etc. Nos. 812–13, 21–2 October 1814.
7. *Report from the Committee on the Petition of Owners of Collieries in South Wales*, 7 June 1810. Ev. of Henry Smith.
8. Llanelly Public Library.
9. Nevill, Druce Documents, National Library of Wales, Deeds, etc. No. 26, 1 August 1769.
10. *Sketch of Bynea Farm as surveyed by Mr. John Thornton for the executors of the late Chauncey Townsend*, 1772. Mansell Lewis papers, Stradey Castle.
11. Ibid., No. 409, 6 November 1786.
12. J. Hopkin Morgan, 'Llanelly', op. cit.
13. *A Plan for the Continuation of Genl. Warde's Canal*, 1821, MS. Llanelly Public Library.
14. W. O. Harriss, MS. 'History of Loughor', Llanelly Public Library.
15. Llanelly Public Library.
16. Richard Cort, *A Letter to John Taylor* . . ., 1824, Llanelly Public Library.
17. J. Hopkin Morgan, 'Llanelly', op. cit., himself quoting an unidentified indirect source.
18. J. Hopkin Morgan, 'Llanelly', op. cit.
19. Nevill, Druce Documents, National Library of Wales, MS., Vol. 4, Letter 2 January 1805.
20. Ibid. Deeds, etc. No. 124, 15 August 1811.
21. Nevill, Druce Documents, National Library of Wales, MS., letter 8 March 1798.
22. *Trans. Carm. Antiq. Soc.* Vol. 50, p. 70, and *J.H.C.* Vol. 32, p. 693.
23. Letter from William Hopkin to Lady Stepney, 24 July 1793, Stepney Estate papers, Llanelly Public Library.
24. See Stepney Estate papers, Llanelly Public Library and *Hereford Journal*, 3 April, 1 May, 29 May, 28 August, 11 September, 27 November 1793, 1 January and 12 February 1794, and 24 October 1798.
25. A. Rees, *Cyclopaedia*, 1819, art. *Canal*, and *Hereford Journal*, 9 September 1801.
26. 42 Geo III *c.* 80.
27. *Hereford Journal*, 30 November 1803. Two miles were reported open in Barnes's Report of 28 July 1803 to the company. Llanelly Public Library.
28. S. Lewis, *A Topographical History of Wales*, 1840, art. *Carmarthenshire.*
29. B.T.C. Historical Records, Carmarthenshire Railway report, 31 January 1805, etc.
30. J. Hopkin Morgan, 'Llanelly', op. cit.
31. Walter Davies, *General View of the Agriculture . . . of South Wales*, 1814.
32. Diaries of L. W. Dillwyn, National Library of Wales, 4 November 1818.
33. Richard Cort, *A Letter to John Taylor*, op. cit., 1824, Llanelly Public Library.
34. It is so marked on a sketch map accompanying the prospectus of the Kidwelly & Llanelly Canal dated 5 October 1811. B.M. Maps 24 e. 16. The creek is called Pil-towyn on the 1830 Ordnance map.
35. See Ashburnham Documents, 338, 339, 340, and accounts of Pembrey colliery in Ashburnham collection, Vol. 10, National Library of Wales.
36. This is called Bowser's Canal on Green's map of the Kidwelly & Llanelly Canal, 1833, B.T.C. Hist. Recs., but on other maps the name of Bowser's is given to another coal level.

37. 52 Geo III *c.* 173.
38. In B.M. Maps 24 e. 16.
39. 58 Geo III *c.* 75.
40. *Carmarthen Journal*, June 1824.
41. It is not marked on Green's map of 1833, made to show the navigations in use, though it appears on the Ordnance Survey map of 1830.
42. S. Lewis, *History*, op. cit., art. *Pen-brey*.
43. British Records Association Document No. 45, National Library of Wales.
44. Ashburnham Document No. 935, National Library of Wales and plan attached.
45. *Hereford Journal*, 9 June 1824. The entry may refer to the Kidwelly & Llanelly Canal.
46. 6 Geo IV *c.* 115.
47. Nevill, Druce Documents, National Library of Wales, Vol. 6, letter 10 November 1824.
48. Nevill, Druce Documents, National Library of Wales, Vol. 6, letter 16 February 1825.
49. Ibid. Letter 19 February 1825.
50. Ibid. Letters 5 March, 12 March 1825.
51. *Trans. Carm. Antiq. Soc.* Vol. 50, p. 49.
52. See Nevill, Druce correspondence quoted above.
53. Llanelly Custom House Records, letter from Robert Bowser, 7 May 1832. It had been partially opened at the beginning of June 1831. See *Cambrian*, 4 June 1831.
54. For James Green in the Westcountry see my article, 'James Green as Canal Engineer', in the *Journal of Transport History*, May 1953.
55. B.T.C. Historical Records.
56. *Cambrian*, 8 August 1835.
57. Ibid., 8 July 1837.
58. Printed Report, B.T.C. Hist. Recs.
59. I have worked out the rises of the three inclines from the deposited plan of 1865. In Green's Report they are given as 52 ft. 6 in., 53 ft. 6 in., and 85 ft.
60. Evidence of G. F. P. Sutton on the Carmarthenshire Railway Bill of 1864.
61. Op. cit.
62. Carmarthenshire Railway Bill, 1864. Ev. of J. P. Luckraft and D. Watney.
63. Kidwelly & Burry Port Railway Bill of 1864, ev. of G. F. P. Sutton.
64. *Cambrian*, 6 February 1836.
65. Carmarthenshire Railway Bill, 1864, ev. of G. F. P. Sutton.
66. Ibid.
67. Ibid.
68. Information from Mr R. S. Craig, who has made a special study of shipping and related developments in this area.
69. For similar craft in Scotland, see *British Canals*, 2nd. ed., pp. 112, 167; for a plan by Outram on similar lines for the Somersetshire Coal Canal, see *The Canals of Southern England*, p. 154.
70. 28 and 29 Vic. *c.* 218.
71. *Hereford Journal*, 7 August 1805.
72. 53 Geo III *c.* 183.
73. S. Lewis, *History*, op. cit., art. *Llanelly*.
74. *British Almanac*, 1835, p. 248.
75. *Report to the Trustees of the Kidwelly Trust*, 9 January 1829, House of Lords Record Office.

76. S. Lewis, *History*, op. cit.
77. See the deposited plan of the Pen-clawdd Canal, Glamorgan County Records where it is marked.
78. Ibid.
79. 51 Geo III *c.* 106.
80. Letter, 1858, from Townsend Kirkwood, Custom House, Llanelly.
81. Diaries of L. W. Dillwyn, National Library of Wales, 5 February 1825.
82. *Cambrian*, 22 February 1840.
83. This account is largely derived from Mr F. V. Emery's article, 'The Penclawdd Canal', in *Gower*, 1952, and from information given by him. In the map on p. 41 the canal should be shown running north of Gowerton.
84. From Charles Hassall, *General View of the Agriculture of Pembroke*, 1794, p. 59, and information given by Mr R. E. Bowen.

Notes to Chapter III

1. D. G. John, 'An Economic and Historical Survey of the Development of the Anthracite Industry, with special reference to the Swansea valley', thesis, University of Wales, 1923.
2. Permission to build it was given by the Duke of Beaufort in 1783, and it was partly built in 1784. Duke of Beaufort *v.* Smith, Court of Chancery Case, 1842, in Corporation of Swansea MSS., quo. J. M. Davies, 'The Growth of Settlement in the Swansea valley', thesis, University of Wales, 1942.
3. W. H. Jones, *History of the Port of Swansea*, 1922, p. 119.
4. *Report from the Committee on the Petition of Owners of Collieries in South Wales*, No. 344, 1810. Evidence of H. Smithers.
5. Swansea Vale Railway Letter-book, 2 May 1845, B.T.C. Hist. Recs.
6. J. M. Davies, 'Swansea Valley', op. cit.
7. B.T.C. Western Region Deeds and Records.
8. Ibid.
9. Ibid.
10. *Railway Magazine*, April 1939, pp. 292–3.
11. *Case of the Duke of Beaufort and the other Noblemen and Gentlemen on the proposed Swansea Canal.* Swansea Public Library. Morris's Canal is shown on an accompanying plan.
12. *Swansea Canal Case.* Swansea Public Library.
13. Ibid.
14. Glamorgan County Records, Dep. Plan No. 4.
15. I have been helped by the account of the Swansea Canal by Harold Pollins in the May 1954 issue of the *Journal of Transport History.*
16. For the economic background see J. M. Davies, 'Swansea Valley', op. cit.
17. *Swansea Canal Case*, loc. cit.
18. Ibid.
19. W. H. Jones, *Swansea.* I think the date of 1780 given on p. 106 is a misprint for 1790.
20. *Hereford Journal*, 17 April 1793.
21. *Swansea Canal Case*, loc. cit.

22. Ibid.
23. W. H. Jones, *Swansea*, op. cit., p. 106.
24. *Swansea Canal Case*, loc. cit.
25. *Case of the Duke of Beaufort . . .*, op. cit.
26. S. Lewis, *A Topographical History of Wales*, 1840, art. *Glamorganshire.*
27. 34 Geo III, *c.* 109.
28. J. M. Davies, 'Swansea Valley', op. cit.
29. A. Rees, *Cyclopaedia*, 1819, art. *Canal.*
30. Swansea Canal Proprietors' Minute Book, 2 July 1799.
31. *Hereford Journal*, 4 September 1799.
32. Thomas Martyn, *An Account of a tour of Wales made in* 1801 . . . MS. National Library of Wales 1340 C.
33. *Hereford Journal*, 27 February 1805.
34. W. H. Jones, *Swansea*, op. cit., p. 120.
35. *Cambrian*, 25 February 1804.
36. See my *The Canals of Southern England*, 1955, p. 86.
37. *Cambrian*, 1 September 1804.
38. Swansea Canal Proprietors' Minute Book, 3 July 1804.
39. Prospectus of Kidwelly & Llanelly Canal, 5 October 1811.
40. I am indebted for this information to the maps accompanying J. M. Davies's thesis on 'The Growth of Settlement in the Swansea Valley', and to the 25-in. Ordnance plans.
41. *Cambrian*, 22 February 1840.
42. Swansea Vale Railway Committee Minute Book, 1 September, 3 November 1845.
43. Swansea Canal Proprietors' Minute Book, 10 October 1846.
44. J. M. Davies, 'Swansea Valley', op. cit.
45. Ibid.
46. There is a plan in the *Cambrian*, 8 May 1830.
47. Neath & Brecon Railway Minute Book, 3 May 1864.
48. Ibid., 26 October 1864.
49. See B.T.C. Historical Records, M.P.S. 2/61.
50. J. M. Davies, 'Swansea Valley', op. cit.
51. 35 and 36 Vic. *c.* 152.
52. J. M. Davies, 'Swansea Valley', op. cit.
53. Swansea Canal Committee Minute Book, 2 April 1805.
54. Diaries of L. W. Dillwyn, National Library of Wales, 10 December 1822.
55. Samuel Lewis, *Dictionary*, op. cit., art. 'Devynock'.
56. Dillwyn, Diaries, op. cit.
57. T. Jones and Sir J. R. Bailey, *A History of the County of Brecknockshire*, 1909–30. IV 92, and see Swansea Canal Proprietors' Minute Book, 5 July 1825.
58. *Hereford Journal*, 28 May 1828.
59. See some sale particulars in Neath & Brecon Railway papers, B.T.C. Historical Records.
60. John Lloyd, *The Great Forest of Brecknock*, 1905, p. 111.
61. John Brunton's Book, 1939.
62. *Hereford Journal*, 11 September 1833.
63. W. H. Jones, *Swansea*, op. cit., p. 283.

Notes to Chapter IV

1. D. J. Davies, *The Economic History of Wales prior to* 1800, referring to thesis by D. G. John, 'Contributions to the Economic History of South Wales'. University of Wales, 1930.
2. D. R. Phillips, *The History of the Vale of Neath*, 1925, p. 327, also Penlle'r-gaer Documents, National Library of Wales, Section B, Parcel 7, No. 58.
3. Phillips, *Vale of Neath*, loc. cit.
4. S. Evans, 'An Examination of Sir Humphrey Mackworth's Industrial Activities', thesis, University of Wales, 1950, quoting William Waller, *An Essay on the Mines of the late Sir Carbery Price*, 1698, and *First*, *Second*, and *Third Abstracts* (Mine Adventurers), 1700.
5. Ibid., quoting frontispiece to *A View of the Advantages arising to the Copartners, or Company of the Mineral Manufacturers of Neath*, 1720.
6. Called Lady Mackworth's Canal. Glen A. Taylor in *Trans. Neath Antiq. Soc.*, 2nd Series, Vol. 2, p. 9, quoting the Diary of Herbert Evans of Eaglesbush.
7. D. R. Phillips, *Vale of Neath*, op. cit., p. 327.
8. Glen A. Taylor, *Trans. Neath Antiq. Soc.*, op. cit., p. 88, quoting Herbert Evans.
9. Neath Canal Minute Book, 7 December 1797.
10. *British Chronicle & Hereford Journal*, 28 July 1790.
11. Penlle'r-gaer Documents, National Library of Wales, Section B, Parcel 7, No. 59, letter 10 February 1791.
12. *British Chronicle* (Hereford), 13 October 1790.
13. Penlle'r-gaer Documents, No. 59, loc. cit.
14. *Report from the Committee on the Petition of Owners of Collieries in South Wales*, 7 June 1810. Ev. of Dr. R. Griffiths and Richard Bevan.
15. 31 Geo III *c.* 85.
16. Inf. from Neath Public Library.
17. Penlle'r-gaer Documents No. 59, loc. cit.
18. Neath Canal Proprietors' Minute Book, 11 August 1791.
19. Ibid., 1 October 1795.
20. 38 Geo III *c.* 30.
21. Glen A. Taylor, *Trans. Neath Antiq. Soc.*, op. cit., p. 9.
22. Neath Canal Letter Book, 1804–16, Memorial to Customs, 1813.
23. *Glocester Journal*, 3, 17 September 1792.
24. *Plan of a Canal and Railway for forming a junction between the Glamorganshire and Neath Canals* . . . by John Dadford, 1792. Glamorgan County Records.
25. Neath Canal Proprietors' Minute Book, 4 July 1799.
26. *Plan of the intended Aberdare Iron Co's Canal, Tram, or Rail Road to the Glamorganshire and Neath Canals*, 1800. Glamorgan County Records.
27. Neath Canal Letter Book, 17 May 1805.
28. Ibid., 21 January 1805.
29. Ibid., 9 September 1806.
30. Ibid., 15 September 1806.
31. Neath Canal Records, Agreement of 1 October 1807.
32. *Cambrian*, 2 May 1807.
33. See letter of James Tappenden with particulars of the tramroad and the financial position in John Lloyd, *The Early History of the Old South Wales Iron Works*, 1760–1840, 1906, pp. 120–1.
34. Neath Canal Letter Book, 20 May 1807.
35. L. S. Pressnell, *Country Banking in the Industrial Revolution*, 1956, p. 308.

36. Neath Canal Letter Book, 20 May 1807.
37. Ibid., 10 January 1809.
38. Ibid., 12 November 1809.
39. Ibid., 14 December 1809.
40. Ibid., 22 January 1810.
41. Ibid., 16 October 1810.
42. D. R. Phillips, *Vale of Neath*, op. cit., pp. 329 *et seq.*
43. Ibid.
44. Neath Canal Letter Book, 24 December 1805.
45. Letter from George Tennant to Sir William Garrow, 28 September 1822.
46. Prospectus of the Kidwelly & Llanelly Canal, 5 October 1811.
47. C. F. Cliffe, *The Book of South Wales*, 1847, p. 129.
48. Letter in Swansea Public Library (466) 19 December 1836.
49. Neath Canal Proprietors' Minute Book, 7 August 1845.
50. *South Wales News*, 31 March 1924.
51. Vale of Neath Railway Directors' Minute Book, 8 November 1845.
52. Ibid., 3 December 1845.
53. Neath Canal Proprietors' Minute Book, 28 July 1853.
54. Neath Canal Letter Book, 5 May 1875.
55. Neath Canal Committee Minute Book, 10 July 1873.
56. Ibid., 19 January 1816.
57. Glen A. Taylor, *Trans. Neath Antiq. Soc.*, op. cit., p. 9, and original MS. in Neath Antiquarian Society's collection.
58. Neath Canal Committee Minute Book, 11 January 1866.

Notes to Chapter V

1. In the library of the Royal Institution of South Wales: quoted by D. R. Phillips in his *History of the Vale of Neath*, 1925, pp. 327 *et seq.*
2. Rev. J. Oldisworth, *Swansea Guide*, 1802.
3. *British Chronicle* (Hereford), 26 May 1790.
4. Oldsworth, *Guide*, op. cit.
5. D. R. Phillips, *Vale of Neath*, loc. cit.
6. George Tennant, *Neath and Swansea Red Jacket & Neath Canals. Narrative of some Particulars relating to their formation, etc.*, 1824.
7. George Kirkhouse, grandfather of William, had come from Gateshead with Chauncey Townsend to prospect for him in the Llansamlet, Swansea and Neath areas. For the Kirkhouse family see E. Phillips, *A History of the Pioneers of the Welsh Coalfield*, 1925, ch. xxiv, 'The Kirkhouse Family of Mining Engineers'.
8. Neath Canal Committee Minute Book, 21 October 1819 and Proprietors' Minute Book, 6 July 1820.
9. *Report from the Committee on the Petition of Owners of Collieries in South Wales*, 1810. Ev. of Richard Bevan.
10. George Tennant, op. cit.
11. Neath Antiquarian Society's collection.
12. George Tennant, op. cit.
13. From George Tennant's notebook, Tennant Estate papers.
14. Neath Canal Proprietors' Minute Book, 24 October 1822.

15. Diaries of L. W. Dillwyn, National Library of Wales, 20 December 1822.
16. Tennant Estate papers.
17. Tennant Estate papers, letter to Law Life Assurance Society.
18. George Tennant, op. cit.
19. J. M. Davies, 'The Growth of Settlement in the Swansea Valley', thesis, University of Wales, 1942.
20. Tennant Estate papers.
21. Capt. Martin White, *A Chart of Swansea Harbour and Port Tennant*, 1826. Tennant Estate papers.
22. James Abernethy: *Plan of Proposed Port Tennant Docks*. Tennant Estate papers.
23. Map of G.W.R. Swansea Harbour & Docks, 1931.
24. George Tennant, op. cit.
25. Dillwyn, op. cit., 29 April 1826.
26. Ibid., 24 May 1826.
27. 7 Geo IV *c.* 102.
28. Tredegar collection, National Library of Wales, 2nd Group, Box 84, Nos. 219–20.
29. S. 19 of 25 and 26 Vict. *c.* 193, for which S. 19 of 26 and 27 Vict. *c.* 130 was substituted.
30. Neath Canal Proprietors' Minute Book, 1 July 1824.
31. Tennant Estate papers, letter 4 April 1830.
32. *Cambrian*, 25 September 1830; 5 March 1831.
33. Vale of Neath Railway Directors' Minute Book, 4 March, 11 August 1846, 30 April, 7 October 1847.
34. Ibid., 16 January, 25 November 1851.
35. William Kirkhouse's Letter Book, Swansea Public Library, No. 466.
36. H. R. de Salis, *Bradshaw's Canals and Navigable Rivers of England and Wales*, 1918.

Notes to Chapter VI

1. Generally see J. Lloyd, *The Early History of the Old South Wales Iron Works*, 1760–1840, 1906; C. Wilkins, *The History of the Iron, Steel, Tinplate and other Trades of Wales*, 1903; and John P. Addis, *The Crawshay Dynasty*, 1957.
2. E. L. Chappell, *Historic Melingriffith*, 1940.
3. Charles Wilkins, *The History of Merthyr Tydfil*, 1908, p. 68.
4. See lease of 14 October 1777 from Ann Richard to A. Bacon of 'the Land under the Canal', listed in J. Lloyd, *South Wales Iron Works*, op. cit., p. 49.
5. C. Wilkins, *The South Wales Coal Trade*, 1888, pp. 67–8.
6. Charles Dupin, *Force Commerciale de la Grande-Bretagne*, 1826, Vol. II, p. 250.
7. The 1767 road is not certain. See D. E. Fraser, 'The Development of the Road System in Glamorgan up to 1844 . . .', thesis, University of Wales, 1940.
8. See Enid Walker, 'The Development of Communications in Glamorgan . . . between 1760 and 1840', thesis, University of Wales, 1947.
9. W. H. Smyth, *Nautical Observations on the Port . . . of Cardiff*, 1840.
10. *British Chronicle* (Hereford), 5 May 1790.
11. 30 Geo III *c.* 82. It does not appear that the Bill was introduced before 1790, in spite of the statement in E. L. Chappell, *History of the Port of Cardiff*, that it was first introduced in 1784.
12. Guest papers, Address of W. Taitt to landowners, 28 January 1799. Glamorgan County Records.

13. E. L. Chappell, *Melingriffith*, op. cit., pp. 33–4.
14. Charles Wilkins, *Coal Trade*, op. cit., p. 180.
15. The above from Guest papers, loc. cit.
16. J. G. Wood, *The Principal Rivers of Wales*, 1813, p. 55.
17. Guest papers, loc. cit., Letter Book, 1782–94, letter 14 March 1791 to Samuel Homfray.
18. Ibid., letters 7, 23, 28 March and 7 May 1792.
19. Glamorganshire Canal Minute Book, 5 June 1793.
20. Ibid., 1 June 1791.
21. Enid Walker, 'Communications in Glamorgan', op. cit.
22. Clifford Davies, 'The Evolution of Industries and Settlements between Merthyr Tydfil and Abergavenny from 1740 to 1840', thesis, University of Wales, 1949, quoting Cyfarthfa Ledgers No. 1, 1790–98, p. 17, Cyfarthfa Castle Museum, Merthyr Tydfil.
23. J. Phillips, *A General History of Inland Navigation*, 4th ed., 1803, p. 585.
24. D. E. Fraser, 'Road System', op. cit.
25. 36 Geo III *c*. 69.
26. See Glamorganshire Canal Minute Book, 14 January 1796.
27. Ibid., 13 December 1794.
28. Thomas Martyn, *An Account of a tour of Wales made in* 1801 . . ., MS., National Library of Wales, 1340 C.
29. Glamorgan County Records.
30. Letter of R. Hill to J. Powell, 13 February 1794, Cardiff Public Library.
31. *Case*, Bute MSS., Cardiff Public Library.
32. Glamorganshire Canal Minute Book, 17 February 1798.
33. *Glocester Journal*, 24 September 1798.
34. Ibid., 1 October 1799.
35. Monmouthshire Canal Committee Minute Book, 21 December 1798.
36. *Glocester Journal*, 21 January 1799.
37. Glamorganshire Canal Minute Book, 27 March 1799.
38. S. Lewis, *A Topographical History of Wales*, 1840, art. 'Glamorganshire'.
39. For the history of the Penydarren tramroad see S. Mercer, 'Trevithick and the Merthyr Tramroad', *Trans. Newcomen Soc.*, 1948, Vol. XVIII, and the *Railway Magazine*, March 1951, where there is a map.
40. E. L. Chappell, *Melingriffith*, op. cit., p. 57. For a survey of the water supply of the canal, see Bute Collection, National Library of Wales, Box 141, Parcel 6, Report dated 26 March 1842 by William Blackadder on the water-power of the Taff.
41. Cyfarthfa Papers, National Library of Wales, Letter Book 1, Letters 34, 68.
42. See Glamorganshire Canal Minute Book, and *Case*, Bute MSS., loc. cit.
43. Glamorganshire Canal Minute Book, 20 September 1821.
44. Ibid., 7 March 1822.
45. Ibid., 3 June 1818.
46. Ibid., 10 May 1821.
47. Ibid., 7 February 1822.
48. *Case and Opinion*, 26 January 1822, Bute Collection, loc. cit., Box 31, Bundle A
49. Cyfarthfa Papers, loc. cit., Box 1, Letter 209(b), 5 March 1825.
50. Ibid., Letter 209(a), 3 March 1825.
51. B.T.C. Historical Records, *A Plan and Section of an Intended Railway or Tram Road from or near the Navigation House . . . to . . . Cardiff with a Basin and Canal from thence to near the Mouth of Ely River . . .*, 1823.

52. Cyfarthfa Papers, loc. cit., Box 1, Letter 252, 13 January 1824.
53. Guest Papers, loc. cit., D/DG Section G, Box 1.
54. Glamorganshire Canal Minute Book, 11 February 1824.
55. Ibid., 2 June 1824.
56. Bute MSS., loc. cit., printed judgement of 17 December 1824.
57. Bute Collection, loc. cit., Box 104.
58. Glamorganshire Canal Minute Book, 8 November 1827.
59. Bute Collection, loc. cit., Letter Book 1847–48, Box 70, letter 18 September 1847 to William Crawshay.
60. Ibid., Letter Book 13, Box 70, letter 15 August 1839 to William Cubitt.
61. Bute MSS. (MS. copy).
62. *Cambrian*, 22 January 1831.
63. Charles Wilkins, *Coal Trade*, op. cit., p. 74.
64. Cyfarthfa Papers, loc. cit., Letter Book 3, Letter 216.
65. Ibid., Box 2, letter 642, 5 August 1832.
66. Ibid., Letter Book 3, Letter 342, 19 December 1833.
67. Ibid., Letter 354, 14 March 1834.
68. W. H. Smyth, *Port of Cardiff*, op. cit., pp. 8 ff.
69. Cyfarthfa Papers, loc. cit., Box 2, Letter 642, 5 August 1832.
70. Ibid., Letter 817, 20 March 1834.
71. Ibid., Letter 838, 20 July 1834.
72. Ibid., Letter Book 3, Letter 376, 16 July 1834.
73. *Hereford Times*, 26 October 1833.
74. L. T. C. Rolt, *Isambard Kingdom Brunel*, 1957, p. 81.
75. See *Railway Magazine*, June 1941, 'Some Early Welsh-Built Engines'.
76. *Hereford Times*, 4 August 1832.
77. *Cambrian*, 30 June 1832.
78. See also Lieutenant Dornford's statement of the expenses of loading in the canal, 8 November 1844. Bute MSS., loc. cit.
79. Taff Vale Railway Proprietors' Minute Book, 12 October 1835.
80. Diaries of L. W. Dillwyn, National Library of Wales, entries of 1, 3, 7 March, 9 and 16 May 1836.
81. Bute Collection, loc. cit., Box 70, Letter Book 13, 15 March 1836 to W. Cubitt.
82. 6 Will. IV, *c.* 82.
83. Taff Vale Railway Co. 1st printed Report, 16 September 1836.
84. 1 Vic. *c.* 70.
85. Taff Vale Railway Co. 1st printed Report, 16 September 1836.
86. Bute Collection, loc. cit., Box 70, Letter Book 13, 28 April 1838 to Captain Smyth.
87. Ibid., 13 August 1841 to Robert Stephenson.
88. Ibid., 14 August 1841.
89. Ibid., 26 August 1841.
90. Ibid., 19 December 1843.
91. Taff Vale Railway Committee Minute Book, 16 August 1844.
92. Ibid.
93. Bute Collection, loc. cit., Box 70, Letter Book 13, 8 July 1845.
94. Ibid., 20 November 1844.
95. Quoted Enid Walker, *Communications in Glamorgan*, op. cit.
96. Glamorganshire Canal, MS. Reports, Cardiff Public Library.
97. Glamorganshire Canal Minute Book, 6 June 1850.
98. Cyfarthfa Papers, loc. cit., Box 6, letter 28 May 1864.

99. See *South Wales Daily News*, 8 February 1888.
100. Taff Vale Railway Report, 31 January 1884.
101. Glamorganshire Canal Minute Book, 12 August 1885.
102. E. L. Chappell, *Port of Cardiff*, op. cit.
103. Bute MSS., MS. Report, loc. cit.
104. Railway & Canal Traffic Act: Returns made to the Board of Trade, 1888 and 1898.
105. C. S. Howells, *Transport Facilities in the Mining and Industrial Districts of South Wales and Monmouthshire*, 1911.
106. Ibid.
107. H. R. de Salis, *Bradshaw's Canals and Navigable Rivers of England and Wales*, 1904.
108. For this canal, in addition to de Salis and the minutes of the Glamorganshire Canal, see 'Morien', *History of Pontypridd and Rhondda Valleys*, 1903, and John Charles, *Pontypridd Historical Handbook*, 1920.
109. J. Lloyd, *South Wales Iron Works*, op. cit., p. 114.
110. Guest Papers, loc. cit., Letter Book, 1782–94.
111. *Plan of a Canal and Railway for forming a junction between the Glamorganshire and Neath Canals* . . ., John Dadford, 1792. Glamorgan County Records.
112. 33 Geo III *c*. 95.
113. D. E. Fraser, 'The Development of the Road System in Glamorgan up to 1844', thesis, University of Wales, 1940.
114. Aberdare Canal Minute Book, 20 June 1793.
115. D. E. Fraser, 'Road System', op. cit., and Enid Walker, 'Communications in Glamorgan', op. cit.
116. J. Lloyd, *South Wales Iron Works*, op. cit., pp. 125–6.
117. *Glocester Journal*, 29 September 1800.
118. Glamorganshire Canal Minute Book, 18 July 1801.
119. *Glocester Journal*, 22 March 1802.
120. Aberdare Canal Minute Book, 25 March 1823.
121. Ibid., 9 August 1826.
122. Ibid., 19 June 1827.
123. Ibid., 29 January 1840.
124. D. S. Barrie, *The Taff Vale Railway*, 1950, p. 14.
125. Vale of Neath Railway Directors' Minute Book, 16 October 1850, 9 May 1851.
126. Ibid., 11 November 1851.
127. E. T. MacDermot, *History of the Great Western Railway*, 1931, Vol. II, p. 11.
128. Vale of Neath Railway Directors' Minute Book, 9 January 1854.
129. Ibid., 23 October 1854.
130. Aberdare Canal Minute Book, 9 August 1849.
131. Ibid., 15 September 1875.
132. C. S. Howells, *Transport Facilities*, op. cit.

Notes to Chapter VII

1. C. S. Howells, *Transport Facilities in the Mining and Industrial Districts of South Wales and Monmouthshire*, 1911.
2. *British Chronicle* (Hereford), 21 December 1791.

3. Ibid., 29 February 1792. See also Tredegar Collection, National Library of Wales, 2nd Group, Box 53, No. 65, *Case of the proprietors, landowners, etc., for the Monmouthshire Canal.*
4. J. M. Scott, *The Ancient and Modern History of Newport*, 1847, p. 62.
5. 32 Geo III *c.* 102.
6. Preamble to the Act of 1792.
7. Monmouthshire Canal Committee Minute Book, 2 August 1796.
8. H. R. de Salis, *Bradshaw's Canals and Navigable Rivers of England and Wales*, 1918.
9. C. J. Evans & John Britton, *A Topographical & Historical Description of the County of Monmouth*, 1809.
10. Monmouthshire Canal Committee Minute Book, 10 July 1792.
11. Charles Wilkins, *The South Wales Coal Trade*, 1888, p. 162.
12. Monmouthshire Canal Proprietors' Minute Book, 20 October 1794.
13. Ibid., 2 May 1804. J. Phillips, *A General History of Inland Navigation*, 4th ed., 1803, p. 586, says 2 March.
14. See *A Plan of the Intended Extension of the Monmouthshire Canal below the Town of Newport*, by Thomas Dadford, 1796 (Monmouthshire County Records), which shows it running down past Jack's Pill to curve round by the river bank and end at Pillgwenlly.
15. 37 Geo III *c.* 100.
16. See Monmouthshire Canal Proprietors' Minute Book, 15 May 1797, and letter from Sir Charles Morgan in explanation, 1 June 1797, in B.T.C. Historical Records, M.N.R.C. 8/2.
17. Preamble to Act of 1797.
18. See *Plan of the Monmouthshire Canal in the Town of Newport*, 1804, B.T.C., Western Region Deeds and Records.
19. Monmouthshire Canal Proprietors' Minute Book, ND, April 1799.
20. Walter Davies, *General View of the Agriculture and Domestic Economy of South Wales*, Vol. II, 1814.
21. Monmouthshire Canal Committee Minute Book, 18 March 1802.
22. Ibid. Proprietors' Minute Book, 16 October 1797.
23. Ibid. Committee Minute Book, 7 February 1798.
24. Ibid. Proprietors' Minute Book, 2 May 1821.
25. I have not seen a copy of the original report. There is an extract, which I have used, in the B.T.C. Historical Records, Gen. 3/37.
26. W. Coxe, *An Historical Tour of Monmouthshire*, 1801, p. 202.
27. 27 Geo III *c.* 13.
28. See *Report from the Committee on the Petition of Owners of Collieries in South Wales*, 7 June 1810. Ev. of Dr R. Griffiths, T. Protheroe, P. Reece.
29. See above, and letter of 1 June 1797 from Sir Charles Morgan, B.T.C. Historical Records, M.N.R.C. 8/2.
30. *Report from the Committee*, etc., op. cit., 1810, Appendix 3.
31. Monmouthshire Canal, half-yearly report, May 1817.
32. J. W. Dawson, *Commerce and Customs. A History of the Ports of Newport and Caerleon*, 1932, p. 51.
33. 42 Geo III *c.* 115.
34. J. Lloyd, *The Early History of the Old South Wales Iron Works*, 1760–1840, 1906, p. 140.
35. Ibid, p. 142.
36. Monmouthshire Canal Committee Minute Book, 19 March 1800.

37. Extracts from Monmouthshire Canal Minute Book, 19 December 1800, Monmouthshire County Records.
38. Monmouthshire Canal Proprietors' Minute Book, 1 November 1809.
39. 42 Geo III *c.* 115.
40. *A Plan of an intended Rail Way, or Tram Road, from Sirhowy Furnaces . . . by Tredegar Iron Works . . . to communicate with the Monmouthshire Canal and the River Usk at or near the Town of Newport.* David Davies, Surveyor, from a line marked out by John Hodgkinson, Engineer. Newport Public Library.
41. That this date is not later is confirmed by George Overton in *A Description of the Faults or Dykes of the Mineral Basin of South Wales*, Part I, 1825. who says: 'This road has been in use for more than twenty years.'
42. D. S. Barrie and Charles E. Lee, *The Sirhowy Valley and its Railways*, 1940, p. 9.
43. The agreement is in the Monmouthshire County Records. See also Monmouthshire Canal Proprietors' Minute Book, 7 November 1810 and 5 November 1817.
44. W. L. Meredith, *A Century of Railway Development in South Wales and Monmouthshire*, Permanent Way Institution, 1913.
45. Barrie & Lee, *Sirhowy Valley*, p. 9, op. cit.
46. Monmouthshire Canal Letters, B.T.C. Historical Records, M.N.R.C. 8/103 and Monmouthshire Canal Committee Minute Book, 6 June 1823.
47. *Plan of the Extension of the Monmouthshire Canal below the Town of Newport*, 27 September 1805, by John Hodgkinson. Monmouthshire County Records.
48. Monmouthshire Canal Committee Minute Book, 2 June 1807.
49. James Matthews, *Historic Newport*, 1910, p. 165.
50. Monmouthshire Canal Proprietors' Minute Book, 24 December 1816.
51. Monmouthshire Canal Committee Minute Book, 17 February 1826.
52. See original agreement, 15 January 1793, Monmouthshire County Records.
53. Information given by Mr P. G. Rattenbury.
54. Ibid. Proprietors' Minute Book, 24 April 1817.
55. John Lloyd, *South Wales Iron Works*, op. cit., p. 181.
56. Brecknock & Abergavenny Canal Committee Minute Book, 26 June 1817.
57. Monmouthshire Canal Committee Minute Book, 5 November 1817.
58. Ibid., 16 January 1818.
59. *Cambrian*, 19 February 1831.
60. Ibid., 6 February 1830.
61. *Plan of the Monmouthshire Canal Company's part of Sirhowy Tram Road with the intended branch from Risca to Crumlin . . . Produced to the committee*, 18 *Dec.* 1823. B.T.C. Western Region Deeds and Records.
62. See letters 1824–7 complaining of water shortage from the *Ebbw Vale Letter-book*, quo. Clifford Davies, 'The Evolution of industries and settlements between Merthyr Tydfil and Abergavenny from 1740 to 1840', thesis, University of Wales, 1949.
63. T. Jones, *A History of the County of Brecknock*, Glanusk ed., 1909, Vol. II.
64. Monmouthshire Canal Proprietors' Minute Book, 5 May 1830.
65. Ibid., Committee Minute Book, 16 September 1829.
66. For locomotives generally on these lines see Barrie & Lee, *Sirhowy Valley*, op. cit., p. 18 *et seq.*, and *Railway Magazine*, June 1941, 'Some Early Welsh-Built Engines'.
67. Monmouthshire Canal Committee Minute Book, 26–28 July 1831.
68. This summary is made from a *Plan of the Canals and Railroads communicating with the Town of Newport*, by T. Morris, 1839. B.T.C. Historical Records, M.P.S. 3/35.

69. D. S. Barrie, *The Brecon & Merthyr Railway*, 1957, gives information.
70. Taken from a *Plan of the Monmouthshire Canal Company's Tram Roads and Canal*, 1835. B.R.B. Western Region Deeds and Records.
71. Monmouthshire Canal Proprietors' Minute Book, 4 March 1830.
72. E. M. E. Davies, 'The Port Development & Commerce of Newport, Mon.', thesis, University of Wales, 1938.
73. *The Port of Newport*, 11 January 1833. B.T.C. Historical Records.
74. E. M. E. Davies, 'Newport', op. cit.
75. *Hereford Journal*, 3 November 1830.
76. *Hereford Times*, 16 November 1833.
77. Monmouthshire Canal Proprietors' Minute Book, 6 May 1840.
78. Prospectus in Newport Public Library.
79. *Hereford Journal*, 18 January 1843.
80. B.T.C. Historical Records, M.N.R.C. 8/167. Dated 28 November 1842.
81. Monmouthshire Canal Committee Minute Book, 2 May 1843.
82. Prospectus of 1844 in Newport Public Library.
83. For particulars of these diversions of traffic, see *New Monmouthshire Railway*, 1844 (a paper for the Board of Trade) in Railway Pamphlets IV, Newport Public Library.
84. Ibid.
85. Newport Public Library.
86. Monmouthshire Railway Co.'s Report, 23 December 1846. Newport Public Library.
87. 8 & 9 Vic. *c.* 169.
88. James Brown, *The Present State and Future Prospects of the Monmouthshire Canal Company considered* . . ., 1847. Newport Public Library.
89. 11 and 12 Vic. *c.* 120.
90. Monmouthshire Canal Proprietors' Minute Book, 2 November 1850.
91. Ibid., 2 April 1851.
92. Printed note from Richard Blakemore to meeting, 12 June 1850, Newport Public Library.
93. Report to half-yearly meeting, 19 November 1851.
94. Report of committee to meeting, 2 March 1852.
95. Ebbw Vale company's notice, 10 February 1852. Newport Public Library.
96. Report of committee to meeting, 17 November 1852.
97. James Matthews, *Newport*, op. cit., p. 190.
98. Report, 16 November 1859.
99. Report to meeting, 19 March 1873.
100. Ibid.
101. James Matthews, *Newport*, op. cit., p. 193.
102. For further information about the Monmouthshire Railway see E. T. MacDermot, *History of the Great Western Railway*, 1931, Vol. II, pp. 103–24.
103. Photograph (M 000626), Newport Public Library.
104. *Reminiscences of George Jobbins*, 1935, MS., Newport Public Library.
105. *Hereford Journal*, 5 June 1793.
106. Maybery Papers, National Library of Wales, Box 42, letter from Daniel Williams, 12 July 1794.
107. *Hereford Journal*, 7 December 1803.
108. Generally, see Barrie & Lee, *Sirhowy Valley*, op. cit., and John Lloyd, *South Wales Iron Works*, op. cit.

Notes to Chapter VIII

1. *British Chronicle* (Hereford), 29 August 1792.
2. Ibid., 19 September 1792.
3. Ibid., 26 September 1792.
4. John Lloyd, *The Early History of the Old South Wales Iron Works*, 1760–1840, 1906, p. 182.
5. Monmouthshire Canal Committee Minute Book, 16 October 1792.
6. *Plan of a Canal from the Town of Brecknock to join the Monmouth Shire Canal near the Town of Ponty Pool . . . by T. Dadford Junr. Engineer*, 1793. Copy in Brecon Museum.
7. *British Chronicle* (Hereford), 7 November 1792.
8. 33 Geo. III *c*. 96.
9. For information about the family and bank see John Lloyd, *Historical Memoranda of Breconshire*, 1903, Vol. 1, and R O. Roberts, "The Operations of the Brecon Old Bank of Wilkins & Co. 1778-1890," *Business History*, Dec. 1958.
10. Walter Davies, *General View of the Agriculture and Domestic Economy of South Wales*, Vol. II, 1814.
11. *Glocester Journal*, 19 November 1792.
12. Spring 1796 according to T. Jones, *A History of the County of Brecknock*, Glanusk ed., 1909. Vol. II.
13. Brecknock & Abergavenny Canal Committee Minute Book, 26 June, 28 July 1794.
14. Ibid. Proprietors' Minute Book, 24 April 1806.
15. Ibid., 16 October 1794.
16. Ibid., 15 October 1795.
17. *Glocester Journal*, advt., 4 February 1799.
18. Charles Wilkins, *The South Wales Coal Trade*, 1888, p. 44.
19. Walter Davies, *General View*, op. cit.
20. Maybery Papers, National Library of Wales, Bundle 14. Report to meeting of 25 March 1800.
21. Ibid., Box 42, statement of 26 April 1804.
22. Brecknock & Abergavenny Canal Committee Minute Book, 31 August 1795.
23. J. Lloyd, *South Wales Iron Works*, op. cit., p. 189.
24. Monmouthshire Canal Proprietors' Minute Book, 4 November 1807.
25. 44 Geo III *c*. 29.
26. Brecknock & Abergavenny Canal Committee Minute Book, 7 February 1812.
27. Edwin Poole, *History of Breconshire*, 1886.
28. J. Lloyd, *South Wales Iron Works*, op. cit., p. 161.
29. Brecknock & Abergavenny Canal Proprietors' Minute Book, 20 October 1814.
30. Information given by Mr P. G. Rattenbury.
31. Maybery Papers, loc. cit., Box 42, paper 26 July 1819.
32. Brecknock & Abergavenny Canal Committee Minute Book, 24 July 1828.
33. Ibid., 27 August 1828.
34. Ibid., Proprietors' Minute Book, 25 April 1833.
35. Ibid., Committee Minute Book, 25 July 1839.
36. Collection of Mr D. S. Barrie.
37. *Hereford Journal*, 6 October 1858.
38. See Breconshire Railway & Canal Co. Minute Book, Maybery Papers, loc. cit. Meeting of Provisional Directors, 1 March 1859.

39. J. Lloyd, *Breconshire*, op. cit., Vol. I, p. 192.
40. *Hereford Journal*, 4 September 1793.
41. Ibid., 30 October 1793.
42. Ibid., 13 November 1793.
43. Ibid., 17 October 1810.
44. Walter Davies, *General View*, op. cit., Vol. II.
45. Brecknock & Abergavenny Canal Proprietors' Minute Book, 18 October 1810.
46. *Hereford Journal*, 7 November 1810.
47. Brecknock & Abergavenny Canal Proprietors' Minute Book, 13 March 1811.
48. J. Priestley, *Historical Account of the Navigable Rivers, Canals, etc.*, 1831, p. 453.
49. 51 Geo III *c.* 123.
50. *Hereford Journal*, 20 March 1811.
51. Ibid., 3 April 1811.
52. Ibid., 18 September 1811.
53. Ibid., 23 October 1811.
54. J. Priestley, *Navigable Rivers*, op. cit., p. 351.
55. 52 Geo III *c.* 107.
56. J. Priestley, *Navigable Rivers*, op. cit., p. 351.
57. *Hereford Journal*, 19 May 1813.
58. Ibid., 13 April 1814.
59. Ibid., 10 March 1819.
60. Ibid., 31 March 1819.
61. Ibid., 5 May 1819.
62. Ibid., 12 May 1819, 19 January 1820.
63. 7 Geo IV *c.* 100.
64. *Hereford Journal*, 23 September 1829.
65. Ibid., 21 July 1830.
66. Severn & Wye Railway & Canal Minute Book, 14 April 1830.
67. *Hereford Journal*, 29 June 1836.
68. For the Newport, Abergavenny & Hereford Railway see E. T. MacDermot, *History of the Great Western Railway*, 1927, Vol. I, pp. 526–537.
69. *Hereford Journal*, 1 January 1845.
70. Ibid., 24 March 1847.
71. Ibid., 20 April 1853.
72. Ibid., 5 August 1857.
73. Ibid., 16 March 1814.
74. Ibid., 5 January 1814.
75. Ibid., 3 May 1815.
76. Hay Railway records.
77. *Hereford Journal*, 19 December 1860.
78. Evidence by John Protheroe before the committee on the Brecon & Merthyr Railway Bill of 1862.
79. John Lloyd, *Breconshire*, op. cit., Vol. I, 1903.
80. Printed notice in Brecon Museum, and *Hereford Journal*, 22 May 1793.
81. *Hereford Journal*, 11 September 1793.
82. Ibid., 22 May 1805, 1 August 1810.
83. Brecknock & Abergavenny Canal Committee Minute Book, 19 December 1810.
84. *Hereford Journal*, 25 July 1810.
85. F. B. Ellison, 'The Hay Railway', in *Trans. Newcomen Soc.*, Vol. 18, and C. R. Clinker, *The Hay Railway*, 1960. See also *Trans. Woolhope Naturalists' Field Club*, 1936–8.

86. Walter Davies, *General View*, op. cit., Vol. II.
87. *Hereford Journal*, 20 February 1811.
88. 51 Geo III *c*. 222.
89. 52 Geo III *c*. 106.
90. Hay Railway Committee Minute Book, 9, 16, 18, 20 March 1812.
91. J. Priestley, *Navigable Rivers*, op. cit., Walter Davies, *General View*, op. cit., gives £50,375 12s.
92. Ellison, 'Hay Railway', op. cit. The *Hereford Journal* implies the 14th, but such implications are not always reliable.
93. *Hereford Journal*, 9 August 1854.
94. Ibid., 1 November 1854.
95. Ibid., 22 November 1854.
96. See Hereford, Hay & Brecon Railway Act, 1860, Brecon & Merthyr Railway Act, 1861, and Mid-Wales Railway Act, 1861.
97. 58 Geo. III *c*. 63.
98. *Hereford Journal*, 22 March 1820.
99. It is described as in existence by George Overton in *A Description of the Fautsl or Dykes of the Mineral Basin of South Wales*, Part I, 1825.
100. *Trans. Newcomen Soc.*, Vol. 18, art. W. A. Young, 'A Stockbook of 1828 and other Finds'.
101. *Hereford Journal*, 4 January 1834, 15 March 1837, 29 December 1841, 1 February 1843, 27 December 1843, 1 January 1845, 28 January 1846.
102. See *Trans. Woolhope Naturalists' Field Club*, 1955–7, art., C. R. Clinker, 'The Railways of West Herefordshire'.

Notes to Chapter IX

1. John Taylor, *Taylor's Last Voyage*, p. 23.
2. T. S. Willan, *River Navigation in England*, 1600–1750, p. 21.
3. See T. S. Willan, 'The River Navigation and Trade of the Severn Valley, 1600–1750', in the *Economic History Review*, Vol. VIII, 1937–8, p. 68, summarizing BM, Wye Navigation, 1622–62, add. MSS. 11,052.
4. 14 Car II P.A.
5. T. S. Willan, *River Navigation in England*, op. cit., p. 65.
6. Special Report on the canals and navigable rivers of Herefordshire, Herefordshire County Council, 1906. Hereford Public Library. See Act of 1695.
7. 7 and 8 Will III *c*. 14.
8. T. S. Willan, *River Navigation in England*, op. cit., pp. 53–5.
9. Ibid., p. 65.
10. T. S. Willan, *Severn Valley*, op. cit.
11. *J.H.C.* xx 784, quo. T. S. Willan, *River Navigation in England*, op. cit.
12. 13 Geo I *c*. 34.
13. T. S. Willan, *Severn Valley*, op. cit.
14. *England's Improvement*, i, 161, quo. T. S. Willan, *River Navigation in England*, op. cit., p. 150.
15. R. Atkyns, *Ancient and Present State of Gloucestershire*, p. 34, quo. T. S. Willan, *River Navigation in England*, op. cit., p. 152.
16. J. U. Nef, *Rise of the British Coal Industry*, Vol. I, p. 98.
17. Daniel Defoe, *A Tour through England and Wales*, Vol. II, p. 52 (Everyman ed.)

18. *Trans. Woolhope Naturalists' Field Club.*, 1946–8.
19. G. F. Townsend, *The Town and Borough of Leominster*, 1862.
20. Ibid.
21. F. G. Blacklock, *The Suppressed Benedictine Minister and other Ancient and Modern Institutions of the Borough of Leominster*, 1898.
22. Special Report, Hereford Public Library, op. cit., says Mordiford, Longworth, and Lugg Bridge.
23. Ibid.
24. W. Gilpin, *Observations on the River Wye*, etc., 2nd ed., 1789.
25. *British Chronicle* (Hereford), 6 January 1790.
26. Ibid., 2, 9 June 1790.
27. *Hereford Journal*, 12, 19 September 1804.
28. Ibid., 28 August, 11 September 1805.
29. 49 Geo III *c.* 78.
30. *Hereford Journal*, 23 January 1811.
31. Ibid., 30 July 1814.
32. Ibid., 3 June 1811.
33. Ibid., 8 February 1815.
34. Ibid.
35. Ibid., 22 November 1815.
36. Ibid.
37. Ibid., 14 September 1825.
38. Ibid., 8 September 1847, quoting from Knight's *The Land We Live In*, Vol. I, p. 246.
39. Ibid., 12 January 1825.
40. Ibid., 30 January 1828.
41. For the bark trade, centred at Monmouth, see W. Coxe, *An Historical Tour Through Monmouthshire*, ed. 1904, p. 240.
42. Grahame Farr, art. 'The Severn Navigation and the Trows', in *Mariner's Mirror*, 1946.
43. John Clark, *General View of the Agriculture of the County of Hereford*, 1794, p. 12.
44. Hereford Public Library.
45. Special Report, op. cit.
46. Herefordshire & Gloucestershire Canal Proprietors' Minute Book, 27 March 1834, Committee Minute Book, 11 April 1838, 13 June 1838, *Hereford Journal*, 22 August 1838.
47. *Hereford Journal*, 25 May 1853.
48. Grahame Farr, Severn Navigation op. cit.
49. Information from "Dean Forester".
50. Report, 20 December 1777 (Hereford Public Library).
51. Letter in *British Chronicle* (Hereford), 15 July 1789.
52. *British Chronicle*, 9 December 1789.
53. Ibid., 27 January 1790.
54. Ibid., 28 April 1790.
55. J. Priestley, *Historical Account of the Navigable Rivers, Canals*, etc., 1831, p. 438.
56. Ibid.
57. J. Rees, *Cyclopaedia*, 1819, art. 'Canal'.
58. *British Chronicle*, 29 December 1790.
59. 31 Geo III *c.* 69.
60. By William Faden, Charing Cross (Hereford Public Library).
61. *British Chronicle*, 13 October 1792.

62. Ibid., 28 November 1792.
63. *Hereford Chronicle*, 11 September 1793, *Hereford Journal*, 11 December 1793, 25 December 1793.
64. Not identified.
65. MS. Life of the elder Rennie by Sir John Rennie, Vol. I, p. 113 (Library of Institution of Civil Engineers).
66. 36 Geo III *c.* 70.
67. *Hereford Journal*, 27 July 1796.
68. Ibid., 7 December 1796.
69. J. Rees, *Cyclopaedia*, op. cit.
70. *Hereford Journal*, advt., 17 May 1797.
71. Ibid., 2 September 1801.
72. Pamphlet, *To the Proprietors of Shares in the Leominster Canal*, 16 May 1803, by John Hodskinson (Hereford Public Library).
73. 43 Geo III *c.* 141.
74. *Hereford Journal*, 7 March, 18 July, 29 August 1804.
75. Ibid., 8 May 1805, 13 May, 11 November 1807.
76. J. Rees, *Cyclopaedia*, op. cit.
77. Anon., *Historical and Topographical View of the Ancient and Present State of Leominster*, 1808, p. 238.
78. *Hereford Journal*, 22 August 1810.
79. Ibid., 17 July, 7 August 1811.
80. Ibid., 16 September 1812.
81. 7 Geo IV *c.* 94.
82. *Hereford Times*, 2 November 1833.
83. Ibid., 11 January 1834.
84. Herefordshire & Gloucestershire Canal Committee Minute Book, 7 February 1834.
85. Staffordshire & Worcestershire Canal Committee Minute Book, 19 February 1835.
86. Ibid., 21 March 1835.
87. *Hereford Times*, 13 October 1838.
88. A Member of the Mechanics' Institute of Kington, *The History of Kington*, 1845, pp. 252–5.
89. Shrewsbury & Hereford Railway Minute Book, 3 June 1845.
90. *Hereford Journal*, 26 November 1845.
91. Ibid., 29 July 1857.
92. Ibid., 24 June, 29 July 1846.
93. Shrewsbury & Hereford Railway Minute Book, 23 February 1847.
94. 10 and 11 Vic. *c.* 266.
95. Ibid., Preamble.
96. Shrewsbury & Hereford Railway Minute Book, 8 June 1855.
97. For full accounts of the lawsuit, see *Hereford Journal*, 15, 22, 29 July, 12 August 1857.
98. Shrewsbury & Hereford Railway Minute Book, 24 November 1857.
99. *Hereford Journal*, 19 May 1858.
100. Shrewsbury & Hereford Railway Minute Book, 10 May 1859.
101. Tenbury Railway Minute Book, 5 September 1860.
102. *Glocester Journal*, 2 January 1775.
103. Report of 20 December 1777. (Hereford Public Library.)
104. *British Chronicle* (Hereford), 9, 23 September 1789, as 'Ledbury Canal'.

105. Ibid., 24 March 1790.
106. *To the Gentlemen Promoters of a Navigable Canal from the City of Hereford, by way of the Towns of Ledbury and Newent, to the City of Gloucester*, 27 April 1790 (Gloucester Public Library).
107. *The Report of the Committee for the Herefordshire and Gloucestershire Canal shewing some of the advantages . . .*, 1790 (Hereford Public Library).
108. *British Chronicle*, 26 January 1791.
109. 31 Geo III *c.* 89.
110. Herefordshire & Gloucestershire Canal Proprietors' Minute Book, 14 July 1791.
111. *British Chronicle*, 8 August 1792.
112. 33 Geo. III *c.* 119.
113. *Hereford Journal*, 26 June 1793.
114. Herefordshire & Gloucestershire Canal Committee Minute Book, 5 November 1794.
115. Ibid., 8 June 1795.
116. *Hereford Journal*, 23 October 1793.
117. Herefordshire & Gloucestershire Canal Committee Minute Book, 23 April 1794.
118. *Hereford Journal*, 4 November 1795.
119. Herefordshire & Gloucestershire Canal Committee Minute Book, 9 November 1796.
120. *Eddowes's Salopian Journal*, 31 August 1796.
121. Herefordshire & Gloucestershire Canal Committee Minute Book, 2 February 1797.
122. Ibid., 9 November 1796.
123. J. Phillips, *A General History of Inland Navigation*, 4th ed., 1803, pp. 587–8, based on *Hereford Journal*, 4 April 1798.
124. Herefordshire & Gloucestershire Canal Committee Minute Book, 23 May 1800.
125. Ibid., 26 November 1812.
126. Ibid., Proprietors' Minute Book, 24 May 1829.
127. *Hereford Times*, 8 November 1834.
128. *Hereford Journal*, 27 April 1836.
129. Ibid., 7 June 1837.
130. *Hereford Times*, 4 August 1838.
131. 2 and 3 Vic. *c.* 26.
132. *Hereford Journal*, 24 July 1839.
133. Herefordshire & Gloucestershire Canal Committee Minute Book, 18 July 1839.
134. Ibid., 1 October 1839.
135. *Hereford Journal*, 22 April 1840.
136. Ibid., 28 February 1844.
137. Herefordshire & Gloucestershire Canal Proprietors' Minute Book, 28 March 1844.
138. *Hereford Journal*, 2 October 1844.
139. Ibid., 3 July 1844.
140. Herefordshire & Gloucestershire Canal Committee Minute Book, 10 May 1845.
141. *Hereford Journal*, 11 November 1846.
142. Staffordshire & Worcestershire Canal Committee Minute Book, 20 March 1847.
143. Herefordshire & Gloucestershire Canal Proprietors' Minute Book, 13 May 1847.

144. *Hereford Journal*, 9 June 1847.
145. Herefordshire & Gloucestershire Canal Committee Minute Book, 28 June 1855.
146. Ibid., 13 November 1869.
147. *Report of the Select Committee on Canals*, 1883, Q. 2069.
148. See my *British Canals*, 2nd ed., p. 211, for notice of closing.
149. This section has greatly benefited from the courtesy of "Dean Forester" in putting their manuscript account of transport in the Forest of Dean at my disposal.
150. *Hereford Journal*, 18 November 1800.
151. *Glocester Journal*, 19 January 1801.
152. Ibid., 14 September 1801.
153. Ibid., 12 October 1801.
154. Ibid., 2 October 1801.
155. *Hereford Journal*, 27 January, 10 February 1802.
156. *Glocester Journal*, 27 December 1802.
157. Gloucester & Berkeley Canal Minute Book, 25 August 1806.
158. Ibid., 30 July 1807 and *Hereford Journal*, 29 July 1807.
159. B.T.C. Historical Records, MPR 430/1.
160. Ibid., printed paper of 24 September 1811.
161. 49 Geo III *c.* 159.
162. *Trans. Newcomen Soc.*, Vol. 18, p. 200.
163. See Advt. *Glocester Journal*, 24 September 1792.
164. 50 Geo III *c.* 215.
165. Severn & Wye Railway & Canal Minute Book, 16 March 1813.
166. *Hereford Journal*, 24 March 1813.
167. Severn & Wye Railway & Canal Minute Book, 18 January 1820.
168. Ibid., 23 December 1840.
169. Ibid.
170. *Railway Times*, 4 February, 10 June 1843.
171. Much information on the relationship between the Forest tramroads and railways and the Wye, and also the Lydney and Pidcock's canals, can be found in H. W. Paar's *The Severn & Wye Railway*, 1963, and *The Great Western Railway in Dean*, 1965.
172. H. G. Nicholls, *The Forest of Dean*, 1858, reprinted 1966, and information from Mr Alec K. Pope.

Note on Sources

The following are the principal collections of useful records in the hands of public authorities:

Authority	*Records*
British Transport Historical Records	Kidwelly & Llanelly Canal (few), Carmarthenshire Tramroad (few), Swansea Canal, Monmouthshire Canal, Brecknock & Abergavenny Canal, Herefordshire & Gloucestershire Canal, Severn & Wye Railway and Lydney Canal.
National Library of Wales	Glamorganshire Canal, Ashburnham Collection, Nevill, Druce Documents, Tredegar Collection, Maybery Papers, Cyfarthfa Papers, Bute Collection.
Glamorgan County Records	Deposited plans, Guest Papers, Ynyscedwyn Papers.
Monmouthshire County Records	Deposited plans, Monmouthshire Canal (few), Sirhowy Tramroad (few).
Cardiff Public Library	Bute MSS., Glamorganshire Canal (few).
Newport Public Library	Monmouthshire Canal (few).
Llanelly Public Library	Llandeilo & Llandovery Canal project, local maps.
Swansea Public Library	Swansea Canal, Tennant Canal (few).
Hereford Public Library	Herefordshire & Gloucestershire Canal, Leominster Canal, Wye River.
Gloucester Public Library	Herefordshire & Gloucestershire Canal (few).

Other records are in the hands of Mr A. J. S. Coombe-Tennant (Tennant Canals), the Neath Canal Company (Neath Canal), the Bute Estate (Aberdare Canal), and Mr R. Trevor Griffiths of Hay (Hay Railway). The British Museum has a good collection of canal maps. The Minutes of Evidence before Parliamentary Committees in the House of Lords Record Office should be consulted. The principal newspaper files are those of the *Cambrian*, the *Hereford Journal* and the *Glocester Journal.*

The books consulted can be found in the Notes to each chapter.

APPENDIX I

Summary of Facts about the Canals and Navigations of South Wales and its Border

A. *Rivers Successfully Made Navigable*

River	*Date of Act under which Work was begun*	*Date Wholly Opened*	*Approx. Cost at Opening*	*Terminal Points*
Neath	None	*c.* 1750	Not known	Aberdulais–Ynysygerwyn
Wye*	1662	*c.* 1727	*c.* £18,000	Severn River–Hereford, later Hay
	1809 (towing path)	1811	£5,000	Lydbrook–Hereford

B. *Rivers with Uncompleted Navigation Works*

River	*Date of Act under which Work was begun*	*Money Spent*	*Terminal Points Authorized*	*Length on which Work was done*
Lugg	1662	Not known		Probably between Leominster and the Wye

* I have classified the Wye to Hereford under this heading, but it is almost unclassifiable.

Length including Branches	*Greatest Number of Locks*	*Size of Boats Taken*	*Date of Disuse for Commercial Traffic*	*Whether bought by Railway and Present Ownership, if any*
1¼ miles	2	Not known	*c.* 1794	—
Severn–Hereford 69½ miles towing path 37 miles	—	(*c.* 30 tons)	*c.* 1860, except for lower 37 miles	No.

Greatest Number of Locks	*Size of Boats Taken*	*Date of Abandonment of Works*	*Later Events*
At least three half-locks, probably more	Not known	Probably soon after 1756	Probably navigable between 1727 and *c.* 1860 on bottom 5 miles up to Lugg Bridge

C. *Canals, the Main Lines of which were Completed as Authorized (including Private Canals)*

Canal	*Date of Act under which Work was begun*	*Date wholly Opened*	*Approx. Cost at Opening*	*Terminal Points*	*Branches Built*
Aberdare	1793	1812	£26,220	Glamorganshire C. at Abercynon–Tŷ-draw	—
Ashburnham's, Earl of	None	*c.* 1796	Not known	Ffrwd-Gwendraeth Fawr estuary	Near Ffrwd-Coed
Brecknock & Abergavenny	1793	1812	*c.* £200,000 inc. tram-roads	Monmouthshire C. at Pontymoile–Brecon	—
Cinderford	None	1795	Not known	Broad Moor–Cinderford Iron-works	—
Cyfarthfa	None	*c.* 1776	Not known	Canaid brook–Cyfarthfa	—
Doctor's	None	1813	Not known	Glamorganshire C. at Denia–Treforest	—
General Warde's (Dafen)	None	*c.* 1769	Not known	Llwynhendy–Dafen pill	—
General Warde's (Yspitty)	None	*c.* 1770 extended *c.* 1787	Not known	Yspitty–Bynea	From near Bynea to Pencrug

Length	*Greatest Number of Locks*	*Size of Boats Taken*	*Date of Disuse for Commercial Traffic*	*Whether bought by Railway and Present Ownership, if any*
6¾ miles	2 and stop-lock	60 ft. by 8 ft. 9 in.	1900	No. Various
1½ miles (br. ¼ mile)	Not known	Not known	Pen-y-bedd–estuary *c.* 1816 Rest probably *c.* 1867	No.
33¼ miles	6	64 ft. 9 in. by 9 ft. 2 in.	*c.* 1933	Bought in 1865 by Monmouthshire company: sold with that company to G.W.R., 1880. British Transport Commission.
c. 1¼ miles	—	Not known	Not known	No
2 miles	—	Not known	*c.* 1835	No.
1 mile	—	60 ft. by 8 ft. 9 in.	*c.* 1910	—
¾ mile	—	Not known	Probably soon after 1808	No.
1 mile (br. ¼ mile)	—	Not known	*c.* 1820	No.

Canal	*Date of Act under which Work was begun*	*Date wholly Opened*	*Approx. Cost at Opening*	*Terminal Points*	*Branches Built*
Giant's Grave & Briton Ferry	None	*c.* 1825	Not known	Giant's Grave–Briton Ferry	—
Glamorganshire	1790	1794 (extension 1798)	£103,600	Merthyr Tydfil–Cardiff	—
Glan-y-wern	None	1790	Not known	Glan-y-wern–Red Jacket	—
Herefordshire & Gloucestershire	1791	1845*	£248,000†	Gloucester–Hereford‡	Oxenhall
Hopkin's	None	Not known	Not known	Townsend's Pill, Yspitty–towards Bryn-Carnafon	—
Kymer's	1766	1769	Not known	Kidwelly–Pwllyllygod	—

* Gloucester–Ledbury 1798: Ledbury–Hereford 1845.
† Gloucester–Ledbury £106,500; Ledbury–Hereford £141,500.
‡ Originally Gloucester: later Over on the western branch of the Severn.

Length	*Greatest Number of Locks*	*Size of Boats Taken*	*Date of Disuse for Commercial Traffic*	*Whether bought by Railway and Present Ownership, if any*
½ mile	—	60 ft. by 8 ft. 10 in.	Not known	No.
25½ miles	51 and sea-lock*	60 ft. by 8 ft. 9 in. 90 ft. by 24 ft. sea-lock to Cardiff	1945†	No. Cardiff Corporation
3½ miles	—	Not known at first, later *c.* 60 ft. by 14 ft.‡	*c.* 1910	No. Jersey Estate
Main line 34 miles§ Branch ¼ mile	22**	70 ft. by 7 ft. 6in.††	1881	Leased by West Midland and G.W.R. 1862: bought by G.W.R. 1870
½ mile	—	Not known	Not known	No
3 miles	—	Not known	*c.* 1867	Leased to Kidwelly & Llanelly C., 1835. Canal bought 1865 by Kidwelly & Burry Port Rly, formerly Kidwelly & Llanelly Canal Co.

* One of these, New Lock, next above sea-lock, was built well on in the nineteenth century when the canal was connected to the Bute docks.

† Abercynon upwards 1898, Abercynon-Pontypridd 1915, Pontypridd-Cardiff 1942, sea lock pound 1950.

‡ They were 60-ton craft. I have assumed the probable size.

§ For a short time before 1800 there was also a ¾ mile section between the east and west branches of the Severn. Gloucester–Ledbury 16 miles.

** These locks were unusually deep: 19 of them had an average fall of 10 ft. 10 in., 3 an average fall of 12 ft. 6 in.

†† The canal was built to take this size of craft: those working on to it from the Midland canals were of course the standard 70 ft. × 6 ft. 10 in. boats.

Canal	*Date of Act under which Work was begun*	*Date wholly Opened*	*Approx. Cost at Opening*	*Terminal Points*	*Branches Built*
Llansamlet	None	*c.* 1784	Not known	Llansamlet–Foxhole	—
Lydney	1810	1813	£20,000	Lydney–Nass Point	—
Mackworth's	None	*c.* 1700	Not known	Neath River–Melyn works	—
Monmouthshire	1792	1799 (extend. *c.* 1814)	*c.*£220,000*	Newport–Pontnewynydd (extend. in Newport *c.* 1814)	1. Crindai (Malpas)–Crumlin. 2. Potter Street–downwards) (private)
Morris's	None	*c.* 1790	Not known	Landore–Fforest works	—
Neath	1791	*c.* 1795 (extend. 1799)	*c.* £40,000	Glynneath–Giant's Grave	1. Maesmarchog 2. Cnel Bach 3. Court Sart (All private)

* Including tramroads.

Length	*Greatest Number of Locks*	*Size of Boats Taken*	*Date of Disuse for Commercial Traffic*	*Whether bought by Railway and Present Ownership, if any*
3 miles	Not known	Not known	*c.* 1852	No.
1 mile	Tide lock and single sea-gates	100 ft. by 24 ft.	Open	Built by Severn & Wye tramroad company. Subsequently became a railway company. Taken over by G.W.R. & Midland Rlys jointly, 1894. British Transport Commission.
⅛ mile	—	Not known	Before 1720	No.
Main line 11 miles (inc. ext. 1¼ miles) Crumlin branch 11 miles Potter Street branch ½ mile (private)	* 42 (main line) 32 (branch)	64 ft. 9 in. by 9 ft. 2 in.	Pontnewynydd–Pontymoile 1849 and 1853	Canal company became railway company also, 1845: bought by G.W.R. 1880. British Transport Commission.
1 mile	—	Not known	*c.* 1794	Incorporated in Trewyddfa Canal
Main line 13 miles Maesmarchog branch ¼ mile Cnel Bach branch ¼ mile Court Sart branch ¼ mile	19	60 ft. by 8 ft. 10 in.	1934	Neath Canal Co.

* Potter Street was added later as lock 43.

Canal	*Date of Act under which Work was begun*	*Date wholly Opened*	*Approx. Cost at Opening*	*Terminal Points*	*Branches Built*
Pembrey	None	1824	Not known	Kidwelly & Llanelly C. near Tŷ-gwyn–Pembrey old harbour	—
Pen-clawdd	1811	1814	*c.* £7,000	—	—
Penrhiwtyn	None	*c.* 1793	£600	Penrhiwtyn furnaces–Giant's Grave	—
Pidcock's	None	*c.* 1780	Not known	Lydney Pill–Middle Forge	—
Red Jacket	None	1818	(See Tennant C.)	Glan-y-wern C.–Tawe River	—
Swansea	1794	1798	*c.* £55,000	Swansea–Trewyddfa C. at Landore, and Trewyddfa C. at Fforest–Hen-neuadd	1. Ynys-gedwyn 2. Ystaly-fera 3. Cilybe-byll 4. Pontar-dawe (All private) 5. In Swansea parallel to North Dock

Length	*Greatest Number of Locks*	*Size of Boats Taken*	*Date of Disuse for Commercial Traffic*	*Whether bought by Railway and Present Ownership, if any*
2 miles	1	Not known	*c.* 1843	No. Part of site used for South Wales Railway.
3⅝ miles	? 2	Not known	*c.* 1818	No.
1⅜ miles	None	Not known	1798*	—
1½ miles	3	Not known	Not known	No.
1⅞ miles†	2 river locks	*c.* 60 ft. by 14 ft.‡	*c.* 1922	No. Mr A. J. S. Coombe Tennant.
Main line 15⅛ miles Ynysgedwyn branch ½ mile Ystalyfera branch — short Cilybebyll branch ¼ mile Pontardawe branch — short Swansea branch ¼ mile	36	69 ft. 2 in. by 7 ft. 6 in.	1931§	Bought 1873 by Great Western Railway. British Transport Commission.

* Absorbed in Neath Canal.

† And 2⅛ miles of the Glan-y-wern Canal.

‡ They were 60-ton craft. I have assumed the probable size. That at Red Jacket was later enlarged.

§ Lower 6 miles only in use in 1904. No trade to Hen-neuadd for over twenty years before that.

Canal	*Date of Act under which Work was begun*	*Date wholly Opened*	*Approx. Cost at Opening*	*Terminal Points*	*Branches Built*
Tennant*	None	1824	c. £20,000†	Red Jacket C.–Neath C. at Aberdulais	1. Dulais 2. Vale of Neath Brewery (private) 3. Neath 4. Neath Abbey (private) 5. Neath River (Crown works) 6. Tir-isaf (private)
Trewyddfa‡	1794	c. 1796	Not known	Swansea C. at Landore–Swansea C. at Fforest	—
Wern	None	c. 1795	Not known	Copperhouse Dock, Llanelly–Wern colliery	§

* The name now includes most of the Red Jacket Canal and part of the Glan-y-wern Canal, giving a length of 8½ miles, Aberdulais to Swansea.

† This sum includes building the Red Jacket Canal, and enlarging the Glan-y-wern Canal, but not the building of Port Tennant or the purchase of land.

‡ See Morris's Canal.

§ There may have been a short branch; see text.

Length	*Greatest Number of Locks*	*Size of Boats Taken*	*Date of Disuse for Commercial Traffic*	*Whether bought by Railway and Present Ownership, if any*
Main line 4⅞ miles Dulais branch 1/16 mile Brewery branch 1/16 mile Neath branch — Neath Abbey branch 1/16 mile Neath River branch 1/16 mile Tir-isaf branch 1 mile	1 1 on Dulais branch 1 river lock on Neath branch 1 river lock on Neath river branch	60 ft. by 8 ft. 10 in.	Main line *c.* 1934 Tir-isaf branch *c.* 1910 others much earlier	No. Mr A. J. S. Coombe Tennant.
1⅜ miles	—	*c.* 65 ft. by 7 ft. 6 in.	1931	Bought 1873 by Great Western Railway British Transport Commission.
1 mile	—	Not known	*c.* 1810	No.

D. *Canals, the Main Lines of which were not Completed*

Canal	*Date of Act under which Work was begun*	*Date Opened*	*Approx. Cost at Opening*	*Authorized Terminal Points*	*Terminal Points as Built*
Kidwelly & Llanelly	1812	1816 *c.* 1838	£74,500	Kymer's C. at Spudder's-Bridge–Llanelly; from ¼ m. short of north end of Kymer's C.–Cwm-mawr	Kymer's C. ¼m. below Spudder's Bridge–Burry Port; upper part of Kymer's C.–Pontyberem*
Leominster	1791	1796	£93,500	Kington–Stourport	Leominster–Wharf House near Mamble

E. *Canals Partly Built but not Opened*

Kilgetty Canal, begun *c.* 1792.

* See text. From Pontyberem to Cwm-mawr the canal seems to have been built, but to have been used only as a water-channel. Kymer's Canal was leased in 1835.

Branches Built	*Length*	*Greatest Number of Locks*	*Size of Boats Taken*	*Date of Disuse for Commercial Traffic*	*Whether bought by Railway, and Present Ownership, if any*
Moat Farm (Trimsaran)	9 miles† (branch ⅜ mile)	5 and 2 inclined planes‡	Not known§	*c.* 1867	Canal company became railway company in 1865, and used track for lines. British Transport Commission.
—	18½ miles	16	70 ft. by 6 ft. 10 in.	1858	Bought by Shrewsbury & Hereford Railway, 1858.

F. *Canals Authorized but not Begun*

None.

† Kymer's Canal–Burry Port 4¼ miles; Kymer's Canal–Pontyberem 4¾ miles. The unfinished portion from Pontyberem to Cwm-mawr was 2¼ miles.

‡ The third inclined plane at Hirwaun-isaf was partly built, but never worked.

§ 6-ton boats over the planes; *c.* 20-ton elsewhere.

APPENDIX II

Principal Engineering Works

A. *Inclined Planes*

Canal	*Name of Plane*	*Vertical Rise*	*Dates Working*	*Notes*
Kidwelly & Llanelly	Pont-Henry	57 feet	*c.* 1838–*c.* 1867	Worked by water power, method unknown
	Capel Ifan	56 feet	*c.* 1838–*c.* 1867	
	Hirwaun-isaf	84 feet	Never used	

B. *Lifts*

None.

C. *Tunnels over 500 yards*

Herefordshire & Gloucestershire Canal	Oxenhall	2,192 yards
Leominster Canal	Southnet (never used)	1,250 yards

D. *Outstanding Aqueducts*

Brecknock & Abergavenny Canal	Brynich (Usk)
Glamorganshire Canal	Abercynon (Taff)
Herefordshire & Gloucestershire Canal (removed)	Shelwick (Lugg)
Kidwelly & Llanelly Canal	Trimsaran (Gwendraeth Fawr)
Leominster Canal	Woofferton (Teme)
Leominster Canal	Rea (Rea)
Neath Canal	Ynysbwllog (Neath)
Swansea Canal	Ystalyfera (Afon Twrch)
Tennant Canal	Aberdulais (Neath)

INDEX

The principal references to canals and river navigations are indicated in bold type

Stepaside, 44